Please check all items for damages
before leaving the Library.
Thereafter you will be held
responsible for all injuries
to items beyond reasonable wear.

6-16 (5)

The Great American
Railroad War

Also by Dennis Drabelle

Mile-High Fever:
Silver Mines, Boom Towns, and High Living on the Comstock Lode

The Great American Railroad War

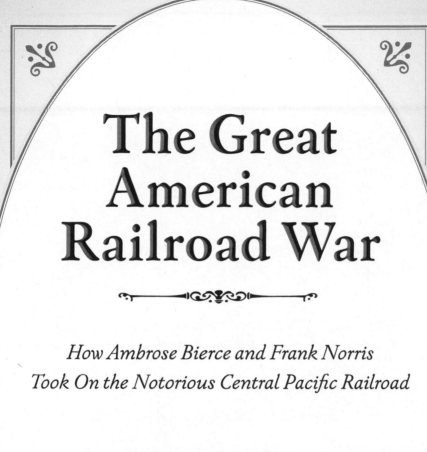

*How Ambrose Bierce and Frank Norris
Took On the Notorious Central Pacific Railroad*

DENNIS DRABELLE

ST. MARTIN'S PRESS ✖ NEW YORK

THE GREAT AMERICAN RAILROAD WAR. Copyright © 2012 by Dennis Drabelle. All rights reserved. Printed in the United States of America. For information, address St. Martin's Press, 175 Fifth Avenue, New York, N.Y. 10010.

www.stmartins.com

Library of Congress Cataloging-in-Publication Data

Drabelle, Dennis.
    The great American railroad war: how Ambrose Bierce and Frank Norris took on the notorious Central Pacific Railroad / Dennis Drabelle.—1st ed.
        p.   cm.
    Includes bibliographical references.
    ISBN 978-0-312-66759-7 (hardcover)
    ISBN 978-1-250-01505-1 (e-book)
1. Central Pacific Railroad Company—History.   2. Railroads—California—History—19th century.   3. Political corruption—Press coverage—California.   4. Bierce, Ambrose, 1842–1914?—Criticism and interpretation.   5. Norris, Frank, 1870–1902—Criticism and interpretation.   I. Title.
    HE2791.C451 D73
    385.0979'09034—dc23

                                                    2012010247

First Edition: August 2012

10 9 8 7 6 5 4 3 2 1

For Jim Drabelle, Joe Drabelle, Jr., and Patti Forrest

contents

Introduction   1

The Great American
Railroad War

⇥ introduction ⇤

The Central Pacific Railroad holds a distinction unique in the annals of American business: It riveted the attention of two great writers at the peak of their artistry. It's one thing for workaday journalists to accuse a firm of such faults as monopolization, bribery, cheating its rivals, and indifference to public safety. Plenty of other companies got the same treatment in the late-nineteenth and early-twentieth centuries, both individually (Standard Oil, for example) and collectively (the insurance industry). But it takes a special kind of ogre to fascinate Ambrose Bierce and Frank Norris, each destined to be a canonical writer, his work enshrined in numerous Classics editions, including the Library of America.

Bierce is best known for the acerbic definitions in his *Devil's Dictionary*, his ghost and suspense stories, and his brutally candid reminiscences of the Civil War (in which he was the only first-rate American writer to have fought). But he made his living in journalism, notably as a columnist for William Randolph Hearst's *San Francisco Examiner*. Far from suffering fools and knaves gladly, Bierce went after them with gusto. He was lucky to live in a scrappy age when words didn't just ring out—they pinched, gouged, slapped, kicked, and pulled hair. Our Victorian-era forebears may have been quick to censor references to bodily functions, but on just about any other subject a writer could sound off with a recklessness that makes even the most outspoken twenty-first-century pundits sound genteel.

Possessed of a large vocabulary, a wide range of interests, a generous supply of allusions, and an extraordinary gift for insult and invective, Bierce made the most of this permissive atmosphere. For more than two decades, he reigned as the West Coast's chief exposer of greed and corruption, its peerless scold of crooks and fools. Though conservative by nature and admiring of great men, in practice he couldn't stop pounding away at the four principals of the Central Pacific—Collis Huntington, Mark Hopkins, Leland Stanford, and Charles Crocker—for the devious way they had amassed money and power, for the arrogance with which they threw both around, for their willingness to accept subsidies while pretending to be self-made. The overbearing and vulgar Crocker, Bierce grumbled (and he could just as well have said the same of the other three), had become obscenely rich "on an original investment of a suspender button and a postage stamp."

The mask of tragedy fit well on Bierce's face, but Frank Norris was all smiles. Born to wealth, blessed with good looks and a fecund imagination, as a young man he seemed headed for a career as an idler. But behind his inconclusive sampling of courses at the University of California and Harvard lay a clear plan. He intended to mold himself into a certain kind of novelist—an American version of the great French naturalist Émile Zola. To his credit, Norris followed through by writing his first masterpiece, *McTeague*. Whereupon he outgrew his Zola phase and tackled a project he could make all his own—a trilogy that would depict modern society by concentrating on one of the world's staples: wheat. And although Norris, too, had an affinity with the wealthy and powerful, his urge to tell a dramatic story put him firmly on the side of capitalism's victims.

Despite their east-of-the Mississippi origins, Bierce and Norris were quintessential Westerners. Their best work can be seen as building on an insight voiced by Mark Twain's character Colonel Beriah Sellers in *The Gilded Age*: "Yes, born East myself, . . . know the West—a great country, gentlemen. The place for a young fellow of spirit to pick up a fortune, simply pick it up, it's lying round loose here." The nineteenth-century West, in other words, was a vast storage locker, full of ore, timber, water, and transportation routes, all ready to be made off with by enterprising men. From this point of view, it's only a hop and a skip to an unsettling corollary. In the remote West, rules were few and sporadically enforced, and the way was open for clever operators to grab far more than their share of those fortunes, especially if they had no qualms about using fraud and force. The Darwinian shibboleth of survival of the fittest applied even better to conditions in the West than elsewhere in the country, and many people seemed to find that right and just.

The Central Pacific had merged with another California-based railroad, the Southern Pacific, and over the years Bierce had tossed an occasional brickbat at the amalgamated firm. In the mid-1890s, however, a series of scheduled events served to concentrate his mind (and that of his politically ambitious boss, Hearst). Back in the 1860s, the Central Pacific had accepted loans from the federal government to subsidize construction. Taking the form of thirty-year bonds, the loans had been issued periodically as the work crews finished laying new stretches of track. With interest, the bonds added up to a roughly $75-million obligation on the railroad's part, and starting in 1896 they would be falling due. Stanford had haughtily expected Uncle Sam to forgive the debt outright, in deference to what he viewed as the Central Pacific's stupendous contribution to the common good. But Stanford was dead now, leaving Huntington as the last surviving member of the Big Four, and he was a more realistic bargainer. He could live with federal legislation that would bundle the debts into a single loan, repayable at, say, 2 or 3 percent interest over a period of, oh, how about seventy-five years? At Hearst's behest, Bierce swung into action against such a betrayal of the public trust, traveling to Washington in January of 1896 as the head of a SWAT team of reporters, cartoonists, and secretaries.

Huntington, who commanded a much larger squad of lobbyists and could dip into a fat purse to keep wavering members of Congress in line, entered the contest as the heavy favorite. Bierce, however, turned himself into a copy-producing dynamo: Over the next five months, he wrote sixty-some articles, most of which Hearst ran on the front page. Laced with stinging epithets, rude similes, and trenchant analysis of law, economics, and politics, these pieces form one of the signal achievements of American journalism, on a par with cartoonist Thomas Nast's campaign against the Tweed Ring and reporters Bob Woodward and Carl Bernstein's pursuit of the truth about Watergate.

A couple of years later, Norris chose to focus the first volume of his wheat trilogy on the means by which the grain entered the stream of commerce—that is, in the freight cars of a thinly disguised version of the Southern Pacific. While conducting background research, he refamiliarized himself with Bierce's campaign against the railroad, but in the end Norris seized upon events from the company's middle age. His title, *The Octopus*, came from an old political cartoon that depicted the railroad as just that, with its tentacles wrapped around and crushing representatives of various sectors of California society. For his climax he worked a powerful variation on a bloody incident from the spring of 1880. The railroad was at loggerheads with settlers in the Mussel Slough region of California's Central Valley over another form of federal subsidy: land grants to be used by the railroad for seeding the farms and communities on which its business would ultimately depend. Instead of working out a deal, both sides dug in their heels, leading to a shoot-out in which seven men were killed. Norris took the version of Mussel Slough least favorable to the railroad and ran with it, transforming this tragedy of errors into an indictment of corporate stubbornness and greed. *The Octopus* is a great American epic, second perhaps only to Melville's *Moby-Dick* in that category. As with Bierce's *Examiner* articles, the much-hated railroad had been the unwitting source of superlative writing by an American master.

And what of the railroad itself? How much it deserved its sinister reputation is a subject best saved for the end of the book, but for now at least this much can be said. Whether or not it was the uncontrollable Octopus vilified by writers and artists, the Southern Pacific did little to gainsay that interpretation. Public relations was in its infancy during the railroad's heyday, and among the Big Four only Huntington voiced an occasional misgiving about how their private profligacy was corroding the corporate image. The Southern Pacific tried to bamboozle the public by paying journalists to do well by it in print—a method that became obsolete the moment publishers realized they could boost circulation and attract advertising by attacking the iron bogeyman. The Big Four could rightfully boast of having achieved a near miracle by building a railroad through some of the roughest terrain in the country. But their record also contains a great failure: They couldn't overcome the widespread perception of their company as a monster that threatened the American republican form of government itself.

The first three chapters of *The Great American Railroad War* set the stage for the main feature—Bierce's and Norris's antirailroad polemics of the 1890s—by telling the story of how the transcontinental railroad was built. The emphasis is on what happened along the West-to-East route punched through the Sierra mountains and across Nevada by the Central Pacific, but since the CP found itself in a race with the westward-building Union Pacific, that company's tactics also figure prominently. Chapters four through six cover Bierce's life up to and including his star turn as scourge of the railroad; chapters seven through nine do the same for Norris; and chapter ten follows the main actors, including the railroad itself, to the ends of their lives.

Mind you, this is not a David-and-Goliath tale. Bierce wrote his dispatches with the backing of the wealthy, brazen Hearst, and

Norris's *Octopus* was published by one of the most respected American houses. Rather, it's a story of countervailing power, of how words—infused with passion, wielded with skill, and disseminated by financially secure media—can make headway against massive economic forces.

Octopus-taming wasn't always pretty. Bierce slanted his material to further the cause for which he fought, and Norris made fiery use of a controversial incident without questioning the superficial version of the story uncovered by his research. Yet for those who rejected Social Darwinism and believed that government should impose some limits on corporate power, the dual crusade was a heartening development. Bierce and Norris formed a kind of tag team. Bierce's acid-tongued rhetoric heaped scorn and ridicule on the Southern Pacific and its last surviving kingpin, while Norris's electric storytelling brought the company's callous behavior vividly to life. Together, the two writers confirmed and sharpened the railroad's reputation as a beast that had to be checked. The rest was up to the political process.

Not the process that had been in place for decades, though. The Big Four had amassed so much power as to call into question government's ability to stand up to them. A generation after Bierce and Norris's fulminations, Californians joined voters in many other states by embracing the initiative, referendum, and recall—at first with a heady sense of progressive accomplishment. In recent decades, however, these reforms have gone sour, at least in California. Today the state finds itself hamstrung by overuse, misuse, and even conflicting uses of the referendum and recall, leading to uncertainty, stasis, and frequent political crises. The Big Four's "greatest" achievement may have been one they could not have foreseen: spooking citizens into unwittingly sentencing themselves and their progeny to lasting governmental failure.

None of this, of course, can fairly be blamed on Bierce or Norris, who are guilty of nothing more than writing as well as they could about the conditions of their time. Today, when newspapers are failing, when bookstores are closing, when the Internet has yet to demonstrate the capacity to give citizens the in-depth information they need to make sound decisions about candidates and issues, when the Supreme Court knocks down limits on expenditures to sway elections, when a career in journalism has lost its luster, when the fiction bestseller lists are dominated by formulaic thrillers and romances, when the artful use of the English language is becoming the province of an elite few—in this volatile and discouraging climate, the amount of trouble stirred up at the dawn of the muckraking era by a veteran journalist and a young novelist is a tribute to the efficacy of an old and honorable combination: a free press and writers eager to give the rich and powerful hell.

⇥ one ⇤

Working on the Railroad

Trains chuffed into the world in the 1820s and '30s, bridging physical and temporal chasms that had held humans back for millennia. The historian Walter A. McDougall has described the upheaval wrought by this revolutionary technology (with supplemental help from the telegraph): "When [Andrew] Jackson entered the White House in 1829, people, goods, and information—even in the most advanced countries—could not travel overland any faster than they did in the time of Julius Caesar. Then all concepts of space, time, and volume exploded." In the following two decades, chain reactions to the explosion rippled through the Eastern, Southern, and Central United States. By the 1850s, almost half of the world's railroad tracks rested on American soil.

Most of that crisscrossed soil, however, lay east of the Mississippi. As the forty-niners could testify, a trip to the West Coast was still circuitous in the extreme: typically by boat from an Eastern port to the Isthmus of Panama, across that sweltering neck of land by whatever means the traveler could afford, and then by boat again to San Francisco. (For inanimate cargo, the most economical way was even longer: around Cape Horn, at the southern tip of South America.) The solution was plain to see. The whole United States should be tied together by rails.

In addition to stimulating trade, both domestic and international (beyond California shimmered the markets of the Orient), a transcontinental line would round out the process of nation building. To leave the vast American midsection uncrossed by the most efficient mode of transportation yet devised, while the alluring West Coast stayed out of reach except via long, arduous, and costly journeys—to stagnate in this way would be to betray the great, ongoing enterprise of territorial acquisition and conquest. Why, the country's very name seemed to cry out for the project: We must be not merely adjacent, but united. As for the work itself, annihilating distance (a catchphrase of the day) was just the sort of challenge for a people who considered themselves blessed with boundless energy and ingenuity.

By midcentury, railroad building had become not just a mission but a mania. Looking back from the vantage point of the early 1900s, Henry Adams, scion of U.S. presidents but brother of a railroad president, had this to say about the task:

> [it was] so big as to need the energies of a generation, for it required all the new machinery to be created—capital, banks, mines, furnaces, shops, power-houses, technical knowledge, mechanical population, together with a steady remodelling of social and political habits, ideas and institutions to fit the new scale and suit the new conditions. The generation between 1865 and 1895 was already mortgaged to the railways, and no one knew it better than the generation itself.

Adams neglected to add, however, that before it could embark on all this remodeling and mortgaging, the railroad generation had to find start-up capital. But the transcontinental job in particular was so massive and risky—laying tracks and constructing bridges, trestles, culverts, tunnels, snowsheds, and depots over almost eighteen hundred miles of sparsely settled plains, deserts, and mountains, while often under the hostile gaze of Native Americans about to be dispossessed—that private investors tended to shy away from it. Hence the near universal opinion held by people of the time: The federal government would have to step in, either taking the initiative itself or giving ample aid to the private citizens who raised their hands to do so.

That much was clear. The railroad's destination, however, was not so manifest. Northerners favored a northern route, from St. Louis or Omaha to somewhere on the West Coast. Southerners advocated a southern route. Behind both preferences stood an ulterior motive: to shape the future of slavery. Northerners hoped to curb the peculiar institution by running the transcontinental line through territory where slavery was unlikely to be welcomed; Southerners wanted to do just the opposite. Jefferson Davis, in his presecession capacity as President Franklin Pierce's secretary of war, ordered a thorough investigation, complete with surveys of five distinct routes. The fieldwork culminated in a report submitted to Congress in 1855 and later published in thirteen quarto volumes. Naturally, it opted for a southern route. (Davis's imprimatur wasn't the only thing the southern option had going for it. Among justifications cited for a major land purchase two years earlier had been the Gadsden strip's potential tie-in with a southern right of way.) While the report assembled scads of information and spurred the growth of local lines, it failed to move Congress to act. A sectional stalemate had developed. It persisted until the outbreak of the Civil War ensured that the Southern Express would not be leaving the station.

By then a visionary named Theodore Judah was lending his considerable talents to planning the project's western leg. The Connecticut-born son of an Episcopal clergyman, Judah had studied engineering at the upstate New York school that has since evolved into Rensselaer Polytechnic Institute. But after the death of his father when the boy was thirteen, his formal education ended, and he went to work for the Schenectady and Troy Railroad. He leapfrogged from project to project and firm to firm, rising so rapidly that while Jefferson Davis's crews were in the field compiling their report, Judah, still in his twenties, was put in charge of a daunting task: threading a railroad through the gorge of the Niagara River. He did so well at that and other assignments that in 1854 he was tapped to go west and help launch the first California railroad, the Sacramento Valley. Already, however, he was daydreaming of a transcontinental line. The necessity for him and his wife, Anna, to reach California the old, halting way (in their case, overland through Nicaragua to reach the Pacific) could only have whetted his appetite.

Judah's Eastern know-how proved adaptable to Western conditions, and on the subject of a continent-spanning railroad he became a zealot, called "Crazy Judah" behind his back. To those with the patience to hear him out, though, he exhibited an impressive mastery of facts and figures. He might be a bit dewy-eyed—in an 1857 pamphlet printed at his own expense, he called for "a people's railroad . . . not a stupendous speculation for a few to enrich themselves with . . . [but] a clean thing, built and owned by the people, for its actual cost and no more"—but he had an unrivaled knowledge of what the project would entail. He was also adept with the levers of power. In 1859, after traveling to Washington to lobby Congress on behalf of his pet cause, he wangled an office in the heart of the Capitol—the old vice president's room, no less—where he set up maps, charts, and sketches (by Anna) in what became known as the Pacific Railroad Museum. A bill to his liking was introduced, but continued bickering kept it from going anywhere.

On returning to California, Judah set out to remedy his plan's chief defect: the lack of a specific, practicable route, especially over its biggest obstacle, the Sierra Nevada, whose granite peaks loomed for hundreds of miles on a north-south axis. Everywhere he looked, the Sierra refused to be overcome in one push; behind each front range lay a valley and then a second thrust of peaks. But Judah got a lucky break in the form of a tip from Daniel W. "Doc" Strong, a druggist in the foothills town of Dutch Flat: Donner Pass, not far from the site of an infamous tragedy in 1847, offered a much-desired one-shot ascent—after which it was downhill all the way to Utah Territory (to which the future state of Nevada then belonged). Not only that, but the summit stood at a "mere" seven thousand or so feet, and the upgrade never exceeded a manageable hundred feet per mile.

Now that he had a feasible plan, Judah thought, rounding up the financing would be a snap. He hoped to enlist a host of small investors—would-be plutocrats need not apply. He gave the venture a name, the Central Pacific Railroad Company of California, and went proselytizing. He had some success in Sacramento, but very little in much wealthier San Francisco, where the establishment viewed the railroad as a threat to existing modes of transportation: ships, toll roads, wagons, stagecoaches, even lesser railroads. (Way up in Alaska, the Sitka Ice Company opposed the project for an equally parochial reason. Ice freighted to the Bay Area from the Sierra would undercut the price of the Alaskan product, which had to make a long north-to-south journey in the holds of ships.) Back to Sacramento went Judah, bound for a rendezvous with four men who were to prove themselves indifferent, if not outright hostile, to his vision of building and running a "clean thing."

To appreciate the temper of the time which allowed—even encouraged—Collis Huntington, Mark Hopkins, Leland Stanford, and Charles Crocker to pile up whopping fortunes at public expense, it might help to know how a bellwether of the era characterized the economic order. Henry Ward Beecher, a man of the cloth famous for his charisma and abolitionist sermons (and also for his adultery), traced the Gilded Age economic-might-equals-right ethic to a divine origin. In an 1877 article commenting on a strike, Beecher asked rhetorically:

Are the working men of the world oppressed? Yes, undoubt-edly, by governments, by rich men, and by the educated classes—not because of selfishness and injustice but because it *must* be so. Only in the household is it possible for strength and knowledge and power not to oppress weakness and igno- rance and helplessness.

Not only that, Beecher went on, but the Christian God was a laissez-faire deity, who "gave me my right to liberty when he gave me myself; and the business of government is to see that nobody takes it away from me unjustly—that is all." (In that case, a sharp observer might have wondered, wasn't the government overreach- ing when it extended a helping hand to private enterprise? Any such objection, however, would probably have been dismissed as petti- foggery.) The human hierarchy, Beecher insisted, reflected "natural law"—a term employed, then as now, to close off debate. It means little more than "the law that comes naturally to people like me." On another occasion, Beecher gave a sermon in which he said, "God has intended the great to be great, and the little to be little." (Beecher, incidentally, has a direct connection with the Central Pacific. In 1884, when the widowed Collis Huntington married for the second time, Beecher officiated.)

Four of the ruggedest individuals to flourish in this God-given, don't-tread-on me world had migrated west around the time of the Gold Rush and quickly noticed something to which most of their fellow fortune hunters were blind: Prospecting was a hit-or-miss occupation, but selling supplies was a sure thing. The most forceful member of the group, Collis Potter Huntington, was such a natural- born entrepreneur that, en route in 1849, he'd made lucrative use of his purgatory on the Isthmus of Panama. While most travelers cooled their heels and fanned their torsos as they waited for passage on a ship to California, Huntington went into action. With money saved by crossing the twenty-four-mile-wide isthmus on foot, the Connecticut native bought items from local suppliers and sold them to his fellow argonauts. After six weeks of dealing, he boarded a boat to San Francisco with $3,000 more in his pockets than when he'd arrived.

Settling in Sacramento, Huntington took advantage of that town's proximity to the Gold Rush by trading in anything the forty-niners might need or want, from grub to blasting powder. Soon, however, he specialized, going partners in a hardware store with Mark Hopkins, an analytical introvert from New York State by way of Michigan who was a whiz at bookkeeping and a scrawny physical contrast to the ursine Huntington.

A decade later, in November of 1860, Judah made a presentation on his favorite subject at a Sacramento hotel. Among his listeners were Huntington and Hopkins; Leland Stanford, a portly, glad-handing wholesale grocer; and Charles Crocker, a hardworking but tactless dry goods merchant—also corpulent. (Assemble the Big Four for a photo, and you would have had to warn the three bossy bears not to crowd out the retiring string bean.) Stanford had been born near Albany, New York, and Crocker in Troy, meaning that the quartet—and Judah, too—all hailed from basically the same part of the world. They had in common, too, their opposition to slavery and loyalty to the Republican Party, which for Huntington included a fascination with backstage political maneuvering and for Stanford a yen to step out front and be a player. (Crocker had just been elected to the state assembly, but just what he might be keen on, or good at, was as yet unknown.) Three of the four were roughly the same age—late thirties—with Hopkins a decade older. Stanford had made a bundle as a mine owner, and the other three had prospered as store-keepers. But none of them was cash rich (Huntington later esti-mated that he was worth about $200,000 in 1862—a lot of money, to be sure, but most of it was tied up in property); nor, as they later admitted, did they know beans about railroading. Yet they were all gifted with the same ability: to make the most of such opportunities as came their way.

Judah had learned something from his rebuff in San Francisco:

Tailor your message to your audience. The sky might be the limit for this project, but why look heavenward when you can point to something much closer and almost as big—the Comstock Lode?

Wedged inside a mountain in the western elbow of Nevada, the lode was yielding great quantities of silver and gold. The rush had started in the late 1850s, when word got out that the "blue stuff" being discarded by scattered gold prospectors as they worked the gulches of Sun Mountain (later Mt. Davidson) was actually silver-bearing ore. Hopefuls by the thousands surged east over the Sierra by stagecoach or on foot, seeking a replay of 1849, albeit one with more staying power. Which is to say that many forty-niners had been victimized by a kind of geological trick. After a year or two of strikes made by small-scale operators using minimal equipment—a pick, a pan, in some cases a rocker—the gold in the California hills had transferred its favors to the well-off. With the easy pickings exhausted, the remaining ore was to be found imbedded in rock, from which it had to be blasted loose by pressurized water shot through canvas hoses. This was hydraulic mining, and it required far more capital than the average roughneck could scrape up. The "little guy" was soon out of his depth in California gold country; but Virginia City, the town that sprang up directly above the Comstock mines, offered a second chance.

Unfortunately, that chance, too, was to pan out for only a few. Comstock silver, it turned out, was even harder to separate from the matrix than second-stage California gold. After being chiseled and hauled out of deep mines, ore-bearing Comstock rock had to be carted to mills: factory-like buildings where it was crushed by steam-driven stamps and subjected to complex chemical processes that ultimately yielded pure silver. All this took capital and organization and a large work force—along with materiel and tools for building and servicing the machines, as well as supplies for booming Virginia City itself. The Comstock frenzy ultimately disappointed almost everyone except a small group of owners and investors (most of them represented by the Bank of California); speculators in mining stocks and especially their San Francisco brokers; and those who had settled into the unglamorous niche of tradesman, including, in the early days, Huntington, Hopkins, Stanford, and Crocker.

That Comstock collision between revived hopes and harsh reality still lay in the future, however. As Judah made his pitch, the wave of mill building was just forming, and would-be prospectors were still converging on Nevada (recently split off from Utah as a territory unto itself), unaware that their lot would almost surely be not to strike it rich but rather to work for someone else at $4 a day. There was no sign of a letup in the influx of either machinery or men, and that night in Sacramento Judah mentioned his railroad's potential as a link in the supply line to Comstock country. Whether and how the new enterprise would plug into a transcontinental route need not be decided now because its first leg would be a bully investment in its own right.

Judah knew railroads, and he seemed well-versed in Washington politics. Several attendees at that first gathering bought small amounts of stock in his fledgling enterprise; Huntington, however, hung back. But he did invite Judah to make a follow-up pitch, which took place the next evening, probably in a spare room above the Huntington-Hopkins store. This time the engineer refined an argument that seems to have tipped the balance: A wagon road running from the Comstock mines to the railroad right-of-way could be built almost immediately, and the tolls collected would reward investors whether the transcontinental phase of the project succeeded or not. The more Huntington mulled it over, the more he warmed to the idea, and it didn't hurt that Abraham Lincoln, the Illinoisan who had just won election as the first Republican president of the United States, was a former railroad lawyer, on record as supporting a transcontinental line. But Huntington came around on his own terms. He urged Judah to concentrate less on rounding up small subscribers and more on lining up a reliable coterie of hands-on investors who would stick with him through adversity. Judah was amenable. His idea had been rattling around inside his head too long, and he was becoming less picky about the means to his end. With contributions from Huntington and a few others, he was ready to take the first step—a field survey. As Anna Judah commented, "It's about time somebody else helped."

In a foretaste of the epic toil to come, the survey proved quite challenging. In June of 1861, Judah wrote to Anna, describing a day's work that beat anything he'd supervised in the Niagara River Gorge. Partway up the Sierra, his men were strung out on a slope he called "the worst place I ever saw":

> the river is 1,200 feet below us, and the top of [the] ridge 700 feet above, in places so steep that if you once slip it is all over. To day the boys carried out ropes, the only way for them to get along being to fasten one end of a long rope around their waists, with a man above holding on with a turn around a tree. . . . They make only a mile all day.

As his party inched forward, Judah tried to rationalize away signs (such as the bent angles of tree trunks) that winter snows might bury the right of way. Finishing up in July, he reported to his backers that getting the railroad to the Nevada border would entail carving out eighteen tunnels and cost an average of $88,000 per mile, for a staggering total of $12 million.

Back East, the Civil War had broken out in earnest (and, in the early going, not much to the liking of the overconfident Union). With Congress bereft of Southerners, the way was clear for passage of a Pacific railroad bill, an idea that seemed more attractive than ever thanks to the new importance of Nevada. The more accessible the territory's silver could be made, the stronger the Union would look, especially when it came to obtaining war loans from European bankers. (In recognition of its economic prowess and solidly pro-Union constituency, Nevada was on its way to premature statehood, which it received in 1864.) The Central Pacific incorporated, with a directorate composed of Stanford as president, Huntington as vice president, Hopkins as treasurer, a Sacramento jeweler named James W. Bailey as secretary, Judah as chief engineer, and Crocker as a member of the board. Stanford had run for governor of California once before and lost; he now threw his hat in the ring again, and his chances looked good. It was a propitious time for Judah to consolidate what he had learned from the survey, return to Washington, and make his best case to Congress.

Backed by so many prominent California Republicans, Judah was soon better-placed in Washington than ever. Not only did he reopen the Pacific Railroad Museum at its old stand in the Capitol, but he had himself appointed clerk to the House subcommittee with jurisdiction over Pacific railroad legislation, secretary to the full House committee, and secretary to the Senate committee—an insider's trifecta over which twenty-first-century lobbyists can only drool. A California congressman marveled at Judah's winning personality: "His manners were so gentle and insinuating, his conversation on the subject so entertaining, that few resisted his appeals." Those appeals may well have been seasoned with boodle. Judah had brought along Central Pacific stock with a face value of $100,000, though actually worth far less. We don't know for sure whether he gave some of it away in an attempt to sway votes, but he wasn't a choirboy anymore. (Even if he did compromise his integrity in this case, however, he wasn't ready to go along with any old thing the Big Four proposed; it wasn't long before they had pushed him too far.) Out in California, the election results were in, and the president of the Central Pacific and the governor of the state were about to be one and the same. Some observers looked askance at this welter of power sharing, insider privileges, and bribes—the label "Railroad Congressmen" was already being applied to certain not-so-esteemed gentlemen on Capitol Hill—but others argued that the main thing was to get tracks on the ground, never mind the niceties of political morality. One of the bill's supporters in the House argued that "the Government must come forward with a liberal hand, or the enterprise must be abandoned forever."

Even with Judah maneuvering as a Congressional insider, it took the better part of a year for a railroad bill to wriggle through the legislative process. The one that emerged, in 1862, treated the Central Pacific as rather an afterthought. Entitled "An Act to Aid in the Construction of a Railroad and Telegraph Line from the Missouri River to the Pacific Ocean, and to Secure to the Government the Use of the Same for Postal, Military, and Other Purposes," the law chartered the Union Pacific Company, which presumably would take the lead in building the new railroad westward (it had a potential competitor, however: the Leavenworth, Pawnee & Western, which ultimately became the Union Pacific's Eastern Division). The starting point would be either Omaha, Nebraska Territory, or Council Bluffs, Iowa (St. Louis had fallen out of contention because of its proximity to the war zone). The choice was left to the president of the United States, and Omaha won out. As an already existing entity, the Central Pacific escaped the detailed oversight to which the law subjected the Union Pacific, and besides, the Central Pacific's share of the project was supposed to be limited to the stretch between Sacramento and the Nevada border. A good indication of how Easterners regarded the line's western branch can be gleaned from a dismissive remark by Pennsylvania Congressman Thaddeus Stevens: "The Western soil is but a platform on which to lay the rails to transport the wealth of the furthest Indies to Philadelphia, Boston and Portland."

Federal aid to the companies was to take two forms: land and bonds. For every mile of track, the railroads would receive 6,400 acres from the public domain, in sections alternating from one side of the right of way to the other. These donations had precedents. Many Eastern railroads had received similar land grants, the idea being for the recipient to divide them up and sell tracts to settlers, thereby dotting the landscape with farms and businesses to help make the railroad self-sustaining. The bonds, however, were something new. The United States would tender them as a kind of loan to the Central Pacific (and the Union Pacific), which would turn around and sell them to investors. The bonds would be issued in $1,000 certificates, and the amount periodically handed over by the government would vary with the degree of difficulty: $16,000 for each mile built across flat or gently rolling land, $32,000 per mile in high plains, and $48,000 in the mountains. Each company could sell these bonds as if they were its own instruments, using the revenues to finance construction, with the federal government paying the bondholders 6 percent interest semiannually. Each company was also entitled to issue and sell its own bonds, but the government's lien had priority, meaning that, in the event of default, holders of government bonds would come ahead of other creditors.

After thirty years, the bill would come due. The companies would owe the government both principal and interest (simple interest, not compound) on the borrowed bonds, minus the value of certain services rendered to the government, such as toting the mail, transmitting official telegrams, and ferrying federal troops. To help the railroads meet their obligations, the Act called for "at least five percentum of the net earnings of said road [to] be annually applied to the payment thereof." In 1875, however, the U.S. Supreme Court found this wording too ambiguous to support the government's contention that the specified 5 percent must be handed over periodically. Rather, the Court decided unanimously, the railroads were free to withhold all payments until the bonds had matured. (This postponement helped build momentum for the epic struggle over the so-called funding bill in the 1890s: Having gotten away with paying back nothing for so long, the railroads had fallen in love with the status quo, while the public was eager for the government to finally start getting its investment back.) In both cases—the land and the bonds—delivery was conditional. The company had to lay a certain number of miles of track and meet certain construction standards before the subsidies would flow. The United States was trying to make sure of getting a quality product.

On paper, the deal looked good for the government. All it supplied was land (of which it had plenty), credit, and the promise to make those interest payments, in return for an eventual recapture of principal and interest. True, some risk was involved, but who better than Uncle Sam to take over and finish the project if the private firms should bungle the job? But the deal looked even better for the entrepreneurs. They had three decades in which to make money by selling bonds and charging for the goods and passengers riding their trains—and, of course, they would each end up owning a railroad.

The law was intricate, to be sure, but at least it was finally on the books. After President Lincoln signed it on July 1, 1862, a jubilant Judah wired his Sacramento backers: "WE HAVE DRAWN THE ELEPHANT. NOW LET US SEE IF WE CAN HARNESS HIM UP."

Congressmen Stevens had added to the difficulty of elephant harnessing by inserting a burdensome clause into the new law: The builders of the Pacific railroad had to use American iron only. This proviso forced the companies to bid against their own government, which needed great quantities of iron (along with locomotives and all the other components of a railroad) for the war. Prices went up accordingly, Judah's cost estimates and engineering decisions were looking dubious, and the Central Pacific's bonds became a hard sell. Even after being discounted, sometimes to as low as 19 cents on the dollar, they weren't moving.

Huntington went to New York on a daunting mission—to convince investors that the Central Pacific was a tolerable risk. After being turned down on Wall Street, he had the wit to approach an old supplier of his store: Ames & Sons, shovel manufacturers whose wares Huntington had peddled to California miners—and with which he had a spotless credit record. To jump-start the railroad, Huntington asked the Ameses for a $200,000 loan. Oliver Ames agreed (think of all the shovels the project would need!), but only after extracting personal guarantees from Huntington and his partners that the interest would be paid. These and other pledges—

conjured almost out of thin air thanks to the arm-twisting and self-confidence that soon became Huntington trademarks—enabled him to start buying rails and locomotives and shipping them west via Cape Horn. His success also anointed him as first among equals in the Big Four, who were already conferring separately from the board that supposedly ran the Central Pacific (the insiders' term for themselves was "the Associates"). Out West, however, the Central Pacific was still a cash-strapped vision for which ground had yet to be broken. Its prospects improved when Stanford stepped in, using his clout as governor to persuade several counties and the state itself to invest in and subsidize the line. In San Francisco, the tactics included vote buying to sway the outcome of a referendum on whether the city should invest. Stanford's brother Philip was reported to have gone around distributing $5 gold pieces so wantonly that voters mobbed his buggy. The election went the railroad's way—but at a hidden cost. Resentful San Franciscans had it in for the Central Pacific almost from its inception.

The toll road, meanwhile—the Dutch Flat and Donner Lake Wagon Road, to give it its full name—was coming along swimmingly. This contrast between the slowly stirring railroad and the burgeoning turnpike gave rise to rumors that all the Associates really cared about was hogging transportation routes to and from the Nevada mines. In this reading, they would lay just enough rails to make the most of their wagon road and then give up. "The Dutch Flat Swindle," detractors were calling it—notably the *Alta California*, a newspaper published in San Francisco. This disdain found some support in the Big Four's history. The shopkeepers had proved their mettle as hunters and hagglers—experts at getting hold of what the customer wanted and selling it to him promptly and heavily marked-up. Nothing in their pasts suggested they might have the vision and stamina to construct a railroad. (As it turned out, the naysayers misjudged the Big Four. Their own greatest leap of imagination was not to see themselves as builders of a new railroad, but as owners of a mature one.) The Associates fought back, with

Stanford using his gubernatorial clout to champion the railroad as best he could—until his two-year term ran out (he was not nominated for a second one). His actions helped ensure that the railroad came into being under a cloud of cynicism that was to hover over it throughout its existence.

Judah was beginning to think he'd thrown in his lot with the wrong fellows. His misgivings deepened as the construction phase got underway. "I knew how to manage men," Charles Crocker asserted. "I had worked them in ore-beds, in the coal-pits, and . . . had worked myself along with them." On the basis of these flimsy credentials, his brethren in the Central Pacific hierarchy awarded the contract to build one of the railroad's first stretches to Charles Crocker & Company, a new entity of which its namesake took charge after resigning from the Central Pacific board to avoid charges of conflict of interest. (This noble gesture was vitiated, however, by the identity of his replacement on the board: his brother.) Crocker later admitted there was no "& Company." There was, however, a potential for sizable profits, along with a tacit commitment to share these with the other Associates.

Since this self-contracting page in the Central Pacific's playbook was soon to be copied by other robber barons—including, most scandalously, the Central Pacific's rival the Union Pacific, which created and funneled contracts to a construction firm called Crédit Mobilier—we had better look more closely at its genesis. The desire to control every aspect of the transcontinental project undoubtedly played a part in the Big Four's thinking, but in his magisterial *Empire Express: Building the First Transcontinental Railroad*, David Haward Bain offers another theory, less obvious but quite sensible. Undercapitalization was a common predicament among fledgling railroads, and a standard remedy had developed: The cash-poor railroad would pay the construction company partly in railroad stock. This ploy held a potential danger, though. The construction firm might go out and buy more shares of stock, eventually accumulating enough to take over the railroad. That very thing had happened to the Sacramento Valley Railroad, and to keep it from happening to them the Big Four hit upon the idea of contracting with themselves.

Judah felt, however, that the arrangement offered Crocker too many temptations: to pad costs, skimp on quality, and indulge in bookkeeping sleight of hand. (All these hunches were eventually borne out, though Judah didn't live to see the damage.) But the energized Crocker waxed eloquent at the groundbreaking ceremony, when it finally took place in Sacramento, on January 8, 1863. "All that I have," he said, "—all of my own strength, intellect and energy—are devoted to the building of this section which I have undertaken." How effective an "all" this might be was still anybody's guess.

Judah was often out of the loop now because he had to be up in the mountains so much of the time, redoing his preliminary surveys. His animosity toward the other board members increased as they made decisions without consulting him. One in particular galled him: a decree that all board members share equally in the costs of building the railroad—and pay up immediately. The trouble was that Judah couldn't command the kind of the assets that his brethren did. The mutual animosity came out in the open, as Judah acknowledged in a letter to that Sierra pathfinder, Doc Strong.

> I had a blowout about two weeks ago and freed my mind, so much that I looked for instant decapitation. I called things by their right name and invited war; but counsel of peace prevailed and my head is still on; my hands are tied, however. We have no meetings of the board nowadays; except the regular monthly meeting, which, however, was not had this month; but there have been any quantity of private conferences to which I have not been invited.

In this fraught climate, another contentious issue arose—the three-tiered bond payments prescribed by the 1862 Act. Judah had his own idea as to where the Sierra Nevada range began (and thus where the top subsidy-rate of $48,000 per mile would kick in): in the foothills, which first revealed themselves in a lift of land twenty-two miles east of Sacramento. And even that, he thought, might be too generous a call. Some years back the California Supreme Court had ruled in a mining case that the range started thirty-one miles out. Neither of these spots suited the Associates. They were angling for a ruling that the mountains came into being a good deal closer to Sacramento, and Stanford, who was still governor at the time, thought he might be able to get it for them. After all, didn't the state geologist report to *him*?

It was Crocker, however, who escorted that official on a field trip one day late in the winter of 1863 and, as Crocker recollected, "did not ask him to do anything except that I wished him to decide where true justice would place the western base of the Sierra Nevadas." Note that wording: not where the Sierra actually began its majestic climb, but where in "true justice" it ought to. The geologist decided that as good a place as any for the birth of the range was Arcade Creek, a mere seven miles east of Sacramento, where the dark soil of the Central Valley touches the red soil of, arguably, the Sierra Nevada—never mind that the landscape, as a commentator wryly put it, is one that "a casual observer would not be likely to call mountainous." Two federal surveyors approved the choice of mile seven, and in September Huntington sent a report to Washington, asking the secretary of the interior and President Lincoln to go along with The Sudden Sierra. Although the report bore the endorsements of that state geologist and those two federal surveyors, it lacked Judah's—he'd been asked to sign on but had refused. (As an experienced engineer, he knew his topography; to have signed would have betrayed his self-image as a professional.) Historian John Hoyt Williams has calculated what this fiddling with the starting line meant to the Central Pacific: "$480,000 more in government bonds than Judah would have awarded his own company and $768,000 more than the state supreme court would have permitted. Helping to pay for the first stretch of construction, these bonds were of crucial importance to the cash-poor company." Not that the bonds would find their way into the Central Pacific's coffers anytime soon. The United States was holding them back until the railroad hit the prescribed marks of progress and quality. But once the president accepted the new geography, as he did the following January, the Central Pacific's prospects brightened considerably.

Stanford and his cronies had scored a coup. A mountain range had slid more than twenty miles west to enhance their financial position. (In Washington, the Big Four's favorite California congressman joked about his successful lobbying of the president: "my pertinacity and Abraham's faith moved mountains.") Yet for all Judah's dudgeon, a charitable analyst might not blame the Associates too severely for this move. Private investment still lagged, the Associates seemed to have bitten off more than they could chew, and weren't those levels of payment in the 1862 law rather arbitrary, especially since it was obvious by now that not even the top rate of $48,000 per mile would suffice to pay for construction in the alpine High Sierra? The nation really did stand to benefit from faster, more reliable coast-to-coast transportation, and three experts had agreed that the mountains might be deemed to begin closer to town than previously supposed. Among the many sins committed by the Central Pacific, this one might be considered venial—not to mention a clever stroke on the part of Stanford and Crocker. On the other hand, Judah had to work with the Associates every day (or at least every day in which they let him know what they were doing), and he probably sensed that this lesser instance of cheating was a harbinger of greater ones to come. However you come out on the Case of the Moving Mountains, though, the Associates had served notice. In the coming scramble, they weren't likely to miss a trick.

By now Judah, however, was fed up with them. He and fellow board member James Bailey tried to coax a San Francisco banker, Charles McLaughlin, into buying controlling interest in the Central Pacific. McLaughlin, who had also sunk money into another unbuilt California railroad, was tempted—until he learned that Huntington was willing to be bought out. "If old Huntington is going to sell out," he explained, "I am not going in." Whereupon Bailey himself sold out. In a rancorous meeting, Judah blasted the Associates for their ethical shortcomings, and they were sufficiently chastened to make a promise: Each would sell his share in the firm for $100,000 if any other director could raise the money. Either they were bluffing, or the railroad had become a hot potato that none of them wanted to hold. Judah and his wife left for the East, where he hoped to line up new-blood investors in what he still liked to think of as "his" railroad. He regarded transportation mogul Cornelius Vanderbilt as the man to see.

Sailing south, the Judahs passed a northbound vessel with a momentous cargo in its hold: the first locomotive destined for the Central Pacific. Farther on, however, Theodore Judah fell victim to one of the hazards of tropical travel—yellow fever. He hung on through the rest of the voyage, even managing to get off a note to Doc Strong. In it, Judah warned that if he failed in his mission to find a white knight with "experience and capital," the Big Four would "rue the day they ever embarked in the Pacific Railroad." Judah clung to life all the way to New York City, but by then he was beyond help. (Note the irony. Had the engineer been able to travel via the railroad he was trying to build, he would have skirted the fever zone.) Not only did his death on November 2, 1863, at age thirty-seven, leave the Associates stuck with carrying out a project toward which they had cooled. It also removed the main obstacle to a number of practices they were soon to adopt on a grand scale: lying, bribery, shoddy construction, looting of the federal treasury, and monopolization.

two

Hell-Bent for Promontory Summit

Judah's death may have given the Big Four a freer hand, but they still labored under multiple burdens. In Washington, legal requirements and bureaucratic inertia (attributable in part to the distraction of waging the Civil War) held up much-needed federal bonds, and during the summer of 1864 the Central Pacific's treasury sat empty for seventeen nail-biting days. Huntington summed up this and other, similar interludes with a bravado that didn't quite hide the shared anxiety: "I have gone to sleep at night in New York when I had a million and a half dollars to be paid by three o'clock on the following day, without knowing where the money was coming from, and slept soundly."

Along with cash flow, the Central Pacific had a backyard rival to worry about: the newly formed San Francisco & Washoe Railroad. Intending to build east from the Bay Area along the south shore of Lake Tahoe to the Comstock mines, the company tried to improve its position by undermining the Central Pacific's. The San Francisco & Washoe made such a fuss over the (alleged) Dutch Flat Swindle that Placer County, which had a stake in the Central Pacific, took notice. The county board of supervisors dispatched two of its members to Sacramento on a mission to examine the Central Pacific's books for signs of irregularity. They found none. (This was the first and last time outsiders were given a peek at Mark Hopkins's ledgers.)

The San Francisco & Washoe now tried a different tack. The Nevada territorial legislature had assembled to draft a constitution for the incoming state. Officials of the San Francisco & Washoe went to Carson City to plump for the appealing notion of competition among railroads. In handing out state aid, they urged, don't single out the Central Pacific by name; instead, be fair—bestow your favors on whichever railroad reaches Nevada first. A clause to this effect was on the verge of being adopted when ex-Govenor Stanford rode to the rescue, appearing before the legislature to tout the Central Pacific's progress and to argue that a race would likely break both companies, thus delaying rail linkage between Nevada and the rest of the Union. The legislature took his point, and the provision was defeated. Huntington was ultimately to turn against Stanford, writing him off as a pompous shirt, and Charley Crocker assessed him as "awful lazy," so it's important to recognize the man's primordial accomplishments. In this case, as a lawmaker acknowledged, "[There was] no earthly doubt that if Governor Stanford had not come over here, this Nevada Constitution would have contained a clause providing an appropriation of three million dollars for the first road that reached our state line." Indeed, at this point, each of the Associates—along with Crocker's older brother E. B. (for Edwin Bryant), who acted as general counsel—was pulling his weight as they forged the working relationship that helped make them an economic and political powerhouse.

In 1864, both the Central Pacific and the Union Pacific had business to tend to in Washington: getting the transcontinental law amended to remedy certain perceived defects. Without much trouble, the two firms won a reversal of priorities as to those bonds. The government bonds were demoted to the equivalent of a second mortgage; now, in case of financial disaster, the holders of the railroads' own bonds would be paid off first. This change was supposed to make the railroads' bonds more palatable to investors, and to an extent it did. Another amendment doubled the federal land subsidy, awarding each railroad 12,800 acres for every mile built. A third benefited the Central Pacific alone. No longer was it required to throw down its tools at the Nevada border. If it got there first, it could keep going, up to 150 miles farther. In private, Huntington made no secret of his intention to disregard even this limit. He, Stanford, and Crocker rushed over to Carson City, where they obtained a franchise to build all the way across the new state. (Two years later, another "mileage" amendment allowed both railroads to raise money ahead of themselves, as it were. They could obtain federal bonds for advance work up to three hundred miles beyond finished, consecutive track.)

On site, Crocker and his crew had laid a good enough first segment of tracks to get the nod to keep going. On June 6, the Central Pacific carried its first passengers. Granted, after a few miles those passengers had to switch to stagecoaches if they wanted to continue; still, this was encouraging progress. How much more could be made, however, was uncertain, thanks to an outbreak of opportunism. Many of the workmen hoped to strike it rich as miners, and they viewed the railroad as an iron means to a silvery end. They would work their way as close to Nevada as possible, then bolt for the Comstock Lode or the new Reese River mining district. Crocker tried importing fresh-off-the-boat Irish immigrants from New York and looked into the possibility of borrowing Confederate prisoners of war, but the "brawn-drain" continued. According to one estimate, 1,900 out of 2,000 workers ran away that summer. Charley Crocker recalled of this bleak period, "I would have been glad when we had thirty miles of road built to have got a clean shirt and absolution from my debts."

But the Dutch Flat road opened for travel on June 14. (Only

modestly successful at first, it eventually grew into a one-million-dollar-a-year cash cow for the Central Pacific—let detractors make of this what they would.) And even with a depleted workforce, Crocker & Company aced its first major physical test: an excavation called the Bloomer Cut—essentially a roofless tunnel blasted through rock to a depth of sixty-three feet and a length of eight hundred feet. Crocker could now be heard crowing about the bang-up job he and his men were doing. As the line neared the (actual) Sierra slopes, however, the degree of difficulty rose accordingly; and work crews continued to melt away. At the end of 1864, the Central Pacific was still in dubious battle.

Early in the new year, though, Crocker solved his manpower problem. Thousands of Chinese had emigrated to California for the Gold Rush, but racism and resentment of their willingness to work for low pay had fueled widespread discrimination. Stanford had contributed to this ugliness while governor, lashing out at the "dregs of Asia," but where else could Crocker turn? Over the objection of his construction chief, a profane Irish-American named James Strobridge, Crocker hired fifty Chinese workers to haul dirt. They performed this and a succession of increasingly hard tasks so well that Strobridge came around. Crocker's agents rounded up more Chinese workers in California and did some recruiting in China; by the end of the year 7,000 Chinese were on the payroll. Their wages of $30 a month were less than what their white counterparts made, but back in China the cost of living was such that a man who saved up a few hundred dollars could come home and retire on it. As a rule, however, the most skilled labor—carpentry, masonry, and rail laying—was reserved for white men, with the Chinese wielding the picks and shovels.

At first, outsiders tended to denigrate the Chinese—here is one reporter's description of the "Celestials" (from their faith in a celestial kingdom) at work: "They are laying siege to Nature in her strongest citadel . . . the rugged mountains look like stupendous ant-hills. They swarm with Celestials, shoving, wheeling, carting, drilling and blasting rocks and earth, while their dull, moony eyes stare out from under immense basket hats in shape and size like umbrellas." Yet the supposedly cloddish Chinese set a hygienic example by bathing daily and drinking hot tea; they stayed healthy while many of their white co-workers, who shunned baths and drank unboiled water, came down with dysentery. Four years later, after the Chinese had helped conquer the Sierra, another reporter took a closer look. He saw:

> hosts of Chinamen, shortening curves and ballasting the track. Nearly four thousand are still employed in perfecting the road. They are all young, and their faces look singularly quick and intelligent. A few wear basket hats; but all have substituted boots for their wooden shoes and adopted pantaloons and blouses. . . . They are tractable, patient, and thorough; they do not get drunk, nor stir up fights and riots.

Basket hatted or not, the Chinese made all the difference in keeping the Central Pacific rolling. In his annual report for 1865, the railroad's chief engineer concluded that "their quiet efficiency was astounding. The experiment has proved eminently successful."

The Associates' acceptance of the Chinese (up to a point) is of a piece with their abolitionism. The Associates were less prone to racial prejudice than most of their peers, and Huntington in particular, after getting rich, made contributions to black churches and to Booker T. Washington's Tuskegee Institute. He opposed Jim Crow laws in the South and, not long before his death in 1900, spoke out against bigotry at a Southern Pacific gathering: "If we deny to the individual, no matter what his creed, his color or his nationality, the right to justice which every man possesses, there will be no enduring prosperity and [the nation's] decline will surely follow." That someone with no qualms about fleecing his fellow man en masse could deal broad-mindedly and generously with many of them as individuals speaks to the complexity of the human heart, even a robber baron's.

Late in 1865, the outlook for the Central Pacific improved. The first installment of government bonds had come through, along with financing from other sources. In Washington, Huntington took advantage of the anguish and confusion surrounding President Lincoln's assassination to put one over on the secretary of the interior. At Huntington's suggestion, that official approved a map on which the Central Pacific's route stretched all the way to Salt Lake City, in contravention of the statutory language telling it to cease and desist 150 miles into Nevada. (A year later, Huntington persuaded Congress to eliminate all doubt, amending the law once more so that the Central Pacific could build eastward until it met up with the Union Pacific—subject to the approval of route maps by the secretary of the interior. With this change, the transcontinental project became a head-on race. Every mile of track laid by one party entitled it to another helping of federal subsidies and deprived the other party of the same amount. The Union Pacific, however, wasn't overly concerned. They figured the Central Pacific would be bottled up in the Sierra for years.) A federal inspector was sent out to rate the quality of the Central Pacific's construction thus far; he submitted a report so glowing that the railroad reissued it as an advertising pamphlet. Revenue from freight and passengers was trickling in as the line reached Auburn and beyond. Elsewhere in California, a development of great import for the Central Pacific occurred. A new railroad company came into being: the Southern Pacific, with a charter to build south from San Francisco to San Diego, then swing east and join up with a putative railroad expected to arrive from the East. Although no one knew it at the time, the Central Pacific and the Southern Pacific were on course to merge.

The here-and-now Central Pacific, however, was still bogged down on the Sierra's western slope. Dutch Flat loomed ahead, and beyond that symbolically charged town the terrain took a quantum leap in ruggedness, throwing up one gnarly obstacle after another:

steeper grades to be negotiated, thick stands of redwood to be felled, monumental rock formations to be circumvented or removed or tunneled through, punishing high-altitude weather to be endured. The roster of required tunnels had slimmed down to fifteen, but some of these would require Herculean effort, especially Summit Tunnel, overlooking Donner Lake, to be bored through granite to a length of 1,659 feet and followed by six more tunnels in the next two miles. The Central Pacific sent a party ahead to get started on Summit, where the rock was so defiant that a whole day's efforts might produce one inch of forward movement. The best way to attack the formation, it was decided, was by tripling up—chiseling away simultaneously from the front, back, and top. To help with removing chunks of granite and maneuvering timber needed for shoring up the tunnel's walls, Central Pacific mechanics converted an old locomotive into a steam-powered hoisting engine. In the interest of better explosions, nitroglycerin replaced blasting powder for a short time. But the liquid behaved so erratically—going off without warning at a cost of human limbs, organs, and lives—that the experiment was halted. Strobridge himself lost an eye to nitro, prompting the Chinese to refer to him as "one-eye bossy man."

Even lesser Central Pacific tunnels were marvels of engineering. Historian John Hoyt Williams pulled together their typical specifications:

On average, a Central Pacific railroad tunnel was sixteen feet wide at the bottom, sloping gently upward and inward to a height of at least nineteen feet. All tunnels were at least partially lined with stout timber . . . and all were roofed with boarding almost three inches thick. The tunnels' side timbers (braces) were commonly twelve-by-twelve-inch, or even twelve-by-sixteen-inch, redwood—heavy, hard-to-maneuver supports that were held to the walls by long three-quarter-inch-thick iron bolts. The Central Pacific had three sawmills working full time on tunnel supports and crossties. To complicate matters, most of the Sierra tunnels were set on both curves and grades.

Given the challenges involved, the railroad kept a reduced crew working on tunnels throughout the winter of 1865–66.

And what a winter it was—the first of three brutally cold ones in a row. In late September, snow began falling in earnest, effacing the landscape, bogging down the crews, and causing the other Associates to nag Charley Crocker for the way his crews poked along. After making a field trip, however, Stanford sympathized. "The snow would fall sometimes five to six feet in the night," he reported. "I believe in one case that nine feet fell in a single night. It obstructed all the roads, and made it almost impossible to get over the mountains." To help keep the right-of-way open, carpenters built elaborate snowsheds that resembled elongated versions of New England's covered bridges. Eventually, thirty-seven of the top forty miles of Sierra right-of-way were roofed in this fashion.

Far to the east, the Union Pacific was off to a queasy start. Its leadership was given to jockeying for position and quarreling over the best route to take, and the seeds of scandal were already in place, sown by its construction company, Crédit Mobilier. Not only was there substantial overlap between the two firms' boards of directors, but several members of Congress had been roped in as Crédit Mobilier investors. Among them was Representative Oakes Ames, a Massachusetts Republican who belonged to the shovel-manufacturing clan from which Huntington had obtained early credit for the Central Pacific. It was one thing for legislators to accept hard-to-trace cash payments for carrying out a company's wishes (the Huntington method), quite another for them to commit themselves on paper to owning part of the action (the most damning paper was a page in a little black book kept by Congressman Ames). Of more immediate concern was a series of Native American raids. So numerous and fierce were the attacks on whites by the Sioux, Cheyenne,

Arapaho, and other Plains tribes that the Union Pacific had been hard put to finish its field surveys.

As for the construction itself, hardwood for railroad ties didn't grow where the Union Pacific work crews needed it. The solution was to "Burnettize" the flimsy cottonwood that was available. This was a mechanized process for extracting water from the wood and replacing it with a zinc solution that acted as a toughening agent, resulting in a board that might fool federal inspectors but could lead to accidents in the long run. At this point in the two lines' histories, it might have been a toss-up as to which had the greater handicaps to work with: the Central Pacific with the steep contours, adamantine granite, and punishing weather of the High Sierra, or the Union Pacific with its shaky organization, weak wood, and vulnerability to mayhem on the Great Plains.

The following summer, the Central Pacific reached the emotionally fraught crossroads of Dutch Flat. Stung by the swindle charges, the Associates were not about to quit there. They celebrated by throwing a party on July 4, 1866, and exulted some more by naming the next station up the line Alta—a dig at the *Alta California*, the newspaper that had cried "swindle" the loudest. With Alta bagged, the line now stretched 69 miles from Sacramento and attained an altitude of 3,602 feet.

Another milestone was marked in November, when the line made it to the town of Cisco, only a dozen miles short of Donner Summit (as mentioned, the Summit tunnelers were working ahead of the rail layers, and, still farther along, grading crews were already gentling the down slope beyond). At 5,911 feet above sea level, the Central Pacific was temporarily the highest railroad in the land.

Several hundred miles to the east, however, the Union Pacific was finally picking up steam. With the U.S. Army making its presence felt (a presence that included a cavalry contingent led by

Colonel George Armstrong Custer), the Native American threat dropped to a bearable level. The company's leadership had achieved a tenuous singleness of purpose; its stock and bonds were selling like mad; and its construction bosses had organized the various tasks into clockwork, as reported in the *New York Herald*: "[The men toiled] with the regularity of machinery, dropping each rail in its place, spiking it down, and then seizing another. Behind them, the locomotive; before, the tie-layers; beyond these the graders; and still further, in the mountain recesses, the engineers. It was civilization pressing westward. . . ." Amid all this bustle, quality control was not a priority. As one higher-up slyly instructed the workers, "Make it as perfect as possible consistent with the rapidity of construction demanded."

Had they been aware of the Union Pacific's fast, if mechanistic, pace, the Central Pacific crews—shivering in the mountains, stopping to build snowsheds, wrestling with boulders and domes and scarps, having to settle for their daily inch—would have chafed all the more at their near stasis. They also would have envied the Union Pacific crews their vices. A swarm of tent- and wagon-based diversions—whiskey, women, and gambling dens—had attached itself to the Union Pacific like a parasite. Whenever the track head got too far beyond this red-light zone, the "entertainers" would break camp, load everything up, and circle around to the new nucleus. A wag called the phenomenon "Hell on Wheels," contributing a phrase to the American vernacular.

For the comparatively wholesome Central Pacific workers, the winter of 1866–67 was even harsher than the one before. Even so, work on Summit Tunnel continued, and a breakthrough occurred when workmen excavating vertically hit grade level, where they could start chipping out horizontal passages toward the front and rear. An observer left a vivid description of how the Chinese tunnelers coped with that winter: "[they] lived practically entirely out of sight of the sky . . . their shacks largely buried in snow. They dug chimneys and air shafts and lived by lantern light. They tunneled their way from the camps to the portal of the tunnel to work long underground shifts. A remarkable labyrinth developed under the snow."

Far above ground, one snow-pompadoured cliff posed such a hazard that something had to be done. An intrepid volunteer climbed to the top of the fixture, deposited a powder keg, and lit the fuse. As described by an eyewitness, there ensued one of the most striking scenes in Central Pacific annals. "A white column shot up a hundred feet, and then the whole hill-side was in motion: it came down a frozen cascade, covered with glittering snow-dust for spray. It was a rare sight, for snow-slides are so rapid and noiseless that comparatively few are seen."

As winter sputtered out, One-Eye Bossy Man agreed to give nitroglycerin another try. This time it exploded on schedule, without maiming anyone, and nitro was in. Not so with another proposed innovation: steam-powered drills. Stanford thought they were worth a shot, but Strobridge said no, and Charley Crocker backed him up. E. B. Crocker lamented this failure to adopt what soon became standard equipment around the world: "It puts me out of all patience to see how that drilling machine matter was mismanaged. . . . The truth is things have got to such a pass that there can't be a thing done unless it suits Stro. Whenever a man gets Charles' confidence, he swears by him and all he says or does is right."

At roughly the same time, the Central Pacific needed a fresh infusion of federal bonds, but gaps in the tracks blocked the way. The amended Pacific Railroad law seems to have reflected a congressional attempt to crawl into the road builders' minds and figure out how they might cut corners—by, for example, slapping down a token segment of tracks far ahead of the advancing line and then claiming bonds commensurate with the full distance. Such a gambit was undesirable because, should the company fail, the government could get stuck with having lent money for a gap-filled and unusable road. Hence the statutory provision permitting the railroads to collect bonds for up to three hundred miles beyond the railhead, but only if the tracks leading up to that point were continuous. The rule might sound more suited to a board game than to a construction project, but it did have a rationale.

Viewed in this light, the Central Pacific's division of laborers, with a party or two working miles ahead of the main body, might be efficacious, but it was also limiting. Until the railroad caught up with itself, it would be in straitened circumstances. Yet—and here the reader can only gasp at the Associates' daring and resourcefulness—this was also the period when the firm began assembling its monopoly. Somehow over the next several months, they scraped up the cash and credit either to buy outright or gain control of one California railroad after another: the Western Pacific, the Yuba, the Southern Pacific, and others. These acquisitions were not made without some gulping, especially by Hopkins, who worried about the financial risks. But by now the Big Four plus E. B. Crocker had established strong bonds of mutual trust (if not a great deal of demonstrable affection) and settled into an executive rhythm. Their solidarity allowed them to weather—and hide from outsiders—this new period of near bankruptcy. Nonetheless, in the midst of it all the normally unflappable Huntington found himself flapped. "It costs a fearful amount of money to pay all the bills," he wrote Hopkins from New York on March 12. "I sometimes think I would change my place for any other in this world."

In June, the Associates met with a check from an unexpected quarter—the Chinese, who struck for higher wages and shorter hours. Charley Crocker had let himself get emotionally invested in the payment process. Once a month, he made a ritual of mounting a horse carrying leather saddlebags that bulged with coins. He would ride out to meet his workmen in the field, take out a sheet of paper, and read names aloud. Then, according to historian Oscar Lewis:

As each stepped forward he dipped into the saddle-bags—gold on one side, silver on the other—and dropped the coins into the lifted palm. It was a chore he insisted on doing himself. Riding up the noisy canyon with a hundred and fifty pounds of gold and silver in his saddle-bags appealed to his sense of the dramatic, and its distribution periodically confirmed a pleasant sense of power.

Having already raised pay for the Chinese to $35 a month, Crocker took the walkout as a personal affront. He cut off supplies, food included, and let the Chinese stew for a week. Then he went out to parley. He offered to cancel the fines they would otherwise have had to pay for not working, but beyond that he would not go. They could take $35 or leave it. They blinked and took it. With his firmness, Crocker had prevailed, but his triumph may have done the Associates a disservice. Over time his tough negotiating stance was to harden into a rigid refusal to give ground under any circumstances—a trait that landed him and his partners in trouble on at least two later occasions.

For now, though, Crocker was entitled to preen a little. He could indeed manage men, and the other Associates happily left that chore to him while continuing to perform their respective roles. In the West, Stanford was the public face, Hopkins juggled the money, and E. B. Crocker interpreted the law. In the East, Huntington raised capital, obtained credit, procured needed materiel, and peddled influence. Oh, and one more task would have appeared on his job description: intelligence gathering, especially on what the Union Pacific was up to. (One of his secret agents was John Boyd, a doorkeeper at the Capitol, who will reappear as Huntington's faithful "tapeworm" in the funding-bill controversy of 1896–97.) This proliferation of duties made Huntington the hardest-working Associate (though E. B. Crocker would have run him a close second), and his displays of energy can put even the best twenty-first-century workaholics to shame. When Congress was in session, he often spent four days of the week in Washington, followed by two in New York and one in Boston.

In contrast to this smooth pooling of efforts, the Union Pacific's hierarchy had fallen into disarray again, with warring factions running to court and seeking injunctions against one another. (They did have an advantage denied the Associates, however. In the fall of 1866, their chief engineer, Grenville Dodge, had been elected to the U.S. House of Representatives from a district in Iowa; along with Oakes Ames, that gave them two House members in the "family.") Out in the field, not snow but rain was beleaguering the westward-building road, washing out bridges and bringing supply trains to a halt. The Union Pacific had supposedly been allotted the easier portion of the West to build through, but in the wet spring of 1867 they might have contested that point.

Courtesy of Huntington's spies, the Associates had a pretty good idea of the Union Pacific's plans and woes. Rumor had it that, as the two rivals edged toward the battleground of Utah, the Union Pacific would gallivant hundreds of miles ahead of its consecutive line, slap down a segment of tracks, and claim all the intervening territory—no matter what the law said. This disturbing possibility got E. B. Crocker to thinking, and in a July 11, 1867, letter to Huntington, the lawyer proposed one of the responses the Central Pacific ultimately made:

> We will of course go right on in good faith, grading a reasonable distance in advance to keep the tracklayers steady at work. If in so doing we should meet a company of Union Pacific graders, or a portion of road graded by them, not connected with a continuous line, we should keep right on, grade our road right alongside their grading until we should "meet & connect" with their continuous line of track.

The Central Pacific, in other words, would be the arbiter here.

In early August, the Donner Summit drama reached a climax. After a nitro blast at the western end of the tunnel died away, the men clearing out the rubble felt a breeze on their faces. A passageway now stretched unclogged from east to west, joining what had been three converging shafts. The result deviated from its blueprint dimensions by a mere two inches, and at 7,042 feet above sea level the line had reached its highest point. Much hollowing out remained to be done, and the tracklayers had to catch up, but in the words of historian David Haward Bain, "It was beginning to look like a railroad there." Central Pacific bonds were now being advertised for as much as 95 percent of par, and the Associates amused themselves by poring over maps and playing comparative geography. True, the Union Pacific had thrown down about five hundred miles of track, nearly five times the Central Pacific's total. But numbers could be deceptive. By the Associates' reckoning, they had put their hardest miles behind them, whereas the Union Pacific was about to enter the highest altitudes—with the severest weather—of its route. "I tell you," E. B. Crocker assured Huntington, "we have got the Union Co. as tight as bricks." He might have been over-emoting, but by the fall of 1867 the Central Pacific could be forgiven for feeling its oats.

That year, incidentally, the Union Pacific played its own version of Magic Mountain. It was time to pinpoint the spot where the Union Pacific's subsidy rate would rise to the top bracket of $48,000 a mile, and the Andrew Johnson administration dispatched someone to make the call. This was an engineer named Jacob Blickensderfer, who represented the government on the railroad's board of directors; it was up to him to say where the Rocky Mountains begin. Blickensderfer might have been disinterested at the outset, but he didn't stay that way long. The Union Pacific's Utah division needed a planning engineer, and an offer was made. Blickensderfer accepted and promptly obliged his new employers by locating the mountains' origin six miles east of Cheyenne (in what is now the state of

Wyoming), a site that, according to an historian, "no one else had suspected." The Big Four weren't the only magicians who could move mountains.

Back East, Crédit Mobilier was further entrenching itself on Capitol Hill. Not content with the handful of lawmakers who owned stock in that Union Pacific subsidiary, Congressman Ames lassoed nine more representatives and two senators, all but one of them Republicans. Foolishly, they allowed Ames to hold their stock in his name, even though the dividends were paid to them, thereby making it look as if they had something to hide. Those dividends, however, were lavish, and for the time being just about everyone loved Crédit Mobilier. Even the Associates were impressed: In reorganizing Crocker & Company that fall, they picked "California Crédit Mobilier" as the new name. A day later, however, came news that the original Crédit Mobilier, the Union Pacific subsidiary's French namesake, had gone bust. The Associates quickly switched to the less chic "Contract & Finance Company," thereby saving themselves from a malodorous association a few years later.

The Central Pacific celebrated an insiders' milestone on November 30. Stanford, Hopkins, the Crockers, and their wives all came out to watch the Chinese wrap up work on the Summit Tunnel and its tracks, whereupon a locomotive entered the passageway on the west side and exited on the east. The normally staid Hopkins captured the event's significance in a bubbly letter to Huntington: "At last we have reached the summit, are on the downward grade & we rejoice. The operators & laborers all rejoice—all work freer & with more spirit—even the Chinamen partake of our joy."

As 1867 came to a close, however, the euphoria gave way to a sense of stark reality. Once again, the Associates had stretched their assets parchment thin, and costs continued to mount. The advance parties on the east side of the Sierra needed heavy hardware, such as rails, freight cars, and locomotives; but this wasn't always to be obtained and, even when it was, had to be rolled on logs across gaps in the line, at great expense. The company later reported that it had spent more than $4 million to overcome the seventeen most arduous miles of the Sierra but that the government subsidy for that stretch had amounted to only $816,000—and was not handed over until a year after the work was done. The Central Pacific could now boast of having more men on the east side of the Sierra than on the west, but its attention was still divided among three sections of track, at least two of which must be linked before more federal subsidies would flow. Another winter was setting in, and the supposedly easy hundreds of miles across the flats and gentle inclines of Nevada were beginning to look like the grapes of Tantalus, poised to spring out of reach just as they looked close enough to pluck.

E. B. Crocker had come to share Hopkins's willies about the buying up of other railroads. "We are expanding too much—getting too much on our hands—too much of the grasping monopoly," the lawyer had complained to Huntington in September. A few days later, Crocker elaborated on his theme: "We can't expect to monopolize all the good things in the State [of California]. We will make enemies by it." Sage advice—but it was not to be heeded. Certainly not by Huntington, who was now working at peak efficiency— ingratiating himself with legislators in Washington, procuring hardware in New York, and lining up credit wherever he happened to be. On December 27, he wrote Crocker a letter that fairly steamrolled over the latter's misgivings: "I think if 1868 should be financially [the same] as 1867, I can supply you with what money you will need to lay 350 miles of Road, and if so, can you do it?" The brashness of this prediction becomes clear when one takes note of how many miles of track the Central Pacific had laid in all of 1867: thirty-nine. (In the event, the Central Pacific did meet its goal of laying 350 miles in 1868, plus a few more for good measure.)

The Union Pacific received unwelcome attention in the new year. Its bonds were selling well, and stock in Crédit Mobilier even better, but its poor workmanship was becoming hard to ignore. The company had been caught violating a federal standard by laying a mile of track on only 1,091 ties instead of the prescribed 2,400. Many of its ties consisted of Burnettized cottonwood, and the use of sand as ballast made the roadbed liable to shift and sag. Even in the pro-railroad 40th Congress, anti–Union Pacific sentiment was growing, and Huntington fretted about a possible spillover effect in a letter to E. B. Crocker:

> As the Union Co. are so very corrupt, it has to a considerable extent demoralized all the Road being built under the Pacific R.R. Act—and I should not be surprised if Congress should order a committee to overhaul all the Co's., and while I know everything is All Right with the C.P., I would be very careful that the Co's. Books should make it so plain that any one could so see it.

By comparison, the Central Pacific may have been doing fairly decent work, but that could change at any time, as witness an instruction from Huntington to Charley Crocker: "when a cheap road will pass [inspection], make it cheap." When not writing admonitory letters, Huntington continued to maneuver with remarkable skill. He coaxed a $500,000 loan out of German investors. At one point in the summer of 1868, he had thirty ships at sea carrying supplies and equipment for the Central Pacific. On learning that the Union Pacific sought 60,000 tons of iron for rails, he bought every scrap of available iron, cornering the market for a while. He tended to members of Congress in need of campaign funds for the fall election, among them Senator William Morris Stewart of Nevada.

Huntington's lobbying skills attracted the notice of Washington reporter Emily Briggs, who left a memorable portrait of him as a one-man devil-fish (octopus):

> Floating in Congressional waters . . . at all hours of the legislative day may be seen the burly form of Huntington, th·

great, huge devil-fish of the railroad combination. . . . He ploughs the Congressional main, a shark in voracity of plunder, a devil-fish in tenacity of grip; for once caught in the coils of the monster for the helpless victim there is no escape. At the beginning of every session, this representative of the great Central Pacific comes to Washington . . . secures his parlors at Willard's [Hotel], which soon swarm with his recruits both male and female. . . . Every weakness of a Congressman is noted, whilst the wily Huntington decides whether the attack shall be made with weapon of the male or female kind.

Briggs didn't say so, but one of Huntington's techniques was bribery. This is not just an educated guess—the man himself admitted as much. As early as 1866, after passage of the amendment to cancel the 150-mile limit on the Central Pacific's incursion into Nevada, Massachusetts Senator John B. Alley had accused Huntington of paying members of Congress to vote his way. Huntington shot back that he had indeed brought money with him to the Senate gallery but, on peering at the Senate floor through a spyglass, concluded that only one lawmaker was corruptible. "And," he concluded, "you know devilish well I didn't try it on *you!*"

With time and practice, Huntington developed a philosophy of corruption, which he expressed as follows:

circumstances arise sometimes when power gets into the hands of corrupt men, who withhold justice and are perfectly willing to ruin others to sustain themselves . . . and when the only possible way of obtaining justice is by the use of influence in whatever form is essential and inevitable; in such cases bribery may be the last and only means left to honest men.

There is also a tacit corollary: The one who makes the call is none other than the briber himself.

Out in Nevada, life proceeded on a less philosophical plane. With no time to worry about his workers' morale, let alone ethics, Strobridge had perfected his own method of robotic construction. His workforce was now laying rails like an army of soldier ants. As described by John Hoyt Williams:

> Under this system, a first gang of tie men placed only every other tie, with a second tie gang following minutes behind to place the rest. These were followed by a crew of levelers, who jostled, kicked, and aligned and seated the ties to a more or less uniform height, and the track men, who were instantly followed by two lines of spikers, one driving half the spikes and the others finishing the job. Under this evolving regimen, Strobridge began hitting his stride, and enjoyed his first two-mile days.

Big news reached the head of the line on June 15: The Sierra gap in the tracks had been closed. This achievement was all the more impressive in light of the obstacles overcome. Gargantuan snow and ice packs left over from another severe winter were broken up and hauled away, and a new crisis with the Chinese was defused—not a strike this time, but a wave of panic. Someone had whispered to them that the way ahead was crawling with murderous Native Americans and gigantic snakes, and many workmen had packed up and left. To calm them down, Strobridge had escorted a small party of Chinese ahead for a look-see; after encountering no hostiles and few vermin, they spread the word, and the exodus stopped.

Newly poised at the head of a continuous stretch of tracks, the Central Pacific was eligible for another infusion of federal bonds. The Union Pacific had long been a darling of the press, but its rival's feats were beginning to draw notice. An Eastern railroad expert pronounced "the crossing of the Sierra Nevada Mountains . . .

the greatest achievement yet accomplished in Civil Engineering."
Far from resting on its laurels, though, the Central Pacific responded
by dividing its forces anew. Charley Crocker sent three thousand
Chinese into Utah to start grading a right-of-way through a clus-
ter of narrow canyons called the Palisades.

The Union Pacific, on the other hand, was being second-guessed.
After conducting a preliminary survey of its work, an outside observer estimated that it would take at least $3 million to bring its
tracks up to standard. Probably goaded by Huntington, Interior
Secretary Orville Browning appointed a commission to flyspeck
the whole Union Pacific line, and the results were alarming. Forget
the $3 million figure; it would cost almost $6.5 million to solve a
laundry list of problems, among them replacing 525,000 weak cottonwood ties. No wonder the Union Pacific had been setting records
of four, six, even seven miles of track laid per day—it was building
rubbish. Further tarnishing the railroad's reputation were the huge
dividends flowing to owners of Crédit Mobilier stock. During one
twelve-month period investors in that enterprise were paid more
than $20 million on an initial investment of $3.75 million.

To appear evenhanded, Browning ordered a similar inspection of
the Central Pacific's work. But one of the assigned commissioners
was so complaisant that he applied a sleep test: If he could doze off
during a ride, the train and its tracks must be safe and sound. Charley
Crocker rose to the occasion, plying the would-be snoozer and his
colleagues with booze. "The train stopped, the engine took a drink,
and so [did] the Commissioners," he recalled. "In truth we became
hilarious. Toasts were called for and drank with vim and enthusiasm, the desert was forgotten, and all went 'merry as a marriage
bell.'" In the end, the Central Pacific was cited for defects that would
cost only $310,000 to fix. This leniency surprised even that arch-
conniver Huntington, who teased Crocker: "I think you must have
slept with [the inspectors]. There is nothing like sleeping with men,
or women either for that matter." Union Pacific officials smelled a
whitewash, and indeed Browning was not very adept at concealing

his bias. (Huntington had curried favor by entrusting his lobbying of Browning to one of the secretary's former law partners.) Browning blocked the release of new bonds to the Union Pacific for several months, only to relent under pressure and let them go toward the end of the year.

With its slipshod methods, the Union Pacific was able to lay 425 miles of tracks in 1868, as opposed to 363 for the Central Pacific (most of the Central Pacific's total came in the second half of the year, after the company had stepped down from the Sierra). Only three hundred miles now separated the two lines, and Charley Crocker was inspired to make a bet with the Union Pacific's influential vice president, Thomas C. Durant (the man who had the title of president was a figurehead): The Central Pacific could lay ten miles of track in a single day. In a more serious vein, representatives of the two sides met from time to time, trying to work out what should happen when their respective vanguards finally met. The discussions were inconclusive.

All the while, the Central Pacific continued to expand and acquire, marching toward octopus-hood. It added two start-ups to its holdings: a ferry company to serve San Francisco Bay and an ice company in the Sierra (thereby confirming the worst fears of those icemen up in Sitka). It also bought the Napa Valley Railroad and ordered surveys for a future San Joaquin Valley Railroad. Yet despite these outlays, the fiscal outlook for the Central Pacific was improving by the month. It was about to connect with the Virginia & Truckee Railroad, which promised to feed robust traffic from the Comstock mines; and tourists were now riding Central Pacific trains to resorts that had sprung up amid Sierra peaks and lakes opened up by the Central Pacific itself. (Despite rumors to the contrary, in the early going the Associates had little luck marketing their federal land grants, although in Nevada they did score a small triumph by auctioning off lots on which the new town of Reno was soon built.)

Early on, analysts had tended to visualize the Central Pacific as forever wrestling with the Sierra tar baby while the Union Pacific romped through Utah and much of Nevada. But now the whole of Nevada was looking like the Central Pacific's bailiwick, and what would happen in Utah was anyone's guess. An exchange of telegrams in mid-April of 1868 reflected this shifting dynamic. After the Union Pacific ran tracks over Sherman Summit in Wyoming Territory, Durant taunted Stanford by wire: "We send you greeting from the highest summit our line crosses between the Atlantic and Pacific Oceans. Eight thousand two hundred feet . . . above the tide water. Have commenced laying the iron on the down grade westward." Stanford's suave reply bespoke a quiet confidence:

> We return your greeting with pleasure. Though you may approach the union of the two roads faster than ourselves, you cannot exceed us in earnestness of desire for that great event. We cheerfully yield you the palm of superior elevation. Seven thousand and forty-two feet . . . has been quite sufficient to satisfy our highest ambition. May your descent be easy and rapid.

But was the Central Pacific really ready to concede a faster approach to the Union Pacific? At this point, Huntington began crossing ethical lines with abandon. As an acquaintance later summed him up, "[There was] something tigerish and irrational in his ravenous pursuit. He was always on the scent, incapable of fatigue, delighting in his strength and the use of it, and full of the love of combat. . . . If the Great Wall of China were put in his path, he would attack it with his nails."

In this case, he used his nails to play amateur lawyer and cartographer. It had occurred to him that technically the law didn't prevent either railroad from working far ahead of its continuous self—only from receiving federal bonds for doing so. Secretary Browning had the authority to establish routes, and Huntington submitted a new map consisting of a red line drawn crudely through a nearly blank expanse across Nevada and into Utah. If the secretary signed off on this, Huntington meant to claim legal sanction for the Central Pacific's overreaching. Its route would be the official one for that segment of the line, the Union Pacific would be left out in the cold, and the Central Pacific could send construction crews ahead (the bonds could wait until the railroad had overtaken itself again). Browning was inclined to grant the favor, but first he covered his derriere by getting an OK from the attorney general. With that in hand, Browning not only approved the map but acceded to Huntington's request to keep the decision from the Union Pacific for several weeks. In effect, one runner in the race had lunged ahead without the other's knowledge. Nor was this enough for Huntington. In a letter to E. B. Crocker, he proposed lying about where they were, sending a party all the way to Weber Canyon in Utah "as soon as we get within say, 400 miles, of course claiming that the distance is inside of 300."

That "of course" should not be overlooked. It indicates that the Associates' most influential member had embraced the perversion of the golden rule later formulated by Standard Oil magnate Henry Flagler: "Do unto others as they would do unto you—and do it first." (And, indeed, who's to say the Union Pacific wouldn't have foisted a dubious map of its own on Secretary Browning and hired his ex-partner as a go-between if they'd thought of it first?) Each side regarded the other not as a proud partner in carrying out a noble endeavor of great value to a vast but sparsely settled nation, but as a rival for grabbing subsidies from Uncle Sam. The two railroads shared that disdain for government which has been a recurring motif in American history, but even more they subscribed to the notion that only chuckleheads curb their appetites when there is advantage to be gained, no matter who might be harmed in the process.

Again, however, Huntington's voracity did not sit well with all the Associates. Responding to a rumor that the Union Pacific might pull the same trick, E. B. Crocker sounded off in a letter of May 23, 1868:

It is in violation of the act of Congress, & is a piece of sharp practice on the part of Durant—which seems to me will not be sustained by Congress or the Sec. of Interior. It places them in the wrong. Will we not be equally in the wrong if we follow suit, & set men at work more than 300 miles ahead of completed road[?] Bear in mind that ours is a national work, that the public are watching us all. Our strength lies in building [the] railroad fast—& keeping within the law, & acting freely and honorably, free from all sharp practice.

This lecture gave Huntington pause. He temporarily backed away from his suggestion that four hundred miles be passed off as three hundred. "I thought we had better take *high ground*," he explained as if the idea were his, "and confine ourselves to the law until we are where we can make more to break it than keep it."

While Huntington and E. B. Crocker discussed ethics, Charley Crocker needed more men in Utah, and the likeliest source was the Mormon stronghold of Salt Lake City. Recruitment was assigned to the glad-handing Stanford, who had to make nice with Mormon leader Brigham Young while concealing a certain decision already reached. The best route went north of the lake, bypassing Salt Lake City, and that was the one the Central Pacific planned to take (the Union Pacific had reached the same conclusion). Huntington bad-mouthed Stanford behind his back, telling E. B. Crocker that they should have sent "a first-class man" to do the job. Yet, although it took him almost six months, Stanford pulled it off: Young delivered the manpower—and then turned around and did the same for the Union Pacific.

That misbegotten outfit continued to display a formidable talent for internecine warfare, with Durant trying to micromanage construction from New York City. The squabbling got so bad that presidential candidate Ulysses Grant was called into service as a referee while visiting the West in the summer of 1868. He sided against Durant, who was told to stop being so meddlesome.

The main problem facing the Central Pacific that summer was more mundane: lack of spikes and other hardware. Charley Crocker pelted Huntington with frantic wires, but he was distracted by an extraneous issue. No sooner had the Central Pacific consummated the purchase of the Southern Pacific than Secretary Browning cancelled the latter's land grants because it had relocated its southbound route inland, from the California coast to the San Joaquin Valley, without so much as a by-your-leave. We'll consider this tussle more fully in Chapter 9. For now, suffice it to say that Huntington persuaded Browning to cancel the cancellation (as Huntington biographer David Lavender coyly put it, "No surviving letters indicate what considerations led to the Secretary's sudden and remarkable change of mind") and Crocker got his spikes, though not before his men had slowed supply trains to a crawl over half-spiked rails for safety's sake. All this had weighed heavily on Crocker, who warned Huntington not to take him for granted: "I will hold my grip until the C.P. is finished—but I give fair warning that there is to be a fairer division of labor when the other roads are to be built—which have been planned & talked over so lavishly. My time & paper have both given out. *Burn this*—I am ashamed of the complaining spirit manifested."

The recipient of that unburned lament was now plotting at a feverish level—and paying for it with chronic headaches. There were days when Huntington took a train from New York to Washington, squeezed in a few hours of lobbying on the Hill or at the Interior Department, caught a northbound train at the end of the day, made a cameo appearance in his Manhattan office the next morning, and then sneaked onto another Washington train—all to hide his machinations from the Union Pacific. In the end, he just couldn't help himself. He told Browning that whopper about the Central Pacific working no more than three hundred miles ahead of its completed line when it was more like four hundred, and the secretary bought it—or rather, the whole Cabinet did, for Browning ran the matter by them. Elated but in a cold sweat, Huntington pleaded with Crocker to make an honest man of him pronto. "By God, Charley, you must work as man has never worked before," he pleaded.

"Our salvation is in you. . . . *Say nothing, lay the iron on the approved line.*" (Three decades later, testifying before a committee of the U.S. Senate, Huntington offered a quite different—and anodyne— explanation for the Central Pacific's near desperate rush to lay tracks. As reported by Ambrose Bierce, Huntington cited the Associates' "deference to the great number of Californians who wanted to go home 'to see the old folks' in the East.")

The Central Pacific had a way of lucking out when it came to inspections, and the one that took place in November was no exception. This time it wasn't drink that befuddled the inspectors but their own gullibility. The *Sacramento Union* had been calling attention to a stretch of poorly built track in Nevada and especially to its ragged culverts. Traveling with the inspectors, Crocker played illusionist as their train neared the section targeted by the *Union*. As he boasted long afterwards, he placed a tumbler of water on the floor of the car and told the inspectors to watch carefully as the train speeded up. The tumbler stayed upright, with little water being spilled.

> "Now, gentlemen," said I, "there is your Sacramento *Union*." And the commissioners all laughed and said that was the strongest proof that had been given. They did not ask for any more; did not want to get out and look at the culverts; they were satisfied that if we could rush over the road at 50 miles an hour and did not tip over a glass of water it was a pretty safe road and well built—and so it was.

For all its hocus-pocus, however, the Central Pacific did not stoop to some of the Union Pacific's most egregious tactics, such as adding needless curves to pad the number of subsidized miles covered or laying tracks over uncleared ice and snow (with the predictable result that one of its trains slid off the tracks, flipped over, and landed upside down in a ditch). Yet the Union Pacific had a legitimate beef about Browning's approval of the Central Pacific's new route map when that action finally came to light. Asserting that the Union Pacific had already and in good faith graded a hundred miles' worth of territory now assigned to the Central Pacific, Grenville Dodge called the approval "an outrage [that] cannot be justified by any reasoning." Browning protested that his action didn't mean what the Union Pacific thought it did. He'd approved a general path, he insisted, not a specific line—which was not, of course, Huntington's view of the matter. As the year came to an end and the Grant administration prepared to take over in March, the vacillating interior secretary must have been looked forward to vacating his hot seat.

Early in 1869, both railroads came under fresh scrutiny. In the prestigious *North American Review*, Charles Francis Adams, brother of Henry Adams and later president of a railroad (the Union Pacific itself), wrote scathingly about the tendency of federal subsidies to find their way into railroad insiders' pockets. Adams had succeeded in uncovering few hard facts about the Central Pacific, which he described as "managed by a small clique in California, [with] its internal arrangements [kept] in about the same obscurity as are the rites of Freemasonry." But he'd learned enough about the Union Pacific to level this indictment against its offshoot, Crédit Mobilier:

> It is but another name for the Pacific Railroad ring. The members of it are in Congress; they are trustees for the bond-holders, they are directors, they are stockholders; they are contractors; in Washington they vote the subsidies, in New York they receive them, upon the Plains they expend them, and in the Crédit Mobilier they divide them. Ever-shifting characters, they are ever ubiquitous—now engineering a bill, and now a bridge— they receive money into one hand as a corporation, and pay it into the other as a contractor.

Newspapers echoed these criticisms, and Browning responded by appointing new commissioners to inspect each railroad and decide where the twain should meet. (The Central Pacific had its eye on Ogden, only about fifty miles from the Utah-Wyoming border; the Union Pacific was angling for something farther west.)

By now advance grading parties from the two railroads sometimes found themselves working side by side. This led to some nasty encounters, as described by Dodge: "The laborers upon the Central Pacific were Chinamen, while ours were Irishmen, and there was much ill-feeling among them. Our Irishmen were in the habit of firing their blasts in the cuts without giving warning to the Chinamen on the Central Pacific working right above them." The resulting rockslides killed a few Chinese, and all-out warfare was only narrowly averted. Nor were the two groups using the same engineering playbook. To bridge one chasm, a Union Pacific crew was erecting what they called the Big Trestle while a Central Pacific crew was shoveling into existence what they called the Big Fill. Unless brought under control soon, the two companies might find themselves not just toiling on duplicative grades but each building a railroad to nowhere.

At the same time, winter weather was hitting the Union Pacific hard. First, snow and ice held up progress; then thaws undermined what little of it had been made. Thawing took place on the Hill, too, as Congress showed signs of addressing the growing Crédit Mobilier scandal. Leading the attack on the Central Pacific's rival was Senator Stewart, who raised so much hell that Huntington thought he deserved a special reward. Once the two railroads had joined up later that spring, Huntington put a recommendation to that effect in writing. "Stewart . . . has always stood by us." Huntington reminded Charley Crocker. "He is peculiar, but thoroughly honest, and will bear no dictation, but I know he must live, and we must fix it so that he can make one or two hundred thousand dollars. It is to our interest and I think his right." Instead of one or two hundred thousand dollars, however, "thoroughly honest" Stewart ended up getting fifty thousand acres of land in the San Joaquin Valley. (He was long to remain a faithful servitor of the railroad—at his constituents' expense. In 1881 a Nevada congressman charged that Stewart had stood by for a decade while the Central Pacific charged Nevadans rates 25 percent higher than those paid by Californians.)

The Central Pacific had run into troubles of its own that winter, including a cholera outbreak among the Chinese and more work-stopping blasts of profound cold in the Sierra Nevada. But Secretary Browning acceded to Huntington's wishes once again by ordering the Union Pacific to cease construction, this time at Echo Summit in Utah (about midway between Ogden and the Wyoming border), beyond which lay turf covered by the Central Pacific's approved map. (Thus, Browning had pulled another of the reversals in which he specialized: Now he was saying, in effect, that the Central Pacific did indeed "own" the right-of-way through that portion of Utah.) At this point, Huntington began pushing a new brainstorm. He was hot to extend the Central Pacific's territory almost to Ogden, where he dreamed of building a new city as the hub of the interior West. (This metropolis never materialized.) The Union Pacific already had men working in the vicinity of Ogden, but Mormon graders under the Central Pacific aegis were out that way, too. Although Huntington had based this series of moves on the theory that the Central Pacific could build ahead with a certain amount of freedom as long as it didn't ask for bonds, he now saw things differently. Surely an approved map triggered the release of bonds—otherwise you would have the wasteful spectacle of two companies simultaneously drawing federal subsidies for laying tracks on separate lines. If Huntington could get Browning to green-light the release of bonds for the contested portion of the line, the effect would be to shove the two railroads' meeting place toward Ogden, with that many more miles' worth of subsidies going to the Central Pacific.

This time, however, Browning dithered. In the waning days of the Johnson administration, the Cabinet approved the bonds' release, the attorney general ruled that Huntington's interpretation of the law was correct, but Browning still had cold feet. He bucked the decision to Treasury Secretary Hugh McCulloch, who also dawdled. Huntington was reduced to making a nuisance of himself by haunting that worthy's anteroom. Late one night, Huntington returned to his hotel room to find a package with the bonds lying on his bed. Amateur lawyer Collis P. Huntington had outfoxed the Cabinet, the Union Pacific, and even his own fellow Associates (Stanford, for one, seems never to have quite grasped Huntington's chain of reasoning in all these transactions).

By April of 1869, the collective brains behind both railroads had reached the same conclusion: better to settle on a meeting place themselves than leave such a vital decision to the government. Accordingly, Huntington and Dodge came face-to-face in the Washington house of a congressman who owned stock in both railroads. They settled on Promontory Summit, overlooking the Great Salt Lake about halfway between the ends of the two sets of tracks as then extant; in deference to Browning's various approvals, however, the Union Pacific would sell to the Central Pacific, at cost, the tracks it had already begun laying between Ogden and Promontory. (The Union Pacific gave in on this point because revelations stemming from a lawsuit brought by Wall Street speculator Jim Fisk had left it embarrassed, weakened, and in dire need of hard cash, even as its leadership was more polarized than ever.) This transfer would leave the Central Pacific owning 744 miles of the transcontinental line, from Sacramento to Ogden; the Union Pacific would own 1,032 miles, from Ogden to Omaha. The following day, Congress passed a joint resolution ratifying the two railroads' decision.

Before the two lines converged, Charley Crocker hastened to make good on his ten-miles-in-one-day bet. (He'd waited until almost the last minute in order to keep the Union Pacific from turning around and outdoing him.) On preimbedded ties, eight Irishmen did the actual rail laying; everything else was left to the Chinese, working together like a single precision instrument. Late on April 28, word of the triumph reached Sacramento by telegraph. Ten miles of track had gone down, plus several more feet for good measure—an improvement of two miles over the Union Pacific's best day. In New York, however, Huntington took a dim view of the stunt. Giving in to months of pent-up frustration, he wrote sarcastically to Crocker on May 10, "I notice by the papers that there was ten miles of track laid in one day on the Central Pacific, which was really a great feat, the more particularly when we consider that it was done after the necessity for its being done had passed."

A couple of weeks after that ten-miler, the Central Pacific mustered surprisingly few dignitaries for the event the nation had been waiting for: the marriage of the transcontinental rails. Huntington was back East, and Hopkins and the Crocker brothers elected to stay in Sacramento, where a shindig was scheduled for the appointed day, May 8. That left Stanford to play his customary role of front man. What the Central Pacific side lacked in mucky-mucks, however, it almost made up for in ceremonial spikes and other trinkets, of which it had toted along plenty. Stanford and his modest entourage reached Promontory Summit by train only to discover that the much larger Union Pacific delegation, en route from Omaha with Durant in charge, would be a day or two late. (The delay was occasioned, in part, by a kind of hostage taking. Workmen halted Durant's train and refused to let it move until they received the back pay they were owed. Money was wired, and the workmen stepped aside.)

It was too late to postpone the festivities in Sacramento, not to mention another bash in San Francisco, both of which went on as scheduled. One of the Sacramento parade floats featured a sign depicting "the Big Five"—Stanford, Huntington, Hopkins, and the Crocker brothers—as the fingers of a gigantic hand. (Add three more digits, and you would have had a semblance of the octopus image that was to haunt the railroad in its later years.) One member of that fivesome, the overworked and overweight E. B. Crocker, had already suffered a minor stroke. A month after the shindig in Sacramento, he had a second, more serious stroke, which caused him to stop working and devote himself to art collecting for the rest of his life (he died in 1875). E. B.'s absence from the Central Pacific's later history has tended to obscure his contributions: During the construction period, he was not only a workhorse but also the closest thing the Associates had to a conscience.

Durant, Dodge, and company finally showed up on the 10th, and the ceremony proceeded more or less as planned. A locomotive from each side approached the other until they stood cowcatcher to cowcatcher. Stanford and Durant picked up hammers to tap the last spikes into place; the track had been wired so that the first blow would telegraph a signal to New York, Washington, and other cities, where huzzahs could then break out. The honor went to Stanford, who swung at a five-and-a-half-inch-long golden spike—and, according to legend, missed. He hit the rail, though, and that triggered the signal, alerting his wired-in countrymen that the marriage had been consummated. Next, Durant took his turn at a silver spike and, as the story goes, missed, too. Neither of these errors, however, may in fact have been committed. Bain notes that the tale of the swings and misses dates from a later period, when both railroads were objects of widespread contumely, and that no contemporary account mentions them.

In any case, the nation's air throbbed with speechifying, both before and after the great event. Clergymen cited the joining of the rails as a divine blessing, and politicians predicted the rosiest of all possible American futures. Among the celebrants at Promontory Summit, Stanford delivered the ultimate in banal remarks: "In conclusion, I will add that we hope to do ultimately what is now impossible on long lines: transport coarse, heavy and cheap products, for all distance, at living rates to trade." So that was what all these years of backbreaking, stroke-inducing labor had been for? Moving coarse and heavy products at "living rates to trade," whatever those might be? Far better was a possibly spontaneous observation by Durant as he and Stanford shook hands afterward: "There is henceforth but one Pacific Railroad of the United States." In distant Massachusetts, where she now lived, Anna Judah reported feeling that "the spirit of my brave husband descended upon me, and together we were there unseen."

Not content with his dreary oration, shortly afterwards Stanford mouthed off at a reception held in his private car. As paraphrased by Dodge, who was there, the ex-governor blasted the federal government for the excessive number of inspections it had inflicted on the Central Pacific and condemned the subsidy program as not a benefit but "a detriment, with the conditions they had placed upon it." Whereupon a Union Pacific official stood up and delivered the perfect squelch: "Mr. President of the Central Pacific: If this subsidy has been such a detriment to the building of these roads, I move you, sir, that it be returned to the United States government with our compliments!"

There was still a lot of mopping-up to do, but less than a week after the gala at Promontory Point, regular through-service began on the "one Pacific Railroad of the United States." Passengers could now ride from Omaha to Sacramento in the astonishingly short span of five days.

⇥ three ⇤

How to Be Very, Very Unpopular

The Associates could be pardoned for strutting and crowing after the linkup at Promontory Point. They had scrounged up money from unlikely sources, demolished the Dutch Flat Swindle myth, defied geography, outmaneuvered their Union Pacific rivals, cut corners, hoodwinked federal officials, managed with aplomb what was probably the largest workforce in American history up to then, and improvised their way past every new obstacle in their path. Moralists might take issue with some of their methods, but more practical onlookers applauded the achievement, all the more impressive for being made by men who had previously been little more than storekeepers. "By engineers of repute, the scheme was pronounced impracticable," Mark Hopkins said of their unlikely triumph; "by capitalists it was ridiculed, and in newspapers and pamphlets it was denounced." Seen in this light, the Central Pacific was more than just a railroad; it was a thumb in the establishment's eye.

In the midst of the euphoria, however, came an annoying distraction. Late in 1869, the *Sacramento Union*, which once led cheers for the railroad, switched sides and went on the attack. The paper's owner traced his about-face to an improper advance by Stanford while he was governor. In return for an undisclosed sum, the *Union* would have been expected to urge one of the railroad's schemes upon the state legislature. "We rejected the offer and opposed the project. . . " the owner huffed. "From that time to this the influence of the company has been used to annoy us and injure us in every possible way. They have descended to means utterly contemptible."

The Big Four, however, attributed the falling-out to quite different causes, the most amusing of which involved a dog. On board a Central Pacific train, the *Union*'s owner had suffered the indignity (to his mind) of being forced to hand over his pet dog, which by regulation had to ride in a baggage car. In this interpretation, his paper's constant sniping was nothing but a petty, personal vendetta.

It was a more serious matter, however, when other, poochless newspapers began to desert the Big Four. Among them was the *Stockton Independent*, which in 1871 characterized them as follows:

No set of men on the face of the globe were ever placed in a more enviable position, or in one where by the exercise of a reasonable foresight, they could have retained their popularity and the friendship of the people. It is now hardly two years since this work was completed, and how remarkable has been the change in public sentiment. Along the whole line of their main trunk road from San Francisco to Ogden, as well as along the various branch roads of this company, nothing is heard but one continuous murmur of complaint. . . .

Over the next decade, that murmur swelled into a roar, until in 1882 G. Frederick Keller, an artist for *The Wasp*, a satirical San Francisco magazine, decorated two facing pages with "The Curse of California," a cartoon depicting the railroad as a giant octopus, its tentacles wrapped around and squeezing various participants in

the state's economy (you can see the cartoon, in color, at http://
nationalhumanitiescenter.org/pds/gilded/power/text1/octopus
images.pdf). The image so perfectly captured what people were
thinking and saying about the Southern Pacific that it stuck, making
"octopus" and "Southern Pacific" virtual synonyms from then on.
The railroad also became a stock villain of American fiction, figuring (sometimes thinly disguised, sometimes not) in three novels
published in the 1880s—with a fourth, and by far the best, Frank
Norris's *The Octopus*, waiting in the wings.

What could have led to such a striking reversal—from widely
anticipated savior to much-maligned monster?

The popular case against the railroad had multiple sources. For one
thing, Westerners soon realized that it was not going to be the
panacea they'd been led to expect. The country was knit together as
never before, but with little effect on the general level of prosperity.
Moreover, the buying of votes, which had perhaps been tolerable
when done to obtain start-up subsidies, became less forgivable when
the grown-up railroad made it a habit. Influenced by cash gifts,
campaign help, and free passes on trains, legislators failed to carry
out such duties as properly supervising the railroad's rates, which
seemed inconsistent, unfair, and just plain high. Nor did the Big
Four help their own cause. They had talent and vigor, but not much
diplomacy. Moreover, for all their plebeian backgrounds, they
lacked the common touch. As if to corroborate the growing suspi-
cion that they had played a stupendous trick on the whole nation,
one by one they began building lavish mansions, touring Europe,
and otherwise flaunting their wealth.

First, however, came a shake-up, followed by a scandal back East
and a desperate move in the West. As mentioned, ill health had
forced E. B. Crocker into retirement. His brother Charley now
proved that his moaning about how the other Associates exploited

his hardworking nature was no bluff: In 1870 he bailed out, selling his share of the Central Pacific to Huntington, Hopkins, and Stanford for $900,000, payable in three annual installments. A year later, however, his former colleagues couldn't scrape together the second installment. Charley shrugged, cancelled the deal, and returned the first installment. The reconstituted Big Four set out to extend their dominance in California and elsewhere.

In September of 1872, during the run-up to the national elections, a bombshell fell. "THE KING OF FRAUDS," read the headline in the *New York Sun*. "How the Crédit Mobilier Bought Its Way Through Congress." The article implicated a dozen or so solons (as journalists were wont to call lawmakers then), some of them big names: Schuyler Colfax, vice president of the United States; James Blaine, speaker of the House; and James Garfield, an up-and-coming Ohio congressman (and future president). With the economy booming, however, the revelations didn't seem to bother the voters much: Grant won reelection handily (though with a new vice president on the ticket). Nevertheless, Congress formed two committees to look into the scandal. Representative Oakes Ames—he of the shovels and the little black book—did himself no good when he went before one committee and offered a weak rebuttal: "I never dreamed [of corrupting my colleagues]. I did not know that they required it, because they were all friends of the road and my friends: if you want to bribe a man you want to bribe one who is opposed to you, not to bribe one who is your friend."

That committee shuffled the deck of suspects. Blaine was dropped, and everyone else was cleared of bribery except Ames and the lone Democrat, James Brooks of New York. Since Crédit Mobilier had unquestionably handed over heaps of money, this result floored anyone who considered "bribe" a transitive verb. Ames used a homely analogy to call attention to the whitewash: "It's like the man in Massachusetts who committed adultery, and the jury brought in a verdict that he was guilty as the devil, but that the woman was as innocent as an angel. These fellows are like that woman." The committee recommended that he and Brooks be expelled from the House; but that body reduced the penalty to censure. The leniency gave the two congressmen little solace, however; disgraced and distraught, they both died within weeks of the censure vote.

In addition to making headlines and begetting committees, Crédit Mobilier and other Grant-era political scandals quickened the imaginations of two neighboring writers in Hartford, Connecticut. One of them, Mark Twain, had been Senator Stewart's secretary in Washington for a short time; the other, Charles Dudley Warner, had once worked as a railroad surveyor in Missouri. They agreed to collaborate on a comic novel that would take aim at the auctioning off of political favors, with a railroad called the Tunkhannock, Rattlesnake and Young-womans-town at the heart of the action. It took the co-authors only three months to crank out *The Gilded Age* (1873), and the haste shows: The novel is far from seamless. Still, it has some good lines, such as one that might have been uttered by a member of the Big Four in his cups: "I wasn't worth a cent two years ago, and now I owe two millions of dollars." Not only did the book sell well; its title gave an indelible name to the corrupt, gaudy era it satirized.

The Crédit Mobilier affair rattled the Big Four. Huntington had been called before one of the special committees; he dodged the toughest questions but afterwards called his interrogators "these hell hounds." The Big Four also faced lawsuits from San Francisco developer Sam Brannan and other Central Pacific stockholders wondering where the dividends were. The answer is that they were being intercepted and pocketed by the Contract & Finance Company, and the Big Four didn't want their incestuous relationship with that entity (their own construction firm) to become widely known. Nor were they keen to make their books public, as a stout defense of the lawsuits would require. What to do? A succinct account of the radical solution they adopted can be found in David Lavender's biography of Huntington:

The ultimate decision was to finish working up a [fictitious] set of figures . . . and then to burn the fifteen volumes of Contract & Finance Company books in the basement of the railroad office. They did it just in time. During the summer of 1873, the New York *Sun* picked up a copy of the Brannan complaint and on July 19 used its figures, somewhat altered, as the basis of a front-page story under the headline "THE ACME OF FRAUD . . . $211,299,328.17—GOBBLED!" Nine days later the Wilson Committee once again put Huntington on the stand, and this time demanded to see the Contract & Finance Company books. There were none, Collis replied sorrowfully. The company was being dissolved and Hopkins, admittedly a peculiar man, had incinerated the records as wastepaper no longer worth saving.

The basement blaze achieved its goal of immunizing the Big Four from scrutiny, but with an added, unforeseen result: They forfeited the benefit of the doubt. In Lavender's elegant phrase, they "condemned themselves to being forever judged by unfriendly figures only."

In their private lives, the Big Four had entered a peacock phase. After Stanford and Hopkins each broke ground for a mansion on San Francisco's Nob Hill, Crocker resolved to outdo them. Commanding a higher spot on the hill, his domicile would be bigger and showier, crowned by a 172-foot-high tower, spreading over 12,500 square feet of floor space, and housing a theater. In surviving photographs, the structure looks like a city hall or a county courthouse. As Ambrose Bierce remarked, "There are uglier buildings in America than the Crocker House on Nob Hill, but they were built with public money for a public purpose; among architectural triumphs of private fortune and personal taste it is peerless." The lord of Crocker Castle sailed to Europe to round up the trappings such an edifice deserved. Unfortunately, however, on his return he got embroiled in a lawsuit brought by the Big Four against one Alfred Cohen for allegedly embezzling bonds while he worked as a lawyer for the Central Pacific. Cohen, who defended himself, could wield a sharp rapier, as when he treated the courtroom to a description of Crocker's physical presence: "being desirous of making the best possible impression on the court and bar, he has reclined back in one of these chairs and with his feet elevated to the rail surrounding the jury-box, has presented to our gaze that portion of his person for which he has the most admiration."

The glib Cohen also mocked Crocker's nouveau-riche pretensions in an imagined soliloquy by the former shopkeeper.

I will drop the obsequious smile with which I used to roll up calico and tape for my customers, and in its place there shall come the arrogant, supercilious grin of oleaginous self-satisfaction. I will build myself a mansion, which I will set upon a hill. I will upholster and furnish it so that visitors shall be filled with doubt whether it is designed for a haberdasher's shop or a stage scene for a modern furniture drama. I will purchase Gobelin tapestries, and employ someone to tell me whether they should be hung upon the walls as paintings or spread upon the floor as mats. I will buy pictures from the galleries of the Medicis and employ Mr. Medici himself to make the selections. I will show the world how an intelligent patron of the arts and literature can be manufactured by the process of wealth out of a peddler of needles and pins. I will visit Europe until I can ornament my ungrammatical English with a fringe of mispronounced French. I will wear a diamond as big as the headlight of one of my locomotives; and my adipose tissue shall increase with my pecuniary gains until my stomach is as large as my arrogance, and I shall strut along the corridors of the Palace Hotel [in San Francisco] a living, breathing, waddling monument of the triumph of vulgarity, viciousness, and dishonesty.

Cohen's thrusts were so accurate that he didn't just exonerate himself in court; afterwards, the Big Four rehired him.

Back on Nob Hill, another domestic folly of Crocker's went far to cement the image of the Big Four as a pack of blackguards. He had foreseen his mansion taking up a whole city block—the one bounded by California, Taylor, Sacramento, and Jones Streets. Barring the way, however, was an undertaker named Nicholas Yung (of Prussian ancestry rather than, as his name might suggest, Chinese), who owned a hilltop parcel with a small house on it. Crocker offered to buy Yung out. Yung said no or, in another version, agreed to sell but changed his mind and demanded more money simply because he thought Crocker could afford to pay it. Crocker upped his offer. Yung still wouldn't sell. Whereupon Crocker is said to have vowed to "seal him in as if he were in one of his coffins!" Getting back in touch with his inner crew-boss, Crocker had workmen isolate the Yung property by erecting a forty-foot-high wood fence on three sides of it, cutting off views, air, and sunlight and limiting access to the north. Known as the "spite fence," it became a symbol of hubris, a tourist attraction, and a butt of jokes. (For a look at the Crocker house and the spite fence, visit http://www.sfgenealogy.com/sf/history/hgoe75.htm.) Crocker's intransigence also played into the hands of San Francisco labor leader Denis Kearney, who held a rally outside the mansion one night, with the spite fence lending a vivid backdrop of plutocratic arrogance. Kearney's rabble-rousing led to the birth of the California Workingmen's Party, which went on to agitate successfully for a new state constitution designed to restrict the power of railroads and other monopolists. (As we shall see, however, the Southern Pacific managed to foil this effort.)

Yung and his family closed the house, moved elsewhere, but refused to sell, and Crocker wouldn't budge either. His death in 1888, after he'd lapsed into a diabetic coma, left the dispute unresolved. (Both houses and the fence are long gone, and the Crocker block is now occupied by Grace Episcopal Cathedral.) Yung had been inconvenienced, but not as much as the Big Four, for Crocker, with his tone deafness to public relations, had brought down ridicule and contempt on them all. Indeed, Cohen had zeroed in on the ostentation atop Nob Hill while fighting that embezzlement charge. "With absence of shame and decency," he asserted, "they parade the results of their crimes in the face of the world by erecting edifices to crown the heights of our city, which, instead of being, as they assert, monuments of honest enterprise, are to the thoughtful mind glaring and conspicuous . . . emblems of shame and dishonor." No wonder the Big Four saw fit to co-opt Cohen by bringing him back into the fold.

Sensitive to the damage caused by all this showing off, Huntington scolded his partners for their lack of restraint. He took care that his palace, when he got around to building it, should not further tarnish the Big Four's image in California—by siting it on Manhattan Island. (Huntington had never felt at home in California, which he scoffed at as a "climate for weaklings.") The Huntington pile went up at Fifth Avenue and Fifty-seventh Street, and Collis and his second wife were on the verge of crashing New York society when he messed up. Ward McAllister, social arbiter, toady to Mrs. Astor, and source of the phrase "The Four Hundred" as shorthand for the East Coast elite, threw a dinner party for the Huntingtons and wangled them an invitation to the Patriarchs' Ball, where they were introduced to the great lady herself. Collis had agreed to a fee of $9,000 for McAllister's services but refused to pay up. Newspapers got hold of the story, and the Huntingtons' crassness became fodder for gossip columnists. Collis and his missus failed in their mission to become numbers Four Hundred One and Two.

All the while, the Octopus was extending its tentacles by picking up new railroads. Railroad economist Stuart Daggett summarized the state of near perfection to which the Associates brought their California holdings.

By 1877 the Central Pacific-Southern Pacific combination was in control of over 85 percent of all the railroads in California. . . . Not only had the associates established the monopoly which they desired, but the operations of their system had reached an extent which they themselves would have thought inconceivable a few years before. The operated mileage of the Central Pacific–Southern Pacific line on June 30, 1877, was 2,337.66 miles, the capitalization $224,952,580, and the gross earnings $22,247,030.

Not just newspapers were squawking about the devil-fish's dominance of the state. Western Union and the Associated Press joined the chorus, spreading material harmful to the Central Pacific because they resented the high-handed way it ran its telegraph business.

The company's most controversial practices, however, had to do with its core function of railroading. According to Daggett, rates charged by the Central Pacific and Southern Pacific were significantly higher than elsewhere in the country. Yet analyzing railroad shipping rates is no easy task. Conditions in California—the difficulty of maintaining track across rugged terrain, for example, and the sparse interior settlement, which could generate losses if the railroad tried to accommodate every town or junction that demanded service—went at least some way toward justifying the differentials. The trouble was that virtually no one outside the inner sanctum of the railroad's employees could make heads or tails of how rates were set.

Perhaps the railroad's single most resented maneuver was doubling back, by which shipping agents required freight headed from the East to, say, the Central Valley to go to San Francisco first. There it would reverse directions—doubling back eastward—to reach its final destination. This wasteful back-and-forth allowed the railroad to exploit its in-state monopoly by charging a noncompetitive, higher rate for the extra leg of the trip. Over in Nevada, the Central Pacific took the double-back a step further. As explained by historian Russell R. Elliott, "the railroad charged Nevadans the traffic for goods shipped from New York to San Francisco and then, additionally, from San Francisco to the Nevada points, although the goods were left off as the train passed through Nevada on the way to San Francisco." The second half of the doubling-back, in other words, was a fiction—and a costly one for the railroad's customers.

The Central Pacific was by no means the only double-backing railroad. The practice was so widespread and resented as to figure in debates over bills to establish the Interstate Commerce Commission in the mid-1880s. But in California, with its great distances and relatively few railroads, the technique seems to have been especially prevalent and irksome—so much so that Frank Norris was able to make devastating use of it in *The Octopus.*

Further imposing itself on customers, the Central Pacific devised the so-called "pink contract," as explained by Bierce.

The railroads . . . raised their rates as much in some instances as 50 per cent. Merchants who would sign these contracts got the old rates, others the new. Needless to say, nearly all signed; the others were ruined. By the contract the merchant was bound to send and receive all his freight by rail and to give no other persons the benefit of the agreed rate under cover of his name. He was bound to have the contents of his packages plainly marked, and, if suspected of containing something falsely named, the packages might be broken open and a double rate charged if the suspicions were verified. The merchant was bound, moreover, to let the railroad officials inspect his books at will.

These and other imperious practices left the Central Pacific with few friends in California—except, that is, for the public officials they paid off. Nonetheless, the Big Four felt dismayed and hurt by their growing unpopularity. They liked to think of themselves as not just decent chaps, but towering heroes who had done glittering things for their country. Instead, they had become living symbols of greed and exploitation.

How much the railroad deserved its reputation for omnipotence, though, is debatable. Only a few years after Promontory Summit, the national economy stalled, with California being particularly hard hit. Historian Richard Orsi has taken a broad view of the state's stagnation during most of the last third of the nineteenth century:

California in the period from 1869 into the early 1900s suffered chronic depression, broken up by sudden speculative flurries and collapses in mining stocks or real estate prices. Despite many real gains, the state's instability signified an unbalanced, immature economy, booming or busting according to the market at a given time for a few commodities: mining stocks, land, or grain.

But few Californians of the era were able to attain such a perspective. Instead they glanced around them and saw the Central Pacific riding high while the rest of the state tended to stagnate. Once trumpeted as an economic godsend, the railroad found itself stuck in the role of scapegoat.

On the plus side, the Southern Pacific was a booster of California agriculture, not just in words but in deeds. In 1884, the railroad helped persuade a federal court to ban the dumping of waste from hydraulic mining; the Southern Pacific also sponsored agricultural research and was one of the early proponents of scientific farming. That these initiatives may have flowed from enlightened self-interest (robust agriculture meant more produce to be carried by the railroad) doesn't negate their beneficial effect on California's economy. Even the political helplessness that so many Californians felt when the railroad did something to vex them may have been overblown, at least by the end of the century. In the 1894 gubernatorial race, for example, both major-party candidates favored a government takeover of the Southern Pacific.

And yet the railroad was indisputably that resented thing, a monopoly; its owners advertised their enrichment by building themselves palaces; its corruption of public officials was pervasive and well-known; and its leadership repeatedly went all out to capture or stymie any governmental entity created to rein it in. On top of all this, the Southern Pacific was oblivious to public relations. Huntington had at least an inkling of this deficiency, as shown when he upbraided his colleagues for all the showing-off on top of Nob Hill. The full truth was brought to his attention in 1895, when he hired one R. B. Carpenter to monitor political affairs in California. "The events of the past year have left the S.P. Co. in a [state] of moral siege with the whole State as the attacking force," Carpenter reported. "In the present conditions and temper of the public, the social, political, and moral elements in human nature must be considered in connection with great vested interests as well as purely commercial desires." Even at the height of its power, the Southern Pacific might have fallen a bit short of full-fledged octopus-hood, but its efforts to combat that image were woefully inadequate.

As Huntington strove to make the most of the Central Pacific, the Southern Pacific, and myriad other interests, he realized he needed help. Hopkins was ailing; Crocker was no strategist; and Stanford had acquired a new fault to go with his laziness and shallowness: a preoccupation with the horses he bred and raced on his Palo Alto estate. (One legacy of this hobby was a series of photographs Stanford commissioned from Eadweard Muybridge to settle a dispute: Are all four hooves of a galloping horse ever off the ground at the same time? Yes, they are.) Enter David Colton, a bumptious friend of Crocker's who liked to be called "General" although his claim to the title rested on nothing more than an uneventful stint in the state militia. Huntington had been serving as president of the Southern Pacific, but he resigned on the understanding that the Associates would name Colton in his place. Instead, however, they chose Crocker, a decision that Huntington found doubly obnoxious. Not only had he been fooled, but the arrangement undercut a fiction they all were supposed to be maintaining: that the Central Pacific and the Southern Pacific were entirely different outfits.

Colton rushed his new colleagues with the zeal of a fraternity pledge. He began referring to "we five" in letters to the other Associates. (Newspapers put him in his place, however, by renaming the group the Big Four and a Half.) In his politics, at least, he made a good fit with the others. In 1878, after Congress had enacted a law requiring both the Central Pacific and the Union Pacific to start transferring a portion of their annual earnings to a sinking fund (something like an escrow account) for the retirement of their debts, Colton gave voice to their indignation: "No government can last long when the rights of the *Individual* are ignored to gratify the many."

With the new law on the books, the situation was this: The railroad might not have to hand over a cent due on those bonds until their thirty-year periods were up, but at least it had to start segregating funds for that eventual purpose. Sharing Colton's indignation, both Pacific railroads sued the United States over the sinking-fund mandate, alleging that by enacting it Congress had tampered unconstitutionally with the original contract (embodied in the laws of 1862, 1864, and 1866) between themselves and the United States. In a decision known (unimaginatively) as the *Sinking Fund Cases*, a majority of the Court upheld the law. But dissenting Justice Stephen Field—a jurist second to none in his championship of big business—saw fit to comment on how low the Central Pacific and Union Pacific had dipped in the public's estimation, not just in California but throughout the land:

I am aware of the opinion which prevails generally that the Pacific railroad corporations have, by their accumulation of wealth, and the numbers in their employ, become so powerful as to be disturbing and dangerous influences in the legislation of the country; and that they should, therefore, be brought by stringent measures into subjection to the State. This may be true; I do not say that it is not; but if it is, it furnishes no justification for the repudiation or evasion of the contracts made with them by the government.

Soon enough, the Associates regretted having ever admitted Colton to the club. Mark Hopkins died in March of 1878, followed by Colton in October. Colton had paid his membership dues by tendering the Big Four a one-million-dollar note; after his death Huntington and Crocker discovered that the new boy had over-reached. Aware of his precarious perch, he'd helped himself to company funds and stocks. Huntington and Crocker offered Colton's widow a deal: If she relinquished all of her late husband's investments in the Central Pacific and associated enterprises, they would cancel the note. For the sake of the General's good name, she accepted. Soon, however, she had second thoughts. The instruments she had given up, she now believed, were worth considerably more than $1 million. In 1882, she filed suit. With the cagey Alfred Cohen leading the defense team, Huntington and Crocker won the case—but at a cost. Numerous letters received by Colton were introduced into evidence and then leaked to the press. They demonstrated for all to see that bribery was a principal tool by which the Big Four got their way.

A pair of letters written by Huntington in 1874 can be stand-ins for dozens more of similar tenor: "Friend Colton," goes the first one. "Would it not be well for you to send some party down to Arizona to get a bill passed in the Territorial Legislature granting the right to build a railroad east from the Colorado River . . . [and] have the franchise free from taxation . . . ?" A follow-up message made the suggestion more explicit. "Cannot you have [Governor] Safford call the Legislature together and grant such charters as we want at a cost of, say, $25,000? If we could get such a charter as I spoke to you of it would be worth much money to us." As items like these found their way into print, Huntington toughed it out. Resorting to what has become standard procedure for anyone caught making incriminating or embarrassing statements, he declared that his words were taken out of context. But unless Arizona had opened a store to sell railroad charters, it's hard to imagine any context that would redeem instructions to pay public officials $25,000 to issue one.

One last letter found among the Colton papers—this one from Huntington to Hopkins, a year before the latter's death—should be quoted from. It shows that, to the Big Four, $25,000 was peanuts. Outlining his latest strategy to defeat a certain Congressman's bill, Huntington wrote: "It costs money to fix things so that I would know that his bill would not pass. I believe with $200,000 I can pass *our* bill." John Hoyt Williams estimates that over the years Richard Franchot, the Central Pacific's most effective lobbyist in Washington, gave lawmakers and journalists a total of $5 million to advance the railroad's causes.

In the winter of 1878–79, Californians brought the Central Pacific into what Justice Field had referred to as "subjection to the State"—or so they thought. That was when a constitutional convention met in Sacramento. The resulting document called for an elected three-member railroad commission to review rates and regulate practices. But the railroad was far from licked. Once the new constitution had been ratified by the voters and the commission was up and running, each initial member betrayed the public trust in his own way: One proved eminently bribable, a second had been financially allied with the railroad for some time and stayed that way, and the third was all talk and no action.

Occasionally in later years, a man of both integrity and gumption made his way onto the commission—only to meet with discouragement. Seldom if ever could a lone commissioner hold his own against the railroad's expert staff when it came to mastering reams of data, following the intricacies of bookkeeping and rate-making, and construing relevant laws. Such inadequacy should have come as no surprise. One of the arguments for creating the commission—made by the San Francisco Chamber of Commerce, no less—had been the need to address this very problem: "no one outside the railroad employ knows anything accurately about the nature of that enormous and most complicated business." Unfortunately, the commission did not get the help it needed to overcome its ignorance. Members came and went over the years, but one thing stayed constant: the commission's ineffectuality. As Bierce summed up the sorry record in 1896, "for [the entire sixteen years of its existence], with the exception of the expired time of the present board, [the Southern Pacific] has owned two of the three commissioners, body and soul, and now owns one." A reform that had seemed to hold so much promise turned out to be just another source of frustration. *The Wasp* reflected the prevailing disgust with the commission's first few years in an 1881 editorial: "The idea of a Railroad Commission might almost have been originated by the C.P. themselves. It is so obviously easier to—ahem—convince three men than a hundred." (The state railroad commission's failures were to inspire some of the most dramatic scenes in Norris's *Octopus*.)

In the mid-1880s, Collis Huntington and Leland Stanford had much to commiserate about. In 1883, Huntington's wife, Elizabeth, died of cancer. A year later, Leland Jr., the Stanfords' only child, died at age fifteen after contracting typhoid fever. (The grieving parents founded Stanford University as a memorial to their beloved boy.) The survivors' rapprochement, however, was short-lived. In 1886, Stanford double-crossed Huntington during the scheming to choose a U.S. senator for an open seat in California (this was the era when senators were elected by the state legislature). After agreeing to support Huntington's choice, former Senator Aaron Sargent, who was trying to make a comeback, Stanford put himself forward as a candidate instead. Huntington wired from New York: "IT IS REPORTED THAT YOU ARE IN THE FIELD AGAINST SARGENT. I CANNOT BELIEVE IT. PLEASE TELEGRAPH AT ONCE." Stanford held firm and was elected.

In the meantime, he, Huntington, and Crocker had reorganized their affairs. They dissolved the Contract & Finance Company and obtained a charter from the state of Kentucky for a holding company called the Southern Pacific Company, with Leland Stanford as president; the new company entered into ninety-nine-year leases with both the Central Pacific and the Southern Pacific railroads. The name given the umbrella firm reflected a couple of truths. First, with Nevada's mines running low on ore, the Central Pacific was carrying less traffic than before; and, second, Southern California was gaining importance as a population center and trade zone. Having subordinated both railroads to a holding company, its owners could divert traffic from one line to the other at will—and thus evade the Central Pacific's sinking-fund obligation. (The law called for the Central Pacific to transfer a percentage of its net revenues to the fund; but traffic shunted to the Southern Pacific earned revenue for that line and not the Central Pacific, allowing Huntington, Crocker, and Stanford to continue enriching themselves by declaring handsome dividends.)

Complaints about both the Southern Pacific and the Union Pacific kept piling up, and in March of 1887 Congress established a three-man commission of its own, with ample powers to hire staff, conduct an investigation, and compel testimony from witnesses. Three of those witnesses were Huntington, Crocker, and Stanford, all of whom suffered convenient memory lapses whenever they faced a hard question. At one point, Stanford put on a brazen act. Far from owing the federal government tens of millions of dollars, he opined, the railroad was due $62 million, a figure that included fanciful savings enjoyed by the government thanks to the breakneck speed with which the railroad was built. Ignoring this fairy tale, one of the Pacific Railroad commissioners showed in his questioning of Stanford that he knew how the Associates worked the magic of self-enrichment:

> . . . it seems to be the general belief that the present weak condition of the Central Pacific Railroad Company is due to the fact

that the contract with Crocker & Co., and the contract with the Contract and Finance Company, and the contracts with the Western Development Company, and the contracts with the Pacific Improvement Company have drained the company of its resources; that certain individuals have procured to be issued to themselves enormous quantities of the stock and bonds of this company, and have paid dividends on the stock, and have made the interest charge on the bonds exceedingly heavy, and the origins of its difficulties lie there entirely, and nowhere else.

That explanation pretty much lays it all out. The commission's final report implicated Huntington in bribery, accused the Central Pacific of trying to walk away from its debts, and predicted that it would be unable to repay its loans when they fell due a decade in the future. Accurate as these findings and warnings might be, however, they had little practical effect. There was no follow-up from Congress, and ten years later, when confronted with the report during the funding-bill battle, Huntington claimed never to have read it.

Huntington hadn't forgiven Stanford for the Sargent double-cross, and in old age each tycoon sniped at the other. The only witticism ever attributed to Stanford dates from this period, when he said he trusted Huntington as far as he could "throw Trinity Church up the side of Mount Shasta." Finally, in 1890, Huntington made his move. Having lined up support from the heirs of Hopkins and Crocker, he ousted Stanford from the presidency of the Southern Pacific Company and assumed that position himself. Immediately afterwards, Huntington poured his excess spleen into an imaginary interview that he had the good sense not to publish. In it, the fictitious questioner wonders whether Stanford's dismissal won't hamper the Central Pacific in its attempts to reach agreement with the federal government on the funding shortfall. Huntington's reply: "Mr. Stanford has about as much to do with this settlement as he has with the revolving of the earth."

Stanford died in 1893, leaving his widow, Jane, to carry out their plans for Stanford University (she did a bang-up job). As the last surviving member of the Big Four, Huntington pursued his multifarious interests with hardly a letup. Among these, however, was a cause that ended up costing him dearly in the funding-bill fight, although ostensibly the two issues had nothing to do with each other: seeking federal funding for a new port in Santa Monica, on land jointly controlled by the Southern Pacific and Senator John P. Jones of Nevada. Other players in the Los Angeles area argued that improving the existing port at San Pedro was the way to go, but Huntington and Jones preferred an outlet that was under their exclusive control. Each side anted up considerable money and power, and the battle was fought in Congress for several years.

Although their mansions were something of an embarrassment, the Big Four had so far kept their private lives scandal-free. Following the death of Hopkins, however, certain events set off a detonation of tongue wagging. His widow, Mary, went on a house-building spree; besides the mansion on Nob Hill, she ended up owning two residences in Massachusetts, one in Manhattan, and a summer place on Block Island. Along the way, she became infatuated with a man two decades her junior, an interior decorator named Edward T. Searles. Over the objections of her adopted son, Timothy, she married Searles in 1887. After her death four years later, it was revealed that she had disinherited Timothy and left everything to Searles. Timothy contested the will. An out-of-court settlement gave him some satisfaction but left Searles with a sizable amount of Southern Pacific stock, which he dutifully voted as Huntington directed. Searles donated the Hopkins mansion to the San Francisco Art Association. The building burned down in the fire that swept San Francisco after the 1906 earthquake; in 1920, the Mark Hopkins Hotel went up on the same site, which it occupies to this day. When Searles died that same year, he left most of his money to his male secretary. And so a fellow who had been earning $50 a week to answer letters and pay bills ended up with a goodly share of the Big Four's millions.

Starting in the 1880s, the Central Pacific could have added a new item to its list of dubious achievements: making unsavory appearances in fiction, where it became a symbol of everything that ailed Gilded Age America. In particular, writers seized upon the railroad's involvement in a tragic 1880 incident at Mussel Slough, in the Central Valley. A full discussion of this episode will appear in Chapter 9; for now, suffice it to say that seven men died in a confusing shoot-out over disputed railroad land—and that, given the Central Pacific's tyrannical reputation, most people were ready to believe it was wholly at fault. Resentment over the incident grew, and its sensationalistic elements became fodder for novelists a decade and a half before Norris started writing *The Octopus*.

First up was journalist William Chambers Morrow, a native Alabaman who had moved to San Francisco. In 1882, the San Francisco firm of F. J. Walker & Co. published Morrow's *Blood-Money*, with a plot centered on $22,000 that has gone missing. The young man who is entitled to the money by inheritance hires a detective to help him find it. The detective, it turns out, is a secret operative of an all-powerful railroad, which the author likens to a certain denizen of the ocean deep: "The tentacles of the octopus were around [the detective's] soul as well as his arms."

Morrow goes on to rage at length against the railroad, calling the detective "one of the cogs in this great wheel that grinds men down to desperation, and that has at last driven them to the wall; where, let it be hoped by every man whose mind has not been clouded over nor soul corrupted, the wounded bear may show his teeth, and like the hounded grizzly of the Sierras, tear with claw and end with teeth whatever seeks its death." "I fear that blood must be spilled," another character declares, and a few pages later Morrow restages the Mussel Slough shoot-out, with the railroad as the out-and-out perpetrator.

Morrow took care to give everyone and everything in *Blood-Money* a made-up name. Not so C. C. Post in his *Driven from Sea to Sea; or, Just a Campin'* (1884). Post edited a newspaper in Chicago, and his novel was published by a Chicago house; nonetheless, he displays an impressive familiarity with California's landscapes and economic conditions. *Driven from Sea to Sea* tells the story of a farm family that is always on the move because, wherever it tries to put down roots, some overbearing corporation—often as not a railroad—comes along, cites a legal technicality or corrupts a local official, and snatches its land away. What sets *Driven from Sea to Sea* apart is Post's willingness to introduce real people into his pageant. Thus we are told that "Stanford, the president of the company, had been Governor of the State, and it was while filling this exalted position that he first began to lay plans for the subjugation of the people, and in Huntington and Crocker he had able partners and unscrupulous allies." At the end of the book, after a rehash of Mussel Slough, Post assures the reader that "the story is not yet finished; but so far as told it is a true story. All of the main incidents have taken place substantially as related. They are part of the history of our country; have occurred to our own citizens, beneath the shadow of our own flag."

The Feud of Oakfield Creek (1887), the third and last novel from the 1880s to exploit Mussel Slough, came from an unlikely pen: that of philosopher Josiah Royce. The son of pioneering California parents, Royce grew up in mining country north of Sacramento. After graduating from the University of California, he studied in Germany, got a Ph.D. in philosophy from Johns Hopkins, and spent the rest of his life teaching at Harvard.

This time the villain is not a railroad tycoon but Alonzo Eldon, a wealthy financier and landowner loosely based on Leland Stanford. The reader gets a preview of the fellow's foul nature courtesy of a "negro janitor": "He didn't see any use for hell, he said, if

Alonzo stayed out of it." Eldon, however, has a little-known progressive side. He intends to build a museum in San Francisco promoting "the doctrine that vast public fortunes are social evils, and that the social order must erelong be so reformed as to make such fortunes impossible." But he is not kindly disposed to the squatters on land he owns in the East Bay. Determined to vindicate his ownership, he calls upon the law to oust them, and a Mussel Slough–style shoot-out ensues. As was true of the actual event, Royce notes that "nobody could ever afterwards be sure whence came the first shot."

None of these three novels was a bestseller. *Blood-Money* is so melodramatic that it probably converted few readers to the antirailroad cause, and *The Feud of Oakfield Creek* is windy and tendentious. (As Royce's colleague George Santayana remarked, "Royce sometimes felt that he might have turned his hand to other things than philosophy. He once wrote a novel, and its want of success was a silent disappointment to him.") Though *Driven from Sea to Sea* is fairly engaging, it never stops waving its anticapitalist colors. These books are important not for their artistic value or political impetus, but for what they tell us about how people of the time viewed robber barons in general and the Central Pacific in particular.

One last antirailroad publication should be mentioned: not a novel but an example of a genre that has disappeared from American life, the polemical pamphlet. Businessman John R. Robinson, the author of one that came out in 1894—"The Octopus: A History of the Construction, Conspiracies, Extortions, Robberies, and Villainous Acts of the Central Pacific, Southern Pacific of Kentucky, Union Pacific, and Other Subsidized Railroads"—was hardly an objective observer. In the early days of California railroading, Robinson had frequently taken on the Big Four—and lost every time. He had strong opinions on their methods and policies, along with the wherewithal to self-publish them. Calling Huntington "a perjurer and a liar," he summed up the tumultuous history of the Central Pacific: "For the past thirty years or more California has been in the grip of a monster. . . ." In Robinson's reckoning, that monster had "stolen and robbed the public of more than $200,000,000."

Huntington could have sneered at most of Robinson's digs as the lies and distortions of a sore loser, but one of them might have hit home. "The people," Robinson charged, "have been and are now contributing, through Huntington, to the ease and support of an indigent and indolent foreigner, to whom he (Huntington) gave several million dollars to marry his adopted daughter to give her an empty title. . . ." This was more or less the truth.

Huntington's foster-daughter, Clara, was a willful young woman who in 1888 had almost managed to travel to Europe by herself. Never mind that she had reached the ripe age of twenty-eight—such an impropriety could not be countenanced. Yet even with a chaperone on one side and a maid on the other, the heiress caught the eye of Prince Francis von Hatzfeldt de Wildenberg, who suffered from a common European syndrome: nice pedigree, empty bank account. He followed Clara around Europe, making himself so charming that she agreed to marry him and announced as much in a letter home. Collis and his second wife hastened across the sea to break this up in person, but Clara stood her ground. The only question was whether Collis would meet the prince's demand for a sizable dowry. The old man resisted for a while but ultimately succumbed. Say this much for the gold-digging prince: He kept up his end of the bargain. According to Lavender, "they evidently lived happily, or reasonably so, ever after."

As Robinson had suggested, in the right circumstances the redoubtable Collis Huntington could be as malleable as any other doting father. But if anyone supposed that this instance of familial weakness meant that he was losing his touch as a marketplace aggressor and statehouse influence-peddler, they misjudged their man. By the time of Clara's marriage, repayment of the Central Pacific's thirty-year-old debt was very much a live issue, and Huntington was preparing for his last great fight.

He was in his mid-seventies by then, the last living Associate.

But with his mind still sharp, he remained indisputably in charge of the great railroad and its well-oiled lobbying machine. The Southern Pacific had won most of its important court cases and had weathered opposition to its policies from newspapers in California and elsewhere. Its control of California lawmakers and regulators was intact. It had swatted away the findings of the Pacific Railroad Commission as one might a mosquito. It had withstood name-calling by one fiction writer after another, along with the pamphleteering of an old foe. As Huntington and his minions set out to at least postpone, and perhaps wipe out altogether, payment of a debt pertaining to a distant sector of the country and dating far back into the past, few sporting men in Washington would have bet against them.

❧ four ❧

Ambrose Bierce at a Low Point

It's easy to get Ambrose Bierce wrong—to pigeonhole him as Bitter Bierce, a mudslinging misanthrope whose psychological development was stunted by a miserable childhood and warped by his service in the Union Army, a physically and mentally wounded malcontent who stood apart from his feckless fellow humans and devoted his literary gifts to mocking them. Though commonplace during his lifetime and even now, that indictment has little truth to it. But getting Bierce right is hard. Not only did he play multiple roles in life (soldier, newspaper columnist, businessman, husband, father, poet, fiction writer, crusading journalist, adventurer); he also showed scant interest in examining and justifying his own motives. The key to understanding him, I think, is to scrape off the veneer of worldly cynicism and uncover one of the most sensitive, most easily wounded men ever to take up a pen for a living—as well as one of the most perceptive.

He was an American oddity from the cradle on. Born Ambrose Gwinett Bierce, the tenth of thirteen children, he shared a feature with every last one of his siblings: a Christian name starting with the first letter of the alphabet. The A's were parceled out in the settlement of Horse's Cave, Ohio, where Ambrose was born on June 24, 1842, and on a farm near the town of Warsaw, Indiana, to which the family moved when the boy was four. Wherever they lived, the paterfamilias, Marcus Aurelius Bierce, barely managed to provide for his large brood (at various times he farmed, kept a store, and served as a tax assessor). But he amassed a sizable library, of which the tenth A made good use—looking back as an adult, he acknowledged that "to [my father's] books I owe all that I have."

Some biographers infer from Bierce's writings that he had a wretched time of it as a kid. It's true that as an adult he groused poetically about the shabbiness in which he grew up:

> With what anguish of mind I remember my childhood,
>   Recalled in the light of a knowledge since gained;
> The malarious farm, the wet, fungus grown wildwood.
>   The chills then contracted that since have remained.
> The scum-covered duck pond, the pigstye close by it,
>   The ditch where the sour-smelling house drainage fell,
> The damp, shaded dwelling, the foul barnyard nigh it. . . .

Nor did he care for the family's pervasive religiosity. In his *Devil's Dictionary* he defines faith as "Belief without evidence in what is told by one who speaks without knowledge, of things without parallel."

Much is made, too, of several short stories by Bierce in which a son knocks off his mother or father or both. Grouped under the heading "The Parenticide Club," the stories are told in a jocular manner that is meant to shock—and does. One begins, "Early one June morning in 1872 I murdered my father—an act which made a deep impression on me at the time." As if to spread the wrath around, Bierce led off another tale with "Having murdered my mother under circumstances of singular atrocity, I was arrested and put upon my trial, which lasted seven years."

But whether these works of imagination bespeak a loathing for the writer's own parents is questionable; given their wild exaggeration, one can just as easily take them as impersonal jabs at that Victorian sacred cow, the family. Bierce once described his parents to a friend as "unwashed savages," but the phrase smacks as much of self-made manhood on display—*I come from rock-bottom origins, but look at me now*—as it does of actual animosity. In fact, clear evidence of Bierce's affection for his parents has come down to us in a pair of beautiful letters that he wrote his mother in 1876, as his father was dying back in Indiana. One of them reads, in part:

> My poor Mother, I cannot write as I feel; you know what I would say; you know how dreadful is this affliction to me, who have not even the consolation of having been a good son to so good a father. It is very hard for us all, but there is nothing for us to do but endure whatever it may please a superior power to inflict upon our helpless hearts. Of us all, you, my poor Mother, are the only one to whom the consciousness of having always performed your every duty with unswerving patience, gentleness and grace will come to temper the bitterness of grief.

> I can write no more for I am blind with tears.

Those do not seem the sentiments of a man nursing a profound filial grudge. On the other hand, Bierce did escape from "the malarious farm" early, dropping out of school at age fourteen to take a job that was an unofficial stepping stone for American writers-to-be: printer's devil.

The Bierces could point to a venerable military tradition—Marcus's father had been with Washington at Valley Forge—and the boy now fell under the influence of, and moved in with, that legacy's latest avatar: Marcus's younger brother, Lucius Verus Bierce. A lawyer with a college degree, Lucius gave his nephew access to an even larger private library. Lucius was a successful politician (four-term mayor of Akron, Ohio) who had won notoriety with a feat out of opera buffe. In 1838, he had led a homegrown militia on an invasion of Windsor, Ontario—the kickoff of a campaign to topple the Canadian government. Though the expedition failed utterly, it appealed to American jingoists, and Lucius Verus Bierce was considered a credit to his grandiloquent name. At his suggestion, Ambrose enrolled in a military academy near Frankfort, Kentucky. There he learned the skills, cartography included, that were to make him so valuable in the Civil War.

Nine months after Ambrose left the academy came the event that overshadowed the rest of his life—the outbreak of that war. Along with his lineage and training, he had his favorite uncle's sympathies to consider. Lucius was not just an abolitionist but a friend of antislavery fanatic John Brown; tradition has it that the swords swung by Brown and his sons on their bloody mission to Kansas in 1856 had been a gift from Lucius. A few weeks short of his nineteenth birthday, Ambrose enlisted with the Ninth Indiana Volunteers. Years afterwards, he gave a straightforward explanation for his decision: "At one point in my green and salad days I was sufficiently zealous for universal and unqualified Freedom to engage in a four years' battle for its promotion. There were other issues involved, but they did not count for much with me."

In his first few months as a soldier, mostly in the Cheat Mountains of what is now West Virginia, Bierce carried a wounded comrade to safety and was promoted to sergeant. Then and throughout his service, he filed away what he had experienced firsthand, along with anecdotes told by his comrades. When he got around to writing about the war, mostly in the 1880s and '90s, he could draw upon a wealth of striking incidents and bewildering ironies to support a theme that has been replayed many times since, perhaps most effectively in Joseph Heller's novel *Catch-22*: up close, war can be mindless, morbid, and funny—all at the same time. So, for example, in Bierce's presence one soldier would come through an attack unscratched, while his neighbor, only inches away, was taking multiple hits. A fellow named Abbott was struck and killed by a cannonball; when the ball was removed, its brand-name came to light—"Abbott." A phenomenon called "acoustic shadow" could confound the senses. "At the battle of Gaines's Mill," Bierce wrote, "one of the fiercest conflicts of the Civil War, with a hundred guns in play, spectators a mile and a half away on the opposite side of the Chickahominy valley heard nothing of what they clearly saw." For all the chaos, however, he tended to look back on his service in the first year of the war as a romantic idyll. In a surviving photograph of him in uniform, we see a young man with features that are regular but not fine, a thick mustache, and a shock of dark hair (had color film been anachronistically available, that hair's reddish-gold tint would have been visible), staring at the photographer with a raptor's intensity.

Early in 1862, the fun came to an end. Bierce's regiment was detached and sent west. In northern Mississippi, the young man was plunged into the most savage fighting of the war to date when the division to which he belonged answered an emergency summons to reinforce General Ulysses S. Grant, whose army had been surprised by a large Rebel force. The battle, which became known by the deceptively sweet name of Shiloh, racked up a death toll surpassing that of the Revolutionary War, the War of 1812, and the Mexican War combined. At Shiloh, Bierce witnessed unremitting carnage and touching comradeship, staggering din and eerie silence, battlefields littered with detritus and offal, and the contorted human wreckage left behind after fire raged through a forest crawling with casualties. His biographer Carey McWilliams believed that Bierce never got over Shiloh. "In those hours . . .," McWilliams wrote, "he saw the pageantry of the heroic go down to unutterable defeat before the ruthless idiocy of chance." Already an agnostic, Bierce drew a lesson from the fighting: Life makes no sense. Instead of dulling his interest in the passing parade, however, that grim epiphany seems to have sharpened it.

He took part in several more battles, including Chickamauga, and the promotions kept coming, to sergeant-major, to second lieu-tenant, to first lieutenant. He joined the staff of General William B. Hazen as a topographical engineer, i.e., mapmaker. Some of Bierce's maps have survived, and they are admirable examples of their kind. Even better are his verbal explanations of what topo-graphical engineering was all about: risking one's life by scouting terrain into which an army was about to advance: "It was hazardous work," he recalled; "the nearer to the enemy's lines I could penetrate, the more valuable were my field notes and the resulting maps. It was a business in which the lives of men counted as nothing against the chance of defining a road or sketching a bridge."

Hazen was a gruff customer, competent, perhaps even brilliant, but given to berating his subordinates and quarreling with his fel-low generals. Bierce called him "the best hated man that I ever knew, and his very memory is a terror to every unworthy soul in the service." As a decidedly worthy soul, Bierce adored Hazen, who in his own way returned the favor. The two men remained friends the rest of their lives.

Bierce's war climaxed in Georgia, at the Battle of Kennesaw Mountain, on June 23, 1864, when a bullet struck him in the head, leaving it, in his words, "broken like a walnut." Hazen gave a fuller, if less colorful, account of what happened after he ordered Bierce to direct an advance of the skirmish line. "While engaged in this duty, Lieut. Bierce was shot in the head by a musket ball which caused a very dangerous and complicated wound, the ball remaining within the head from which it was removed sometime afterwards." Sent home to heal, Bierce recovered enough to rejoin the army in late September but was excused from marching because of lingering weakness, including a tendency to faint. He was discharged on January 16, 1865.

Later, when Bierce was producing journalism at full throttle, resolute optimists ragged him for his testiness and gloom. They had in mind such characteristic sallies as this one, from an 1889 essay called "To Train a Writer." The trainee, Bierce advises, should always keep in mind that "this is a world of fools and rogues, blind with superstition, tormented with envy, consumed with vanity, self-ish, false, cruel, cursed with illusions—frothing mad!" Elsewhere he wrote, "Heaven is a prophecy uttered by the lips of despair, but hell is an inference from analogy." From today's vantage point, after an intervening century blotted by trench warfare, ideological slaughters, the Holocaust, the use of poison gas and nuclear weapons, and suicide bombings, such remarks don't seem unwarranted. In the late nineteenth century, however—when faith in human progress was at its apogee and skeptics were considered heretics—Bierce found himself decidedly out of step. Pep talkers could reassure themselves by writing him off as a misanthrope—"Bitter Bierce" or "The Most Hated Man in San Francisco"—but based on what he'd seen and endured, especially from 1861–65, he might better have been described as "Hawkeyed Bierce." He allowed as much himself, when he came to define a word that stuck to him like an epithet: "CYNIC, *n.* A blackguard whose faulty vision sees things as they are, not as they ought to be."

Yet he bristled at being labeled a misanthrope. In a long reply to a San Francisco critic who had likened him to that "hater of mankind," Timon of Athens, Bierce asked rhetorically, "Do you think it philosophical to judge of one's attitude toward the race by one's attitude toward a few scores of individuals whom rightly or wrongly one regards as unworthy of respect?—and this without a knowledge of one's life associations or friendships?" In the next paragraph, Bierce came as close to sentimentality as he was ever to do in the record of his professional life: "does it really seem to you that contempt for the bad is incompatible with respect for the good?—that hatred of rogues and fools does not imply love of bright and honest folk?" He was no loner and never lacked for friends and protégés; the case for his being a misanthrope does not hold up. Nor is there an entry for "misanthrope" in *The Devil's Dictionary*. Had he written one, however, perhaps it would have gone something like this:

one who can't get over his belief that human beings have it in them to be-
have far better than they all too often do.

After leaving the army, Bierce had taken a job with the Treasury
Department in Alabama, as an agent in charge of confiscated
property—mostly cotton. It turned out to be a wretched few months.
Resentful growers threatened him with death, widespread corruption among his fellow workers smothered what was left of his Union
idealism, and the asthma that had bothered him since childhood
made a comeback in the humid South. Far more to his liking was the
job he filled in the summer of 1866, working under Hazen again, as
topographical attaché to a four-man exploratory expedition from
Omaha to the West Coast. Sometimes debilitating, sometimes a
lark, the journey inspired Bierce to fill a notebook with sketches
and verbal descriptions of what he saw. Whether he knew it or not,
he was becoming a Westerner. The mission ended in San Francisco
that fall.

Bierce had expected to be rewarded for his long and stellar military service by being commissioned a captain in the regular army,
but the commission, when it came, was for a second-lieutenancy.
Offended, he turned it down and stayed in San Francisco while
Hazen moved on. Bierce went to work as a night watchman for the
Treasury Department and devoted his spare time to grooming
himself for a possible writing career. He particularly admired and
learned from the caustic satires of Pope and Swift and the para-
doxical maxims of La Rochefoucauld.

In the late 1860s, San Francisco was riding a second precious-
metal boom (the first, of course, being the 1849 Gold Rush). Wealth
was being siphoned away from the aforementioned Comstock Lode,
which, despite its Nevada location, had become a fiefdom of the
Bank of California and a plaything of San Francisco stockbrokers,
who happily catered to a frenzy of mining-stock speculation. It was

a new town—rich, raw, and semi-isolated—that reveled in reading gossip about its own flamboyant inhabitants. Already it had built up a tradition of irreverent journalism—this being another import from Comstock country, where such jesters as Joe Goodman, Dan De Quille, and Mark Twain had raised the tall tale from barroom braggadocio to an art form that captured the anything-is-possible spirit of the booming West. Spoofs, satires, fables, hoaxes, libelous witticisms, many of them aimed at the city's nouveau-riche class—such were the stock and trade of the San Francisco journalist. (Literary historian Lawrence I. Berkove has shrewdly placed Bierce's most famous story, "An Occurrence at Owl Creek Bridge," in the hoaxing tradition.)

Bierce found all this congenial; yarning and deflating pomposity came naturally to him. But ultimately he was to differ from the likes of De Quille and Twain in one big way: style. Bierce's intellect had been formed by the classics, and his years of military indoctrination had left him with a ramrod disposition toward the English language (after all, a wrong word in the order of the day can cost lives). This can be seen, first, in his prose itself, which tends to both punctilio and elaboration, with none of the vernacular impudence preferred by Twain.

A good example of the Biercean style can be found in the opening of his remarkable story "One Summer Night," in which he dilates with Augustan balance and almost fussily exact diction on a topic that is anything but elegant.

The fact that Henry Armstrong was buried did not seem to him to prove that he was dead; he had always been a hard man to convince. That he really was buried, the testimony of his senses compelled him to admit. His posture—flat upon his back, with his hands crossed upon his stomach and tied with something that he easily broke without profitably altering the situation—the strict confinement of his entire person, the black darkness and profound silence, made a body of evidence impossible to controvert and he accepted it without cavil.

Here we have a poor devil trapped alive underground, and the narrator frets about whether the evidence for it can withstand "cavil." It can be argued that the tale—at a mere page and a half, possibly the greatest story of such compactness in all of literature—gains from the contrast between this ornate lead-in and its brutal climax. That first paragraph, at any rate, is vintage Bierce.

His military habits can also be felt in his advice book *Write It Right: A Little Blacklist of Literary Faults* (1909). A precursor to Strunk and White's *The Elements of Style*, Bierce's manual, as he explained it, is designed

> to teach precision in writing; and of good writing (which, essentially, is clear thinking made visible) precision is the point of capital concern. It is attained by choice of the word that accurately and adequately expresses what the writer has in mind, and by exclusion of that which either denotes or connotes something else. As Quintilian puts it, the writer should so write that his reader not only may, but must, understand.

Following that bossy introduction, the book proper consists of an alphabetized series of proscriptions. Some entries remain useful: "*Allude to* for Mention. What is alluded to is not mentioned, but referred to indirectly. Originally, the word implied a playful, or sportive, reference. That meaning is gone out of it." Others will strike the twenty-first-century reader as prissy and antiquated: "*Laundry*: Meaning a place where clothing is washed, this word cannot mean, also, clothing sent there to be washed." The little book's most salient feature, however, is that in passing along what he'd learned during a long writing career, Bierce stuck to no-nos and threw up barriers against change. H. L. Mencken, who admired Bierce, put it this way: "It never seems to have occurred to him that language, like literature, is a living thing, not a mere set of rules."

Back in the late 1860s, the rudiments of that conservative style were impressive enough to please San Francisco newspaper editors, who began accepting Bierce's freelance submissions. James Watkins, the English-born editor of the *News Letter and California Advertiser*, liked the novice's work so much that he became a mentor and eventually had Bierce take over the paper's gossip column, "The Town Crier." The two were soon great friends, and on stepping down in 1868, Watkins arranged for Bierce to succeed him.

Items to be found in "The Town Crier" of September 25, 1869, encompass a wide spectrum of mischief. There is the insult of a local grandee: Charles DeYoung, a member of the family that published the *San Francisco Chronicle*, is called "' a liar, a scoundrel and perhaps—indeed quite probably—a coward.'" There is the roasting of a national figure:

Is President Grant to be allowed to plunge this country into a war with Spain for the mere gratification of his personal taste? It is plain as a pike staff: Grant wants Cuba for the United States in order that he may get cheap cigars. But we won't have it. As Hamlet very properly observes, "What's a Cuba to him or he to a Cuba that he should weep for her?" There'll be no war; it will all end in smoke.

And there is the calling down of a pox on two houses of worship:

An Episcopal clergyman in New York is endeavoring to prove that there are no essential points of difference between the Catholic and Protestant churches. Nor is there; except in the trifling matter of doctrine. Up to date, however, the Protestants are ahead in the number of their killed and wounded. But there is no telling how the score will stand a hundred years hence.

On the strength of sorties like these—as well as his audacious habit of roasting clergymen by name for their sanctimoniousness and illogic—Bierce became noticed, talked about, and feared.

The San Francisco fogs were playing havoc with his lungs, however, and he frequently crossed the Bay to seek refuge in Marin County, where he met Mary Ellen "Mollie" Day, the handsome daughter of a well-off mine owner and his socially ambitious wife. In spite of Mrs. Day's reservations, Bierce won Mollie's hand; the couple married in late December of 1871.

Five months later, they were off to England on a belated, extended honeymoon, a gift from the bride's parents. Watkins had made London sound like the most alluring city in the world, and some of Bierce's "Town Crier" quips had been quoted in the English press. The young journalist leapt at the chance not just to visit the glittering capital of a great empire but also, perhaps, to conquer it. He'd come a long way from the Indiana boondocks, and he'd succeeded on his own salty terms. In his valedictory as "Town Crier" he issued this glum advice: "Remember that it hurts no one to be treated as an enemy entitled to respect until he shall prove himself a friend worthy of affection. Cultivate a taste for distasteful truths. And, finally, most important of all, endeavor to see things as they are, not as they ought to be."

Londoners wanted to peg Bierce as a wild Westerner. At first he fit the bill, publishing sketches like one about a farm lad who presents his mother with an item retrieved from the meadow outside—his father's severed head (another dead dad!). Under her crisp questioning, the boy explains that "the mowing-machine lopped it off." The mother lectures him for having forgotten himself:

My son, the gentleman whom you hold in your hand—any more pointed allusion to whom would be painful to both of us—had punished you a hundred times for meddling with things lying about the farm. Take that head back and put it down where you found it, or you will make your mother very angry.

But while in London (or in Bristol or Bath, to which the London fogs sometimes drove him), Bierce showed newspaper and magazine readers he could do something that most American literary rough-necks couldn't—produce first-rate topical satire. English publishers cashed in on his growing popularity by bringing out three collections of his San Francisco writings in book form. The sight of them prompted the author to size up his literary strengths and weaknesses in a letter to a friend back home: "Do you know I have the supremest contempt for my books—as books. As a journalist I believe I am unapproachable in my line; as an author, a slouch! I should never put anything into covers if I could afford not to." This avowal presages what became a career-long weakness—Bierce's disinclination or inability to produce sustained work on a single topic, to write cohesive books rather than clusters of short pieces.

While abroad, he and Mollie became parents twice over—first a son called Day, then another son, Leigh. A profound experience of a different kind occurred after the death of Bierce's best British friend, the editor Tom Hood. The two had promised each other that whoever died first would come back from the other world and make himself known to the survivor. One night as Bierce was out walking, Hood seemed to do exactly that. "I need not attempt to describe my feelings," Bierce recalled, "they were novel and not altogether agreeable. That I had met the spirit of my dead friend; that it had given me recognition, yet not in the old way; that it had then vanished—of these things I had the evidence of my own senses." The many ghost stories Bierce wrote in the coming decades can be traced in part to this episode.

Mollie and the boys returned to the States for a visit in the summer of 1875, leaving Bierce behind. When Mollie wrote to let him know she was pregnant again, he knew it was time to go home. Though he was in demand as a writer, British journalists were poorly paid, and he missed his wife and boys. (Not until later did his marriage deteriorate badly enough to coax this definition out of him for *The Devil's Dictionary:* "MARRIAGE, *n.* The state or condition of a community consisting of a master, a mistress, and two slaves, making in all, two.") Even so, he found it hard to leave, and he took so much of the country home with him that new acquaintances often mistook him for an Englishman.

Reestablished in San Francisco, he became a father for the third and last time (a daughter, Helen) and obtained steady work as associate editor of *The Argonaut,* a weekly journal co-owned by Frank Pixley, who had founded it as a vehicle to counteract the influence of labor leader Denis Kearney. In addition to editing, Bierce wrote "Prattle," a salty column in which he commented mostly on local news and personages, and where he published some of his early short stories. He joined the Bohemian Club upon its founding but resigned a few years later to protest what he considered the club's fawning treatment of a visitor, the emperor of Brazil. (Late in life, Bierce dismissed the club as "that aggregation of shop clerks, insurance steerers and literary pretenders.") As a friend, Bierce sometimes reacted so strongly to a slight as to break permanently with the offender, with no chance of reprieve. But if you minded your manners and stayed loyal, he could be a pussycat. "Bierce was the mildest and gentlest gentleman I ever met," recalled an editor who socialized with him regularly, "there is no writer I have ever known whose pen and tongue delivered such wholly dissimilar thoughts and views."

After two years, Bierce left *The Argonaut* and undertook a mission to strike it rich as his father-in-law had: in mining. The mining bug bit many a bookish fellow in the late nineteenth century—along with damn near everybody else—as the Gold Rush and the Comstock Lode were succeeded by Bodie and Cripple Creek and a myriad of lesser precious-metal booms and busts whose remains can be found in the ghost towns that dot the West. If you refrained from dashing off to prospect for gold or silver, you gambled on mining stocks or at least daydreamed about bonanzas hidden somewhere out there in the rocks. Twain himself, geologist and author Clarence King, paleontologist Edward Drinker Cope, Senator William Stewart, and several other prominent writers, scientists, and politicians did themselves great harm by throwing away time and money on foolish ventures while in thrall to a lust that had come over them during sojourns in mining country.

Bierce at least had the sense to take one bad swing at the piñata and quit. This came in 1880, when it was the Black Hills' turn to host a rush. He knew the region from having visited it with Hazen in 1866; through the intercession of an old friend, Bierce was hired to manage a gold-mining operation in Rockerville, Dakota Territory. Although he set out with high hopes, even boasting of being quits with journalism, the mine turned out to be an underfunded fiasco. Not only did Bierce have trouble collecting his salary; afterwards he found himself entangled in a lawsuit over the affair. The indignity of having to slink back to San Francisco in defeat was compounded when *The Argonaut*'s owners declined to rehire their erstwhile employee (Bierce blamed this betrayal on Pixley, whom he bludgeoned in print ever after), and no other offers were immediately forthcoming.

When a position finally turned up, it was a good one: editorship of *The Wasp*, a weekly magazine known for its satire, criticism, and especially its cartoons. It was *The Wasp* that published Keller's octopus drawing, and Bierce began taking potshots at the Southern Pacific in the magazine's pages.

He had brought his "Prattle" column with him, and in it he pursued an idea he'd fooled around with in England: writing acerbic definitions that might go into a perverse dictionary. Among the many gems:

ALONE, *adj.* In bad company.
BRUTE, *n.* See HUSBAND.

IMPUNITY, *n*. Wealth.

MAYONNAISE, *n*. One of the sauces which serve the
   French in place of a state religion.

MISFORTUNE, *n*. The kind of fortune that never misses.

PEACE, *n*. In international affairs, a period of cheating
   between two periods of fighting.

SENATE, *n*. A body of elderly gentlemen charged with high
   duties and misdemeanors.

Some entries are longer than the above, with poems and fables
tacked on, but the short, epigrammatic ones work best. This taut
precision also characterized Bierce's news-of-the-day commentary.
"The personal property of the late Anthony Chabot, of Oakland, has
been ordered sold," began an item written in 1888 (though not for
The Wasp). Then came the swift kick. "This is a noble opportunity
to obtain Senator Vrooman." Bierce insulted his former boss by
writing, "HERE LIES FRANK PIXLEY AS USUAL." As a book
critic, Bierce set what surely remains a record for speedy demoli-
tion: "The covers of this book are too far apart." He saved his utmost
contempt for an odd pair of offending classes, crooked politicians
and amateurish writers. Charlotte Perkins Gilman, author of "The
Yellow Wallpaper," complained of him as "the Public Executioner
and Tormentor."

During these years Bierce lived apart from his family much of
the time, typically in hotels and most consistently in Auburn, a
town in the Sierra Nevada foothills; he gave up his editorship but
stayed affiliated with *The Wasp*, where his influence remained
strong. The ostensible reason for the domestic separation was his
asthma, which plagued him less in the dry air of central California.
But there was more to it. Bierce resented his mother- and brother-in-
law, especially when he perceived them as ganging up on him with
his wife; Auburn became his refuge from a sometimes distasteful
home life.

If Bierce had gone into journalism to right wrongs, for the most part he was thwarted. Early on, at the *News Letter*, he had accused a man named Sullivan, a local employee of the Internal Revenue Service, of blackmailing "bankers, brokers and other gentlemen cursed with incomes." An issue later, Bierce gleefully reported that Sullivan had been canned. But such triumphs were rare. A newspaper columnist lacks direct access to the kind of in-depth information on which a solid case for reform can be built, and a magazine editor has to devote his energy to multiple departments and projects, snatching time for his own writing as best he can. Not until the mid-1890s, when he could draw upon the resources of William Randolph Hearst's first two newspapers, the *San Francisco Examiner* and the *New York Journal*, was Bierce able to mount and direct an effective journalistic campaign—the one against the Octopus.

The association with Hearst came about in a most satisfying way. As Bierce recalled, in 1887, then in his mid-forties, he was living in Oakland (the rest of the family had taken up residence in the Napa Valley) when there came a knock at the door.

> I found a young man, the youngest young man, it seemed to me, that I had ever confronted. His appearance, his attitude, his manner, his entire personality suggested extreme diffidence. I did not ask him in, instate him in my better chair (I had two) and inquire how we could serve each other. If my memory is not at fault I merely said: "Well," and awaited the result.
>
> "I am from the San Francisco *Examiner*," he explained in a voice like the fragrance of violets made audible, and backed a little away.
>
> "O," I said, "you come from Mr. Hearst."
>
> Then that unearthly child lifted its blue eyes and cooed: "I am Mr. Hearst."

The "unearthly child"—newly installed as publisher of a newspaper that his father, a precious-metals millionaire and U.S. senator from California, had given him as a present—wanted to make a splash in journalism, and who better than Bierce to help him send water flying? Hearst made an offer that Bierce found acceptable, with one proviso: that his copy be printed just as he wrote it. Hearst assented to this.

This stroke of good fortune not only made Bierce and his family financially secure; it also gave him a sturdy platform for the next two decades. Once again taking his "Prattle" column with him, in the *Examiner* he consolidated his position as the West Coast's primary scourge of fools and knaves. Hearst was counting on his new star writer to generate wit and stir up controversy, and the star writer delivered. On one memorable occasion he skewered a local vintner. "The wine of Arpad Haraszthy has a bouquet all its own. It tickles and titillates the palate. It gurgles as it slips down the alimentary canal. It warms the cockles of the heart, and it burns the sensitive lining of the stomach." Haraszthy threatened to make trouble unless the *Examiner* printed a retraction, and Bierce obligingly supplied the text. "The wine of Arpad Haraszthy does not have a bouquet all its own. It does not tickle and titillate the palate. It does not gurgle as it slips down the alimentary canal. It does not warm the cockles of the heart, and it does not burn the sensitive lining of the stomach." Although at times Bierce disagreed with the paper's editorial stances, he was rarely muzzled. "[Hearst] did not once direct nor request me to write an opinion that I did not hold," he recalled, "and only two or three times suggested that I refrain for a season from expressing opinions that I did hold, when they were antagonistic to the policy of the paper, as they commonly were."

Obligated to produce only two columns a week, Bierce now had enough free time to write the stories and essays upon which a lasting reputation might rest. During his more than two decades in Hearst's employ, Bierce repeatedly got huffy (the publisher's subordinates did not always abide by his no-edits pledge) and gave notice to quit. Always, however, Hearst found a way to woo him back. Hearst's persuasive charm comes across in a letter he sent to head off one of Bierce's resignations.

> Don't for heaven's sake stop "Prattle." I shall think myself a terrible "hoodoo" if immediately on my return *The Examiner* should lose what is to me its very best feature. I hope you will continue. I don't want to have to stop my subscription to my own paper for lack of interest in the damned old sheet. Shall I appoint myself a committee of one to come up and persuade you?

An editor at the *New York Journal* recalled his one and only attempt to rein Bierce in. The offending passage was a joke about the funeral of an actress who was "always famous for her composed manner [but is] now quite decomposed." Measured against some of Bierce's West Coast assaults on good taste, this was small beer, but the editor reached for his red pencil. "Naturally," he relates, "I cut it out. Bierce instantly resigned and was lured back by Hearst—probably at an increased salary. Thereafter I let his copy alone."

Hearst did some deplorable things in his time, such as using the pages of his papers to help foment the unnecessary Spanish-American War. But when he spotted talent, he acquired it and turned it loose. He ended up giving the world two superlative gifts: George Herriman's "Krazy Kat," the greatest of all comic strips, which, though never very popular, lasted for decades simply because Hearst loved it; and the artistry of Ambrose Bierce, polemicist and short story writer.

Bierce's short fiction, much of which he wrote for the *Examiner* and a magazine called *The Wave* in a sustained burst of creativity from 1887–93, runs to occult content and surprise endings. Finding life as it mundanely is to be amorphous and bland, he channeled his dreams and fantasies through the filter of terror literature as shaped by such forebears as the English Gothic novelists (especially Mrs. Ann Radcliffe and Matthew Gregory "Monk" Lewis) and the American Edgar Allan Poe. Writers as disparate as Henry James and H. P. Lovecraft have done more with the ghost story than Bierce, and O. Henry may have surpassed him as a perpetrator of last-paragraph tricks. But Bierce colonized a territory that remains almost his private preserve.

We might set the stage by quoting Dr. Johnson, who admitted to harboring a constant fear of death. "So much so, Sir," he told Boswell, "that the whole of life is but keeping away thoughts of it." It was otherwise with Bierce. While soldiering, he'd seen and felt more of death—including his own close call at Kennesaw Mountain—than any man should have to. His asthma was also a constant reminder of mortality; the malady can leave you gasping and scared, unsure where your next breath is coming from. Given such a constitution and personal history, Bierce would have been hard put to block out thoughts of death. Rather than try to do so, he put his intimate knowledge of the subject to work for him.

In upwards of a dozen short stories, Bierce zeroed in on a cramped but fascinating psychological state: being about to die, sentenced to die, or left for dead. The best of these stories is the magnificent "An Occurrence at Owl Creek Bridge," in which the ever-hopeful mind of a condemned Confederate soldier eases him through his last moments on Earth by staging an elaborate, thrilling, and wholly imaginary escape just before the hangman's rope does its work. Less well-known but equally powerful is "Parker Adderson, Philosopher," in which the title character, a captured Union spy, reconciles himself to his fate—death by firing squad at dawn. So serenely ready to meet his Maker is the spy that he tosses off one mordant quip after another for the delectation of the Confederate general holding him prisoner. Until, that is, the exigencies of war force the general to scrap the schedule, and the heretofore stoic prisoner—but I mustn't spoil the denouement. "One Summer Night" has already been mentioned: an amazingly condensed performance that none of Poe's tales of being buried alive can match. To these masterpieces one can add "The Coup de Grâce," in which a horribly wounded man's wish to be put out of his misery leads to tragic results for a compassionate comrade; "One of the Missing," about a soldier trapped amid the wreckage of a building in such a way that he must stare, hour after hour, at a loaded gun pointed directly at him and liable to be set off by the least twitch of its "target"; and several others.

Bierce also probed the psychology of being in extremis in his nonfiction, such as an item from his "Prattle" column for *The Argonaut* of December 21, 1878. The subject is military executions, and Bierce recalls being on hand when a condemned soldier, up on the scaffold with a rope around his neck, tried to put a good face on his plight by crying out that he was "going home to Jesus," whereupon a nearby train blew "a loud and unmistakably derisive *Hoot—hoot!*" and the assembled witnesses burst out laughing. When the support boards were removed from under the pious prisoner and an equally doomed companion, they became, in Bierce's words, "the only persons I know in the other world who enjoyed the ghastly distinction of leaving this [one] to the sound of inextinguishable merriment."

Death comes to all men, as the newsreel announcer used to remind us, but Bierce stands virtually alone in his willingness to stare without flinching at its effects on the psychology of the person undergoing it. Having found a subject he could treat better than anyone else, he revisited it again and again with coruscating effect. Few other writers are so closely identified with a particular phase of human life, which in this case happens to be the final and most mysterious one. The irony would not have been lost on Bierce. In focusing intently on death, he earned a measure of immortality.

The prevalence of death in his life and fiction is worth dwelling on because it may have helped Bierce sustain the fierce outspokenness of his campaign against the Southern Pacific. When you've already survived mass carnage, fought asthma to a draw, sublimated your fear of death in your art—when, in short, you've gone steady with death almost your whole life—what's left to fear from a giant corporation. Or from anything at all?

The "deathly" stories, along with many others, were gathered into two volumes, *Tales of Soldiers and Civilians* (1891) and *Can Such Things Be?* (1893). They got good press and served notice that Bierce was more than just a fabricator of journalistic ephemera. The influential William Dean Howells thought so much of these stories that he placed Bierce "among our three greatest writers." Bierce, who had no use for Howell's pedestrian approach to fiction, retorted ungraciously, "I am sure Mr. Howells is the other two."

In the late 1880s, the Bierce family went through two experiences that could only have reinforced the writer's tragic sense of life. The first was the dissolution of his marriage, which occurred after Ambrose discovered that Mollie had received and kept love letters from an admirer. That was as far as the so-called "affair" went, but Ambrose had an exaggerated sense of personal honor to placate; as he wrote in a letter, "I don't take part in competitions—not even in love." He and Mollie separated—a break so clean that afterwards they spoke to each other only twice.

One of those times came after the second blow fell—the tabloid-worthy death of their elder son. Day Bierce was intelligent, handsome, and arrogant. That he had imbibed his father's sense of honor became evident at an early age. His sister recalled seeing "his eyes flashing, quivering with rage, his sensitive nostrils dilated, his whole person flaming with indignation like a Shelley [and saying], 'I wouldn't think of doing such a thing!' when told about some act of dishonesty or petty cheating."

At age seventeen he declared his ambition to be a journalist and left home. He caught on with a paper in Red Bluff, California, and became engaged to a young woman. The night before the wedding, she ran off with and married one Neil Hubbs, the designated best man. Left behind, Day found himself taunted as a cuckold—most woundingly in the pages of the local papers. When the couple returned, Day was lying in wait. He and Hubbs drew guns and began firing. After giving Hubbs a mortal wound, Day turned his gun on himself.

"Nothing matters," Bierce said by way of summing up the episode—although he might have added "except work." His enemy Frank Pixley had the atrocious taste to editorialize on the subject, sneering that Bierce now knew how the victims of his printed barbs must feel. In his next column, Bierce replied more temperately than he might have.

> Perhaps it is because I am a trifle dazed that I can discern no connection between my mischance and your solemn "Why persecutest thou me?" You must permit me to think the question incompetent and immaterial—the mere trick of a passing rascal swift to steal advantage from opportunity.

Not long after Day's death, Bierce met Gertrude Atherton, a promising young novelist who showered him with compliments. He took issue with one of these. "No, I'm not a great man. No one is better fitted to judge of greatness in men than I am, and I know that I am not great. I'm a journalist, past middle-age, without ambition, and have written nothing that measures up to my ideals." Nor to the public's ideals, either, for literary greatness is seldom awarded to miniaturists like Bierce.

That's one of the most striking features of Bierce's *Collected Works*—how choppy it all is. The corpus consists of one small plate after another—essays, stories, fables, poems, sketches, definitions, reminiscences—and it's a rare item that exceeds fifteen or twenty pages of wide margins and large print. The man couldn't get up a head of steam, couldn't take a single theme, develop it, flesh it out, and recapitulate it over a couple of hundred pages. It's possible that his decades of experience as a columnist had disabled him for l ng flights. Or that this was another effect of his asthma; Edmund Wilson suggested such a connection: "His writing—with its purged vocabulary, the brevity of the units in which it works and its cramped emotional range—is an art that can hardly breathe." Bierce not only reconciled himself to making the most of the short hops he took, churning out reams of what his most talented successor, San Francisco columnist Herb Caen, liked to call "three-dot journalism." Bierce also tried to make his lack of stamina into a virtue, especially when it came to fiction.

He never wrote a novel. (The closest he came was a novella, "The Monk and the Hangman's Daughter," a Gothic romance of no originality and little value—it's his reworking of a friend's translation of a story originally written in German.) He purported to explain why novel writing was not for him in an essay called "The Short Story." The problem, as he saw it, was that the novel sinned against the great aesthetic virtue of unity. "An opera, or an oratorio, that can be heard at a sitting may be artistic," he wrote, "but if in the manner of a Chinese play it were extended through the evenings of a week or a month what would it be? The only way to get unity of impression from a novel is to shut it up and look at the covers." Bierce was here echoing Poe who, in a review of Hawthorne's *Twice-Told Tales*, had pronounced "the ordinary novel . . . objectionable" because "as it cannot be read at one sitting, it deprives itself, of course, of the immense force derivable from *totality*." But at least Poe tried his hand at a novel, the not entirely successful *Narrative of Arthur Gordon Pym of Nantucket*. In Bierce's case, it doesn't take a shrink to see that, in classic sour-grapes mode, he was dismissing a genre for which he had either no gift or no patience. A *Devil's Dictionary* entry reinforces that impression: "NOVEL, *n*: A short story padded. A species of composition bearing the same relation to literature that the panorama bears to art."

The definition goes on. "As [the novel] is too long to be read at a sitting the impressions made by its successive parts are successively effaced, as in the panorama. Unity, totality of effect, is impossible;

for besides the few pages last read all that is carried in mind is the mere plot of what has gone before."

This is silly. Obviously, there are novels that sprawl to their detriment, but there are also well-stuffed masterpieces—*Moby-Dick*, *Little Dorrit*, and *War and Peace* come immediately to mind. Moreover, a skilled writer can keep a long or longish novel as tightly reined in as he would a short story: e.g., Henry James with *The Golden Bowl*. Even if we were to grant that unity is the most prized artistic value, Bierce is pretending to be stupid here, unable to retain in his mind the traits with which a good novelist endows her characters as they make multiple appearances in the story, or to recall any of the well-turned phrases she uses to paint a scene or capture a dramatic moment. Bierce's essay and definition add up to a perverse spectacle: someone who can't write novels dismissing with a wave of his hand all those who can.

Nor was Bierce's limited staying power confined to his fiction. It warped his whole career, keeping him from making the best use of his richest literary material when, after long years of rumination, he got around to mining it: the Civil War. Bierce had the distinction of being the most important American writer to have fought on the Union side. No, make that the most important writer, period—the South's number-one candidate, the poet Sidney Lanier, is all but forgotten today. Bierce saw plenty of action, acquitted himself well enough to win multiple commendations and promotions, and by the end had experienced the war in a wide variety of capacities: enlistee, private, officer, aide to a general, mapmaker, wounded man, witness to such storied battles as Shiloh and Chickamauga, underling at strategy sessions presided over by Grant and Sherman. With his extraordinary powers of observation, exacting prose style, and habit of taking nothing for granted, Bierce not only could evoke the din and confusion of battle and capture the emotions of men under fire, he could also grasp nuances missed by lesser observers.

As evidence, consider a column item reprinted as "The Body

Count at Franklin," about one of the battles in which Bierce took part. He zeroes in on those occasions when soldiers yield ground.

> When two lines of battle are fighting face to face on even terms and one is "forced back" (which always occurs unless it is ordered back) it is fear that forces it: the men could have stood if they had wanted to. In our civil war I saw scores of such instances. Sometimes the Federals fled, sometimes the Confederates.

Following up on this observation, he encapsulates the whole course of the war in two crisp but weighty sentences. "As a rule the Confederates fought better than our men. On even terms they commonly defeated us; nearly all our victories were won by superior numbers, better arms and advantages of position."

In his short story "A Son of the Gods," Bierce cites the experience of entering an abandoned Confederate camp to generalize about the larger phenomenon of mythologizing one's enemy.

> The soldier never becomes wholly familiar with the conception of his foes as men like himself; he cannot divest himself of the feeling that they are another order of beings, differently conditioned, in an environment not altogether of the earth. The smallest vestiges of them rivet his attention and engage his interest. He thinks of them as inaccessible; and, catching an unexpected glimpse of them, they appear farther away, and therefore larger, than they really are—like objects in a fog. He is somewhat in awe of them.

In an essay called "Modern Warfare," Bierce pinpoints a phenomenon that Grant noticed soon enough, too: how readily soldiers can get used to the security of fortified positions, so much so that they handicap themselves as a fighting force.

The particular thing that they lose is courage. In long sieges the sallies and assaults are commonly feeble, spiritless affairs, easily repelled. So manifestly does a soldier's comparative safety indispose him to incur even such perils as beset him in it that during the last years of our civil war, when it was customary for armies in the field to cover their fronts with breastworks, any intelligent officer, conceding the need of some protection, yet made their works much slighter than was easily possible. Except when the firing was heavy, close and continuous, "head-logs" (for example) for the men to fire under were distinctly demoralizing. The soldier who has least security is least reluctant to forego what security he had. That is to say, he is the bravest. . . .

Bierce delivers this kind of aperçu again and again—but in scattershot fashion, writing as the spirit moves him. And so "his" war accumulates piecemeal: in an essay here, a poem there, a short story hither, a letter yon, and even the occasional definition for *The Devil's Dictionary*. Surely there would have been a market for a full-blown war memoir by a well-known man of letters who had experienced so much fighting firsthand, but no such thing came from Bierce's pen. It wasn't until 2002, almost a century after his death, that every surviving scrap of his writing on the war was gathered in one place, an anthology called *Phantoms of a Blood-Stained Period*. Although *Phantoms* is a showcase of intelligence and wit, brimming over with trenchant insights into the behavior of men in battle, it looks rather like Norman Mailer's *Advertisements for Myself*, that grab bag of fiction, reflections, criticism, and poetry which owes its existence more to its author's overbearing persona than to anything else. Had Bierce published such a potpourri during his lifetime, readers would probably have found the format off-putting.

Bierce was also hampered by his insistence on giving readers the unvarnished truth. By the time he took up his pen to write about the war, the nation was preoccupied with wound binding. It was the era of memorials and parades and rose-colored reunions in which Union and Confederate veterans showed up wearing their medals and uniforms (or as much of them as they could still fit into) in order to drink, swap stories, refight battles, second-guess their generals, and relive their youths. For the most part, Bierce declined to be among those who reexamined the bloody past through a scrim of nostalgia. To the contrary, with his sharp memory and lax internal censor, he told readers things they might not want to hear about the futility of war and the repugnance of death on the battlefield.

A good case can be made for Bierce's essay "What I Saw of Shiloh" as the grandfather of no-holds-barred writing about war, and its description of a mortally wounded soldier is still unsurpassed for its brutally hard look at the waste left by battle. Commanding a platoon, Bierce halted his men near a sprawl of corpses, among which they noticed

a Federal sergeant, variously hurt, who had been a fine giant in his time. He lay face upward, taking in his breath in convulsive, rattling snorts, and blowing it out in sputters of froth which crawled creamily down his cheeks, piling itself alongside his neck and ears. A bullet had clipped a groove in his skull, above the temple; from this the brain protruded in bosses, dropping off in flakes and strings. I had not previously known one could get on, even in this unsatisfactory fashion, with so little brain. One of my men, whom I knew for a womanish fellow, asked if he should put his bayonet through him. Inexpressibly shocked by the cold-blooded proposal, I told him I thought not; it was unusual, and too many were looking.

Even today, that passage is best read on an empty stomach. Nor were people eager to hear, as Bierce made sure they did, that dead soldiers left unburied were apt to be dined on by feral pigs.

In his story "Chickamauga," Bierce found an unforgettable way to bring home the carnage of war. A six-year-old country boy, who happens to be a deaf-mute, goes out to play and blunders into a grisly exodus: the crawling of innumerable wounded and desperately thirsty men toward a water hole. To the boy this tableau is a game—they are his army, he is their leader, and when one of the maimed men looks up, exhibiting a face with its lower jaw missing, the boy recoils without understanding what's wrong. Not even when he returns home to find his own mother dead and mutilated can the boy make sense of all he has seen but not heard. War is a tale told by a deaf-mute, full of unheard sound and misunderstood fury, signifying less than nothing.

No, Bierce was not the writer for hero-worshipers or Civil War buffs in padded armchairs. More to their liking would have been someone like Stephen Crane, whose 1895 novel *The Red Badge of Courage* combines scenes of terror with a feel-good ending in which the cowardly "youth" turns hero. Bierce must have been raked by the anomaly that the *Red Badge* author wasn't born until five years after the war's end and wrote his great book at the tender age of twenty-four with little more experience of rough stuff than boyhood scrapes and football games. The older man's envy comes across in what is perhaps the lamest witticism he ever uttered. When his friend the critic Percival Pollard mentioned two now-forgotten young novelists whom he considered worse than Crane, Bierce retorted, "I had thought that there could be only two worse writers than Stephen Crane, namely two Stephen Cranes." Pollard endeared himself to Bierce by challenging readers to "show [me] a passage in *The Red Badge of Courage* so vividly and truly descriptive of the wounded crawling over a battlefield as that in Bierce's 'Chickamauga.'" (Crane, for his part, lavished praise on "An Occurrence at Owl Creek Bridge," saying to a friend, "That story has everything. Nothing better exists.")

How Crane pulled off the tour de force that is *The Red Badge of Courage* is not easy to explain. We know that as a boy he'd heard his elders tell Civil War stories and that he read extensively in the source material, including the multivolume *Battles and Leaders of the*

Civil War, a compilation of articles on the conflict by those who had fought it. Then there were the playing fields of Lafayette and Syracuse, the two colleges he attended without getting a degree. The rest came courtesy of his genius, and nothing pleased Crane more than finally to observe combat as a reporter and realize how accurately he'd imagined it. *"The Red Badge* is all right," he boyishly concluded after witnessing fighting in Greece.

"All right," but not airtight. Bierce would surely have spotted a farfetched interlude that comes about halfway through the book. After giving in to his fear and turning tail in a battle, the youth falls in with an inquisitive fellow soldier. "What reg'ment do yeh b'long teh?" the soldier asks. "Eh? What's that? Th' 304th N' York? Why, what corps is that? Oh, it is? Why, I thought they wasn't engaged t'-day—they're 'way over in th' center." It's convenient to Crane's purpose for this random stranger to know where the youth's regiment was posted and what it did or did not do—but also highly improbable. As Bierce had written in 1888,

It is seldom, indeed, that a subordinate officer knows anything about the disposition of the enemy's forces . . . or precisely whom he is fighting. As to the rank and file, they can know nothing more of the matter than the arms they carry. They hardly know what troops are upon their own right or left the length of a regiment away. If it is a cloudy day, they are ignorant even of the points of the compass.

How irksome it must have been to be outshone by a whippersnapper whose familiarity with the Civil War came mostly from books. How irritating to be all but eclipsed by a stripling with a dazzling prose style (e.g., "the furnace roar of the battle") and a prodigious talent for observing and evoking human behavior (a furious officer "continued to curse, but it was now with the air of a man who was using his last box of oaths"). Almost every page of *Red Badge* has something on it to make the reader gasp with pleasure at its combination of unexpectedness and keen observation, and whether the author got every historical jot and tittle right is almost beside the point. Bierce had been scooped right in his own back-yard, as it were.

It was at this low point, with Bierce overtaken and outclassed, that he got the opportunity of a newspaperman's lifetime. A telegram came. It was from Hearst. He wanted Bierce to take on a special assignment—go to Washington and do battle with the Octopus.

⇌ five ⇌

Anatomy of the Funding Bill

That William Randolph Hearst should lock horns with the Southern Pacific Railroad was almost decreed by fate. The Big Four were Republicans, but Hearst's senator-father was an antirailroad Democrat, and for all their wealth and spendthrift ways the Hearsts fancied themselves allies of the working class. (It was in the *Examiner* that Edwin Markham's sentimental poem about an anonymous agrarian toiler, "The Man with the Hoe," first appeared.) San Francisco had been an antirailroad town ever since the blatant corrupting of that referendum by Philip Stanford and his moneybags, and there was plenty of room for antimonopoly journalism in Manhattan, where Will Hearst had obtained a platform by buying the *New York Journal* in 1895. As Hearst saw it, a campaign to keep the Southern Pacific from pulling another fast one on the American public would likely not only boost circulation at both his papers but also further his growing ambition to run for political office.

So deep-seated was Hearst's antirailroad animus that it had caused a sweet deal to go sour. In the early 1890s, the Southern Pacific and the *Examiner* had agreed that for a payment of $30,000 (in installments of $1,000 per month) the company would get to place ads in the paper and receive "fair treatment." As far as the railroad was concerned, the ad component was mostly for show. After the agreement unraveled because Hearst couldn't make himself be consistently "fair" to the railroad, the company's top lawyer wrote to the paper's business manager:

> There can be no question that the chief consideration to inure to the Southern Pacific Company in this transaction was the fair treatment to be accorded by your paper; that it would not have entered into an agreement to [pay] $30,000 for advertising merely, as the benefit to accrue from such advertising alone was grossly inadequate to the sum of money involved.

This calls to mind the story about an old populist senator who left office with his mind made up: No lobbying firm could pay him enough to sully his principles by going to work for it. "And then," he confessed some time later, "I found they *could*." For Hearst, the revelation worked the other way around. He'd assumed the Associates could pay him handsomely enough not to expose their misdeeds. And then he found they *couldn't*.

Other papers, however, were not so well-heeled. When Fremont Older took over as editor of the *San Francisco Bulletin* in 1895, he discovered that the Southern Pacific was slipping the paper $125 a month for "friendliness"—and getting it. This contribution, which made a real difference to the struggling *Bulletin*, was a mere filament in the network of bribes by which the railroad tried to sway public opinion and dictate to public officials. Another method noted by Older was the Southern Pacific's practice of giving out "blue tickets," which entitled friends of the railroad to free rides. Looking back a quarter-century later, Older explained why in good conscience he couldn't let the *Bulletin* keep taking the railroad's money and passes.

The entire state at that time was politically controlled by the Southern Pacific. In order thoroughly to dominate the state it not only controlled the Legislature, the courts, the municipal governments, the county governments, which included coroners, sheriffs, boards of supervisors, in fact, all state and county and city officials, but it also had as complete a control of the newspapers of the state as was possible, and through them it controlled public opinion.

With the defections of the *Examiner* and *Bulletin*, that control became less than ironclad in San Francisco.

That Ambrose Bierce should joust with the railroad, however, was not a foregone conclusion. Not only was he pro-establishment by temperament; he loathed "The Man with the Hoe" and had an almost visceral disdain for labor unions, which often clashed with the Southern Pacific. One of Bierce's biographers, Adolphe de Castro, traces his subject's anti–Southern Pacific bias to a personal source: thwarted ambition. According to de Castro, Bierce had taken that job as mining superintendent in Dakota Territory to pad his resumé for the lucrative post he really coveted: director of public relations for the Southern Pacific. Upon returning to San Francisco, de Castro claimed, Bierce applied to Stanford, who seemed favorably disposed but said he must talk it over with Huntington. When Bierce called on Huntington at his office, Stanford was already there, closeted with his partner, but the door was ajar. Bierce overheard Huntington nix Stanford's recommendation to hire Bierce ("This fellow is uncontrollable," Huntington explained) and slunk away in defeat. From then on, he wasted no opportunity to bad-mouth Huntington and the railroad.

This seems unlikely. In 1894, Bierce took Huntington's side after the Pullman strike hit the nation's railroads and Huntington condemned it as the first step toward mob rule. At Hearst's direction, the *Examiner* supported the strikers, but Bierce disagreed in his

column: "From the point of view of reason and right Mr. Huntington's argument seems to me impregnable at every point to dissent
or depreciation." Bierce came to Huntington's defense again a year
later, when the owner of a new San Francisco newspaper quoted
selectively and misleadingly from a letter written by the railroad
baron. In neither case did Bierce have to speak out as he did (during
the Pullman strike, for example, he could easily have inveighed
against the strikers without giving that shout-out to Huntington);
his willingness to do so belies the notion that his attacks on the
funding bill stemmed from a grudge.

De Castro himself makes a better candidate for someone whose
judgment was warped by personal pique. He was Bierce's co-author
on *The Monk and the Hangman's Daughter*, and the two men were
friends—until they had a falling-out. Yet even without that history
behind it, de Castro's claim would have been suspect. During the
funding-bill fight, Huntington would have gone to almost any
length to silence Bierce, and a plausible accusation that his antirailroad campaign derived from a personal vendetta would have been
a telling blow. For Huntington not to have said a word about it
strongly suggests that no such thing ever occurred.

The truth seems to be straightforward: Bierce called disputes as
he saw them, going after Huntington and his partners for the simple reason that they left him no choice. It wasn't personal (not in
origin, at least). He saw them as conniving bastards who couldn't
stop conniving, and there's nothing a fired-up newsman likes more
than to strip such fellows bare. Indeed, you could hardly have asked
for better villains than "the railrogues" (as Bierce liked to call
them), who were widely thought to have lied, cheated, and bribed
their way to huge fortunes at the public expense. They were strong
and sure of foot—but not infallibly so; often cunning, but sometimes crude and blundering; powerful enough that to beat them
would be a grand triumph, while at the same time culpable on so
many counts that merely to shine a steady light on their misdeeds
might be devastating to their cause. To the battle Bierce would

bring financial assets and manpower (both supplied by Hearst) the likes of which he'd never had at his disposal before. For once, he could weave his great strengths—wit and the power of ridicule—through a solid framework of all the available facts, carefully gathered and systematically interpreted by reporters specially assigned to him. At the same time, his most obvious limitation—piecemeal production—wouldn't matter. The campaign's pace would be set by each day's doings on Capitol Hill, and Bierce would simply have to keep up. He undoubtedly recognized the posting to Washington for what it was: the chance, finally, to make a difference.

In fact, he'd been limbering up for the task for years. In one of the barbs destined for *The Devil's Dictionary*, he'd defined "corporation" as "an ingenious device for obtaining individual profit without individual responsibility." And despite occasionally taking Huntington's side, he'd long been chipping away at the façade of the corporation known as, first, the Central Pacific and, then, the Southern Pacific—taking care (in keeping with the definition just quoted) to chastise the men behind it. Historian Daniel Lindley has combed through magazine and newspaper archives for the years leading up to the anti–funding bill campaign to unearth dozens of examples of Bierce sounding off against the railroad and its four impresarios.

Among the exhibits are a couple of poems. The first, "Ode to the Central Pacific Spade," lampooned the display, at the New Orleans World's Industrial and Cotton Centennial Exposition of 1884, of the tool used to break ground for the railroad a generation earlier. The ode closed with these hyperbolic couplets:

Within thee, as within a magic glass,
I seem to see a foul procession pass—
Judges with ermine dragging in the mud
And spotted here and there with guiltless blood;
Gold-greedy legislators jingling bribes.
Kept editors and sycophantic scribes;

Liars in swarms and plunderers in tribes.
They fade away before the night's advance,
And fancy figures thee a devil's lance
Gleaming portentous through the misty shade,
While ghosts of murdered virtues shriek around thy blade!

Nine years later came a more succinct mock-eulogy to the most pompous member of the quadrumvirate who owned that spade.

Here Stanford lies, who thought it odd
That he should go to meet his God.
He looked, until his eyes grew dim,
For God to hasten to meet him.

In a way, however, Stanford's death must have chagrined Bierce—by putting an end to a graphic name game he'd been playing: stigmatizing the quondam governor and senator by spelling his name Stealand Standfirm, Stealand Landford, or £eland $tanford.

Crocker, too, had made a juicy target. His announcement that he was moving to New York had drawn a breathless—and barely grammatical—reaction from Bierce.

To the removal of himself and all his belongings from among a people whose generous encouragement he has punished by plunder—from a state whose industries he has impoverished, whose legislation he has sophisticated and perverted, whose courts of justice he has corrupted, of whose servants he has made thieves, and in the debauchery of whose politics he has experienced a coarse delight irrelative to the selfish advantage that was its purpose—from a city whose social tone he has done his best to lower to the level of his own brutal graces, and for whose moral standards he has tried to substitute the fatty degeneration of his own heart.—to the taking of his offensive personality out of contact with a community interpenetrated with the unclean emanation that he calls his influence, we trust he will address himself with such energy and activity as two laborious decades of public and private sinning have left him the ability to invoke.

It may not be entirely fair to draw inferences from Crocker's failure to sue for libel over that dithyramb, but the temptation is irresistible. Could it be that Crocker feared being called on to testify in court, in which event he might be forced or tricked into disclosing material damaging to the railroad?

On one occasion in 1884, Bierce all but foresaw the showdown to which he and the railroad were heading when he predicted that the Southern Pacific would not repay its long-standing debt to the federal government. Another time, he took an opportunity to try out an early version of a famous put-down attributed to him in 1896. As Bierce told it, someone from the railroad had sent *The Wasp* a letter asking "the market price of our favor." He answered in his column that the price was payment in full, with the railroad discharging its debts to the feds, the state, and everyone else.

Bierce's railroad baiting had gained him new fans—anti-railroad buffs, they might be called. In 1881, a reader had written in wondering whether any significance should be attached to the recent absence of the Southern Pacific from Bierce's column. In reply, Bierce reassured the reader that he hadn't gone soft.

In assuming that we have either made or abandoned a "fight against the railroad people," you are in error. In the natural course of comment—verbal and graphic—upon public matters we have found, not made, occasion to censure the piratical methods of "the railroad people," and on similar occasions shall do so again, as you are likely soon to observe. That is all there is in it—don't worry about our being "bought off." We are more likely to buy *them* off. That appears to be about the only way to get them to behave.

The attacks continued after Bierce went to work for Hearst—and why not, since this was a subject on which they were in near perfect accord? In one *Examiner* column, Bierce gave Huntington a lesson in monopoly economics. The plutocrat had claimed on behalf of railroads the by-then-standard justification cited for trusts generally: Consolidation would lead to efficiencies, which ultimately would result in lower rates for consumers. "What in the absence of competition," Bierce shot back, "would be the motive in reducing rates?" He got so disgusted with the railroads' behavior that he took the brash step of recommending a government takeover. In 1895, when San Francisco mayor Adolph Sutro called a mass meeting at which he demanded the arrest of Huntington, now the last surviving member of the Big Four, Bierce found himself in sizzling agreement: "in the past twenty years there has been no day when [Huntington] did not deserve to be hanged upon every limb of every tree of every acre of land which he has consecrated to his company's use by the laying on of hands."

The funding-bill controversy, it will be recalled, grew out of the federal government's loans, in the form of bonds, to the Central Pacific. The company was allowed to sell these certificates to the public, with the proceeds going to build the line. The government would take care of the interest due bondholders—6 percent paid semiannually—but at the end of thirty years the bonds would mature and the Central Pacific would have to pay back both principal and interest, minus expenses incurred in performing such services as transporting troops and carrying the mail. (To recapitulate, each mile of track built on flatland brought the Central Pacific sixteen $1,000 bonds; each mile in the mountains, forty-eight of them. As an added source of income, the railroad was authorized to issue and sell its own bonds, which—after the 1864 amendments to the 1862 Act—constituted a first lien, meaning that holders of the railroad-backed bonds had priority over holders of the government-backed ones.) The government-backed bonds should have been attractive investments, but the project was so risky that often they failed to sell at par value. These bonds had been issued at various times in the 1860s, but for most of them the thirty-year period would run out in the year 1897.

Prudent businessmen would have willingly put aside sums at regular intervals in anticipation of retiring that debt. But just to be sure, Congress had drafted the enabling laws so as to require annual interest payments—or so it thought. A unanimous Supreme Court ruled otherwise, holding that, like the principal, the interest wasn't due until the end of thirty years. The final tally was expected to be around $75 million. Meanwhile, the Central Pacific and the Contract & Finance Company were declaring fat dividends—almost $18.5 million in one four-year period alone. Stuart Daggett summed up the situation neatly in his history of the railroad. "To see earnings divided among a group of financiers who were believed to be already overpaid, while the unpaid interest on the government subsidy bonds piled up, was all the more exasperating because of the apparent helplessness of Congress."

In 1878, led by Senator Allen Thurman, a Democratic senator from Ohio, Congress took a step to improve the federal government's chances of getting its money back. It was a good time to be sniping at railroads. During his presidential campaign, Rutherford B. Hayes had been sold to the public as a breath of honest air after the corruption infecting the Grant administration. At the same time, the Southern Pacific—along with other lines—had fallen into disrepute thanks to its cumulative record of deceptive construction practices, cockeyed rate setting, influence peddling, and overall greed. More newspapers were taking potshots at the Southern Pacific, and Huntington thought he knew why: bungled bribery. "I have an impression that nobody ever made more mistakes than our people have made in handling matters political in California," he wrote in a letter some years later. "I think they have paid out large amounts of money [and] paid much of it on the street corners, although of that of course I am not certain. We were paying some vampires, like The Argonaut, Bassett's Standard [and] others, whose pay I cut off [and] of course they snarled back at me like so many hyenas." What a tantalizing passage! It seems to be shaping up as a primer on effective graft—*No street-corner action, no dealing with vamps or hyenas*—only to cut off prematurely. One wishes that the master had been more forthcoming on a subject he knew so much about: How to Grease a Palm.

For all his prowess, Huntington couldn't stave off the Thurman Act. This was the law that created a sinking fund into which the Central Pacific was required to deposit a percentage of its earnings each year—much to the dismay of the Big Four, who bitterly resented any interference with the way they managed their money and juggled their books. Huntington fulminated against the bill's sponsor in a statement given years later to historian H. H. Bancroft:

I know old Thurman well. He expected to be President of the United States by passing the Thurman Act, but he was not honored of course. I don't believe he was in earnest. I don't believe he thought the Act was proper. It was a false contract. There was no warrant in law or equity. He turned demagogue for political purposes.

Stanford became almost apoplectic on the subject, reaching back into English history to compare the Thurman Act to the suppression of the Order of Templars in the reign of King Edward II and the appropriation of religious property in the reign of King Henry VIII.

As noted earlier, in the *Sinking Fund Cases*, the Supreme Court sided with Congress. But heinous or not, the Thurman Act wasn't very effective. The wherewithal for the sinking fund was to come from the Central Pacific's earnings, but these were now running low, partly because its owners were steering business away from it to their other railroads—precisely, it would appear, to evade the Act's requirements. Thanks to the Associates' ingenuity, the sinking fund proved to be a well-intentioned failure.

Over the next decade or so, various governmental bodies investigated the railroad, sometimes grilling Huntington and Stanford when they testified at hearings—and invariably suffered abysmal failures of memory. The culmination of these efforts came in 1887, with the work of the U.S. Pacific Railway Commission. In its report, the commission's majority saw through at least some of the evasions, saying, "It is impossible to read the evidence of C. P. Huntington and Leland Stanford . . . without reaching the conclusion that very large sums of money have been improperly used in connection with legislation." A minority of the commissioners went so far as to recommend that the government foreclose on the debt, take over the defaulting railroad, and run the thing itself. (Even if this had been politically feasible, however—which it probably wasn't—it would have been only a partial remedy, peeling away the Central Pacific unit and leaving the rest of the Southern Pacific's empire intact. What's more, the Central Pacific wasn't what it used to be, and it's doubtful whether even the most astute leadership could have squeezed enough money out of it alone to retire the federal loans within a reasonable period.) The commission's majority proposed a gentler solution: The company should convert the debt as it stood on July 1, 1888, into fifty-year bonds, paying 3 percent interest, to be held by the government. This solution was embodied in the so-called Reilly Bill, named after its sponsor.

Most observers consider this a cushy offer, but Stanford was mightily offended. He rated the railroad's heroic contributions to the national welfare so highly that he plumped for total debt forgiveness. One of his arguments for this favor was so brassy that he deserves a prize for chutzpah. He said that the railroad's speedy construction had given the country the incalculable boon of a transcontinental link years ahead of schedule—as if the main reason for the Central Pacific's breakneck speed hadn't been to increase its share of the spoils at the Union Pacific's expense. A related point was equally unpersuasive. The railroad suggested that, had it built more slowly, it would have had time to cajole the public into buying the bonds at par value. To which the counterargument was simple but powerful: The bonds' selling price had been dictated by the market—which is how things work in a capitalist economy. If these appeals for cancellation should fail (and they did), Huntington and Stanford had a fallback position. The government should accept payment in land—the very land that the government had given the Big Four as yet another incentive to get the railroad built. You have to hand it to these characters. At making self-serving arguments with straight faces, they had few equals.

After Stanford's death in 1893, the federal government sued his estate, seeking $15 million on the theory that Central Pacific stockholders could be held personally liable for its debts. In 1896, a unanimous Supreme Court disagreed, declaring that the authorizing statutes did not contemplate personal liability, at least not vis-à-vis the United States. This was probably for the best, the Court added. Otherwise, "It is not too much to say that . . . the accomplishing of the object Congress had in mind would have been seriously retarded, if not wholly defeated," because potential investors would have shied away. Maybe so, but two points should be made about the decision. First, the fact remained that Stanford and his three cronies had rewarded themselves to the tune of roughly $20 million apiece, at the expense of their fellow taxpayers—shouldn't criminal prosecutions for fraud at least have been considered? (Another possibility might have been a shareholders' suit to recover funds wrongfully pocketed by the Big Four.) Second, Bierce was entitled to an "I told you so." His definition of a corporation—"individual profit without individual responsibility"—had been vindicated. At any rate, whether and on what terms that debt would be paid off were now entirely up to the legislative process.

Out in California, another opponent with money to back him up was adding to the Southern Pacific's troubles: Mayor Sutro. This stubborn cuss had made a fortune in Nevada by punching a three-mile-long tunnel into a mountainside for easier access to the deep mines of the Comstock Lode. With canny timing, he had sold his brainchild just before the Lode began to peter out, and moved to San Francisco. There he poured his money into real estate, ultimately acquiring some 12 percent of the city's area. He first tangled with Huntington over one of the latter's many investments. Huntington had controlling interest in the only streetcar line to Sutro Heights, a tract at the western edge of San Francisco on which Sutro was building various public attractions, including Cliff House and the Sutro Baths. It had been a nasty fight, with Sutro at one point offering patrons a choice: Come on foot and you get in free; ride one of Huntington's cars, and you pay 25 cents. Sutro finally won this round by putting in a streetcar line of his own.

But he stayed on the offensive, running for mayor of San Francisco on an antirailroad platform and, after his victory in 1894, dunning members of Congress with rowdy letters as the funding-bill controversy heated up. The envelopes containing Sutro's screeds were emblazoned with slogans printed in red: "Huntington wouldn't steal a red-hot stove," "Down with the Octopus," "How Huntington fixes up committees," "Oh! What a hog!" When the post office balked at delivering the scandalous red letters, a wag urged Sutro to issue a Bierce-like retraction: "The statement that Mr. Huntington wouldn't steal a red-hot stove is false." Sutro even appealed to the state of Kentucky, where the Southern Pacific was incorporated, urging the state to cancel the company's charter.

Sutro was not alone. The California press continued to desert the Southern Pacific, with several San Francisco papers calling for a federal takeover—an outcome they considered best not only for

California, but for the country as a whole. Even the conservative *Los Angeles Times* editorialized that all it would take was for "just one transcontinental line [to come into] the possession of the Government, operated in the interests of the public, [and] the rest of the lines would be brought to time very quickly." (Huntington complained that Californians had "got a kind of craze on" for government ownership.) To rally readers around its position that the Reilly Bill was too lenient, the *Examiner* ran in its pages a petition opposing the bill; it attracted almost 200,000 signatures and was bound and delivered to Congress as a two-volume set. On February 2, 1895, the House of Representatives bowed to these pressures and returned the Reilly Bill to committee, in effect killing it.

Huntington was pretty sure that the government would never take over the railroad. And he agreed wholeheartedly with Stanford's estimate of the Big Four's contributions to the common good. "If there is anybody who has done more for this country than my associates and myself," he said in an 1887 interview with the *New York Daily Tribune*, "I would like a chromo of them, I would." (A chromo was a chromolithograph, an image that could be mass-produced.) As a realist, however, he probably suspected that ground would eventually have to be given. Still, he just couldn't help himself—he now proposed allowing the railroad to issue bonds to the government on *more lenient* terms than those in the Reilly Bill: 2 percent interest (down from 3) and an eighty-five-year lifespan (up from fifty), at the end of which principal and interest would supposedly be paid in full.

About midway through the ensuing fight, in the *Examiner* of March 19, 1896, Bierce sarcastically took the long view—the very long view—of what might well happen if the railroad's solution went into effect:

The new bonds are to bear interest at the munificent rate of 2 per cent, and when in the sweet by-and-by they mature in the hands of our great-grandchildren, they will doubtless be paid, in their turn, by another issue, bearing as much as 1½ per cent. That a railroad company should ever take up one set of bonds except by the issue of another set is so patent an absurdity that General Hubbard [a Southern Pacific backer] regards it with a mixture of austere disfavor and tolerant contempt. . . . It is a fact that the money subscribed for railroad construction is never, or seldom, paid back by the men who borrowed it, nor by their successors. It is paid by another set of subscribers, who in their turn are paid by another, "and so ad infinitum." But the company does not pay and has never intended to pay. It carries that debt and as much more as it can incur forever.

The federal government, in other words, would have been a damned fool to accept these terms, yet they were essentially the ones embodied in the document that drove the 1896 debate: the so-called Powers Bill, after its sponsor, H. Henry Powers, the Vermont Congressman who chaired the House Committee on Pacific Railroads. The Powers Bill was the "compromise" that Hearst and Bierce went all out to defeat.

⇌ six ⇌

Bierce at War Again

In his first decade as a publisher, it had dawned on Hearst, as it had earlier on his rival Joseph Pulitzer, that a paper's news-gathering effort can be newsworthy itself—or at least a good excuse to toot one's own horn. Hence the front-page treatment given a pair of telegrams in the *Examiner*'s issue of January 21, 1896. Hearst's overture, sent from New York (where the publisher was busy with his new plaything, the *Journal*) to "Ambrose Bierce, Esq." in care of the *Examiner*, read:

> Railroad combination so strong in Washington that seems almost impossible to break them, yet it is certainly the duty of all having interests of the Coast at heart to make most strenuous efforts. Will you please go to Washington for "The Examiner"? I will send Davenport from here, and "The Journal" will use whatever power it has to assist. Please answer quick.

With its call for uphill-struggle heroics, the telegram was as much manifesto as invitation, and Hearst risked nothing in making it public because Bierce had already said yes. His reply, dated the same day as the first wire (January 18), was reproduced an inch or two below: "I shall be glad to do whatever I can toward defeating Mr. Huntington's Funding bill, and shall start for Washington on Monday evening next." This tight-lipped acceptance contrasts with the boasting and mudslinging in the accompanying article—hallmarks of the overheated style that makes nineteenth-century journalism so much fun to read:

> Ambrose Bierce knows the trail he is treading. He has blazed it with his own ax many times. And he knows the game he is hunting. He has chased it howling to its lair frequently. There will be no joy in the Huntington lobby when Bierce gets to Washington. He has whipped some of these rascals naked through the town before, and it is not likely that they have forgotten the castigation. It is fairly probable that they are in wholesome fear of a repetition. The readers of "The Examiner" are assured that these folk will not be disappointed.

Hearst's loan of Homer Davenport, a brash *Journal* cartoonist who happened to be a former railroad brakeman, underscored the publisher's commitment to the cause. Davenport, who had gone to work for Hearst the previous year, is remembered mainly for two things: scrawling dollar signs all over the figure of Mark Hanna in caricatures of that venal McKinley supporter; and making life so miserable for New York state legislators that they considered a bill to ban political cartoons (Davenport fought back in a cartoon captioned "No Honest Man Need Fear Cartoons," and the bill was defeated). Davenport was joined in Washington by another fine cartoonist, James Swinnerton, and a small cadre of *Journal* writers and support staff—perhaps a half-dozen in all. They awaited Bierce at what might be called "Funding Bill Central," a rented suite in the Page Hotel at 723 15th St. N.W., not far from the Treasury Building and the White House. They must have felt a comradely sense of mission as they prepared to take on Huntington and his multiple "hirelings" (Bierce's term), who operated out of another hotel, La-Normandie, a couple of blocks away at 15th and I. The estimated total manpower available to Huntington was twenty-six.

Even for the innately exuberant Hearst, however, that public send-off was hyperbolic. As Bierce traveled east by train (probably via the Southern Pacific and Union Pacific lines), he undoubtedly spent some sobering hours thinking about what he would be up against in Washington.

The president, Grover Cleveland, back for a second term after the interregnum of Republican Benjamin Harrison, was known as a Bourbon Democrat—more inclined to serve the interests of big business than to strike blows for populism. Cleveland had made his reputation as a cautiously progressive governor of New York, where he insisted on honest government and vetoed pork-barrel legislation, but he was no trustbuster. He did nothing to stop his attorney general, Richard B. Olney, from watering down the Sherman Antitrust Act. On the other hand, Cleveland had no particular brief for railroads; in 1887, he had signed with enthusiasm the bill creating the Interstate Commerce Commission. Ultimately, Bierce would have reasoned, Hearst's position as a wealthy and influential Democrat ought to help stiffen Cleveland's backbone. That is, if Congress could be brought around on the funding bill, the president would probably not stand in the way of its decision.

Could Congress be swayed? Antimonopoly sentiment in general and antirailroad animus in particular were growing in the 1890s. But both houses of Congress were in Republican hands. The House in particular had gone Republican by a landslide in 1894; in the Senate, the margin was smaller, and complicated by the presence of a handful of Progressive Party senators. Popular opinion had swung so hard against the Southern Pacific in California that few members of its congressional delegation were likely to favor the railroad's position on the funding bill, but whether they would be listened to was unclear. Supporting big business was the Republican default position, and Huntington had not only money to hand out but also a long record as a Party stalwart to point to. Timing was another factor to keep in mind—this was an election year. Whatever action Congress took (or declined to take) on the funding bill had the potential to affect what happened at the polls in November.

Being a savvy newsman, Bierce would surely have made time to be briefed by California politicos before boarding that train. What they're apt to have told him wouldn't have been encouraging: People in the rest of the country simply don't understand this thing. The funding-bill controversy was thirty years old, harking back to a period in American history that now seemed almost primitive. The central feature of federal loans made in the form of bonds was hard to understand, the sinking-fund provision wasn't much easier, and having to pay $75 million all at once might strike the uninitiated as a heavy burden for any company to bear. Thus, the railroad's central argument—in light of all that we did for the nation, why not put this reckoning off into the indefinite future?—had some appeal. Wasn't that the prudent course for Congress to take in *any* election year— postpone a touchy issue, in this case for such a long time (fifty or seventy-five years) that hardly anyone voting for it would ever have to face it again?

If the antirailroad forces were to stand any chance of winning, Bierce would have been told, they would have to get the rest of the country to focus on a complex, hoary, and geographically remote issue. Tough assignment? Undoubtedly. And yet here, as the train clacked eastward through the wintry landscape, is where a smile might have played across Ambrose Bierce's face. If there was one thing at which he excelled as a journalist, it was getting attention.

Washingtonians eager for a taste of Bierce's vaunted outspokenness would not have been disappointed by his first strike, which appeared on February 1. Under the brand-name headline "Bierce on the Funding Bill," the subhead set a slashing tone that was to hold up throughout the campaign: "He Tells How Huntington in Washington Is Fighting Fiercely, Like a Cornered Rat, With His

Old Familiar Weapons, a Paid Press and a Sorry Pack of Sleek and Conscienceless Rogues."

The text proper begins by calling attention to a fib: Although *The Washington Post* has recently been publishing Huntington-signed telegrams datelined San Francisco, in fact "for three days or more of this week the dromedary head of Mr. Huntington, with its tandem bumps of cupidity and self-esteem overshadowing like twin peaks the organ that he is good with, in the valley between, has been more or less visible in this town." Huntington could get away with this deception, Bierce observes, because "to the general public here the various funding schemes now in discussion by a packed committee of the House are absolutely devoid of interest." (By "packed," Bierce means not "crowded" but "stacked in Huntington's favor," presumably by Speaker Thomas B. Reed.) Underscoring the point, he complains of "an acute public apathy" toward the issue he has been sent east to illuminate. Given such listlessness, why, then, does the *Post* run these messages at all? Because it is on the take. This is not mere speculation, Bierce insists. The other day, a fit of carelessness in the *Post*'s composing room allowed the paper to be printed with "the honest words 'Ad Pacific Railroads' in shooting capitals [within] one of Mr. Huntington's articles."

More telegram trouble lies in wait for the railroad, as Bierce sifts through several wires from Californians to the House Committee on Pacific Railroads. One group of senders claims that "OUTSIDE OF A FEW DISAPPOINTED AGITATORS, THE PEOPLE FAVOR AN EXTENSION OF THE DEBT AT A FAIR RATE OF INTEREST." Bierce questions the ethics of anyone who would make such "monstrous statements" in the face of Californians' massive opposition to the railroad, as manifested recently in his own paper's rousingly successful petition drive, and ends with this suggestion: "If 'The Examiner' would care to blacklist these moral idiots with a view to punishment of their criminal audacity . . . I shall be happy to supply all the names." The invitation elicits a merry rejoinder from the paper's editor: "'The Examiner's' columns are long enough to accommodate all that Mr. Bierce may send."

All of which is quite entertaining, but the best thing in the piece is less flashy. Bierce manages to sum up the funding-bill fight in one powerful clause. To side with Huntington, he says, you have to "believe that a corporation which for thirty years has defaulted in the payment of interest and is about to default in the payment of principal because it has chosen to steal both principal and interest can henceforth be trusted to pay both." "Defaulted" is a loaded word, of course, but Bierce was acting as a lawyer here, calling upon his rhetorical skills to lay out the strongest possible case for the prosecution. Exaggerated or not, that last quotation has a ring—and a sting—to it that signaled trouble ahead for the cocky railroad.

The opening salvo had given readers a taste of Bierce-style polemics—and something more. The piece had meat in it, flavored with attar of righteousness. But now what? Before the controversy was over, the back-and-forth between the Bierce platoon and the Huntington army was to fall into a pattern, with several phases, an evolving rhythm, and the advent of an extraneous issue that became a kind of deus ex machina. But none of these developments was evident to, or even suspected by, Bierce at the outset. Granted, he was a seasoned newsman, but he had done little reporting. Like a field commander approaching a well-fortified position, he had to start probing, firing here, feinting there, with a view toward eventually dislodging and routing the enemy. But time was short. He would have to learn his generalship on the fly.

On the other hand, he wasn't exactly starting from scratch. As we've seen, Collis Huntington, his railroad, and the funding issue were all familiar territory to Bierce. He also brought some philosophical baggage to the endeavor, as evidenced in a think piece he'd written for the *Examiner* shortly after joining the paper. Difficult as it might seem to reduce a gut-level activity like dueling in print to a set of principles, he'd given it a shot. The fight is always personal, he maintains, and fundamentally it's about dignity.

> In a newspaper controversy it is important to remember that the public, in most cases, neither cares for the outcome of the fray, nor will remember its incidents. The controversialist should therefore confine his efforts and powers to accomplishment of two main purposes: 1—entertainment of the reader; 2—personal gratification.

As to purpose #1, Bierce insists that "no rules can be given." You're either a beguiling writer, or you're not (easy for him to say, a man whose pungent irascibility had long since made him irresistible to San Francisco newspaper readers). As for #2, he considers it "accomplishable" as follows: "(1) by guarding your self-respect; (2) by destroying your adversary's self-respect; (3) by making him respect you against his will as much as you respect yourself; (4) by betraying him into the blunder of permitting you to despise him." If all goes well, the "controversialist" will have afforded himself the great pleasure of claiming "moral superiority" to the foe, not just as the battle rages but in years to come.

Note that in the world according to Bierce it's not necessary for the good guy to win, in the sense of being allowed to jeer or dance a jig while the bad guy is led away in handcuffs, his cause in ruins. The important thing is to force the churl to confront his own baseness, to make clear to him how far short of your own gleaming integrity he falls. It's a philosophy that lends itself well to the kind of ad-hominem attacks in which Bierce specialized—e.g., that juicy opening-day line about Huntington's "dromedary head, with its tandem bumps of cupidity and self-esteem." (The image came from phrenology, the nineteenth-century pseudoscience of inferring a person's character from the shape and irregularities of his head.) Yet Bierce's four-part approach seems a bit solipsistic, with the audience (newspaper readers) reduced to little more than a source of extra pressure on the backpedaling opponent.

Whether Huntington had read (or recalled) Bierce's strategic credo is doubtful. Hearst, however, probably knew of it—he didn't miss much of what got into his papers. And it was by no means what he had in mind now. Hearst did not send his star writer to Washington so that Bierce could refurbish his own personal sense of honor. The publisher wanted results. Ideally, the *Examiner* should impress Easterners as more than just a provincial rag; its circulation should rise; Hearst's fame should swell, to the benefit of his political ambitions; and the funding bill should go down to defeat. The *Examiner*'s hometown readers were on board, too. Having long felt the ache of the Southern Pacific's stranglehold on their state, they were eager to see the funding bill quashed.

To accommodate the high stakes on the table, Bierce would have to change his approach. The articles he sent home from Washington would have to be more substantial than the squib fests for which he'd become famous in San Francisco. He and his staff would have to perform the traditional legwork of political reporters: studying the issues, consulting experts, interviewing lawmakers, poring over press releases, and keeping readers apprised of the various bills that addressed the funding problem. In journalism as it's done today, Bierce's opinionated articles would probably appear under the heading "Analysis," and in toto they resemble an episodic legal brief more than they do classic newspaper work. In the late nineteenth century, however, they were nothing out of the ordinary: News with a pronounced slant was not only tolerated but expected.

How well Bierce was able to sort all this out on his own is hard to say. We do know that he had help from the *Journal*'s editors in New York. As the campaign got underway, he and they exchanged private telegrams in which he was tutored on the financial complexities involved. At one point later on, they urged him to give more play to Huntington, who, they felt, had been left out of the picture too long.

Happily, however, there was no reason for Bierce to control his urges to poke fun and call names. On the contrary, his taunts could be all the more valuable as a kind of leavening agent mixed in with the weighty matters under debate. The difference was that the mighty Biercean wit was now harnessed to a larger purpose. In place of the cobbled-together segments of his "Prattle" columns, he had to produce a sustained argument. (His working method may have helped him in this regard. According to Daniel Lindley, Bierce wrote his funding-bill articles "on rolls of brown wrapping paper, which he would tear off when he had produced the number of words requested by his editors." Keyed as a telegram, each article sped west to the *Examiner* for editing. By the time the fight was over, Bierce had gone through enough wrapping paper to generate more than sixty articles; most of which started on the front page and were embellished with cartoons that supersized Huntington, who often appeared in the guise of either an overbearing thief or an outmaneuvered giant.) Instead of tickling readers with gossip, literary allusions, and wordplay, he had to lead them through proliferating thickets of lobbying, political posturing, and congressional maneuvering while also delivering jabs at villains intent on having their way regardless of the cost—not just Huntington but also his numerous trench mice, above all his assistant John Boyd, whom Bierce invariably referred to as the magnate's "tapeworm." Though written in response to daily events, Bierce's articles were supposed to add up to a kind of testament. Its purpose was clear: to deny the Octopus its funding bill.

Telegramgate

As mentioned, Bierce had to get Easterners to focus on a complex set of Western circumstances. The battle would be won or lost in blasé Washington, not in impassioned San Francisco. Hearst ordered that a special edition of each day's *Examiner* be printed and distributed to every member of Congress and other influential Washingtonians, but it was up to Bierce to make that freebie a must read. As it happened, Bierce had hardly gotten settled in Washington when the Huntington forces gave him a sword, which he and his editors were quick to wield.

"HUNTINGTON'S METHODS ALMOST BEYOND BE-LIEF," screamed an *Examiner* front-page headline on Monday morning, February 3; out of the subhead jumped the words "Barefaced Lies." It seemed that two signers of those pro-railroad telegrams reprinted in *The Washington Post* had squawked. They had put their names to no such thing; indeed, their views were quite otherwise. One misspoken-for fellow, an ex-U.S. senator named A. P. Williams, was located by Bierce and his staff in Washington; the other, a businessman, was discovered by *Examiner* reporters in San Francisco. Bierce played up the implications of his find:

> If [Williams] is not guilty [of supporting Huntington], his innocence will be strong presumptive evidence that the names of some of the others who have been so liberally quoted in support of the Funding bill have been used with a similar freedom by the good old man of the late Contract and Finance Company or in his interest.

Huntington's strategy here is easy to discern: Use the telegrams to demote the funding controversy to the status of a provincial nuisance. Lawmakers from the rest of the country might as well save their time and energy by writing it off as a California hobbyhorse; they should accept at face value the claim that nearly everyone of note in the state favors the railroad's position—a consensus that excuses outsiders from having to puzzle out the legal and financial intricacies. To that end, the *Post* trotted out three more Californians in support of the Powers Bill—a move that drew Bierce's scorn on February 4 because he regarded all three as nonentities. ("William Greer Harrison is to the fore . . . as a devout admirer of Mr. Huntington and his policy of evasion. Mr. Harrison thinks—but, really, it does not matter what Mr. Harrison thinks so long as nobody thinks of Mr. Harrison.") What Huntington had done,

Bierce added, was to establish a "literary bureau" tasked with drumming up ersatz or nugatory supporters. Two days later, Bierce caught the "bureau" and the *Post* faking it again. A lengthy subhead quoted the irate reaction of a merchant named Julius Raphael when he learned of the *Post*'s latest miscue: "I was not interviewed on the subject, and the Washington 'Post' was imposed upon when it published what purported to be an interview with me. No one had any authority to send on to that paper the stuff it has printed in connection with my name."

On February 8, the *Examiner* printed the disavowal of yet another alleged signatory, W. B. Curtis, manager of the Traffic Association, a group of San Francisco businessmen who had banded together specifically to oppose the Southern Pacific's dominance. Including Curtis's name was a real boner by the Huntington camp. A man in his position would have been a fool to carry the railroad's water, and indeed Curtis protested that he had "never in my life expressed an opinion on any funding measure for the railroad debt"; what's more, if he had, it would have been anti-Huntington. "I do not see any harm," Curtis wrote the *Examiner*, "in the Government taking control of the Central Pacific and operating it as an independent line between San Francisco and Utah." The headline above this story read, "THE MOST BAREFACED OF ALL." At the same time, Bierce had taken up his editors on their offer to make room for a blacklist of those who favored wiping out the Central Pacific's debt. That list became a kind of running joke, shrinking day by day as additional "members" came forward to say that they had been misquoted and in fact either opposed the funding bill or had no opinion on it.

What a godsend all this must have been! Owing to sloppy staff work and the smug assumption that every Californian of the business persuasion would naturally rally behind the Southern Pacific, the Huntington forces had handed Bierce readymade and amusing material at a time when he'd probably been trying to get his footing and plot his next move. The "Case of the Collapsing Telegrams" had done his work for him. Fresh off the starting block, he had shone as a discoverer of falsehoods, while Huntington made a first impression as not just a liar but an inept one. By embarrassing the *Post*, Bierce and the *Examiner* had served notice that they might not be mere hicks from the Western sticks. Best of all, Bierce was making it hard for members of Congress to dismiss the funding bill as a far-off botheration that they might just as well defer to local sentiment. Local sentiment, in fact, gave every evidence of being hostile to the Huntington cause. Bierce was catching on fast.

Huntington Takes the Stand

While "Telegramgate" was unfolding, Huntington had begun to make his case by testifying on the Hill. His first appearance, on February 1, gave Bierce a capital opportunity to flog the old man. We can't be sure who wrote the headlines for these articles, but the one for February 2 sounds Bierccan:

> HUNTINGTON LYING IN HIS LAST DITCH
> Driven to the Wall by the Exposure of his Infamies, the Magnate Crawls Before the Senate Committee on Pacific Railways and Seeks to Draw the Curtain on His Own Black Record by Calumniating Those Who Would Bring Him to Justice.

In the ensuing critique of Huntington's performance (much of which had been devoted to lambasting his enemy the mayor of San Francisco), Bierce was in clover.

> Mr. Huntington is not altogether bad. Though severe, he is merciful. He tempers invective with falsehood. He says ugly things of his enemy, but he has the tenderness to be careful that they are mostly lies. So Mayor Sutro may reasonably hope to survive Mr. Huntington, though Mr. Huntington's rancor blown about in space as a pestilential vapor will outlive all things that be. It is his immortal part.

That is clever copy, but it could use something more. How about a punchy epithet to fix the first real-time sighting of Huntington in the reader's mind? In the next paragraph, Bierce supplies one, calling his archenemy an "inflated old pigskin."

Huntington, by the way, was to testify several more times, in both the Senate and House. Throughout, however, he managed to make only one solid contribution to his cause—and that by resorting to the crying towel. As imaginary violins played, he would half wail, half brag about the valor and endurance the Central Pacific and its construction crews had displayed in laying track up and down mountains, through the snows and bitter cold of winter, against insurmountable odds, et cetera, et cetera. It might not have been a sour note, but he hit it so often that he began to sound like a broken wax cylinder.

An uneventful week went by—one of those inexplicable lulls that sometimes grip the Hill—before the publication of Bierce's next dispatch of substance (that is on a subject other than Telegramgate). And when he did file, on February 9, he had little to report. Nonetheless, he caused as much trouble as he could, showing the way for journalists of the future, who sometimes devote more inches of copy to capturing the emotional core of a Washington event than to conveying its substance. The previous day had been given over to the testimony of a man named Pierce—a lawyer for the other half of the intercontinental system, the Union Pacific—and seldom has a writer devised a better metaphor for a witness flummoxed by tough questioning than this one of Bierce's: "[Huntington] observed them doing Pierce to a delicate nut-brown, inserting their forks into his incinerated sides, turning him on the iron and basting him in his own gravy." In the same piece, Bierce made fun of Huntington as "the illustrious Kentuckian," a dig at the Southern Pacific's incorporation in that state. (On a later occasion, an anti-Huntington congressman deplored the "farcical" practice of states granting corporate charters to firms headquartered thousands of miles away; the ploy was especially silly in this case, for Kentucky had authorized the Southern Pacific to operate a railroad everywhere *except* Kentucky.) And to clear up any doubts as to what punishment Bierce had in mind for the Southern Pacific's sins, he cited a certain entity's fine performance as temporary custodian of the disgraced Union Pacific: "He who considers the practical management of railroads by the United States Government an untried and doubtful experiment may justly boast that large, conspicuous and salient facts have not the power to take his attention."

In the interim, Huntington's tireless literary bureau had rounded up new (and this time apparently valid) endorsements from prominent San Franciscans. Bierce retorted by again citing the 200,000 souls who had signed the *Examiner*'s antirailroad petition and by harping on the Kentucky theme to call Huntington "the inspired scribe of the Blue Grass Gospel." On the whole, however, the controversy was marking time.

Things perked up a few days later, after Huntington, summoned once again by the Senate Pacific Railroad Committee, "took his hand out of all manner of pockets long enough to hold it up and be sworn" and turned in a (literally) shaky performance. "He was nervous and in a visible tremor," Bierce continued. "At times he was almost inaudible." (Biographer David Lavender wondered if in the interim Huntington might not have suffered a minor stroke.) On hand to watch this performance was a special observer, railroad attorney and Congressman Grove Johnson—a Democrat from California who, it now appeared, was the only member of that state's delegation willing to carry the Southern Pacific's water. After taking time out to charge that Johnson stood alone because he was on retainer from the railroad, Bierce belittled Huntington by purporting to feel sorry for him:

The spectacle of this old man standing on the brink of eternity, his pockets loaded with dishonest gold which he knows neither how to enjoy nor to whom to bequeath, swearing it is the fruit of wholesome labor and homely thrift and beseeching

an opportunity to multiply the store, was one of the most piti-
able it has been my lot to observe. He knows himself an out-
mate of every penal institution in the world; he deserves to
hang from every branch of every tree of every State and Territory penetrated by his railroads, with the sole exception of
Nevada, which has no trees. Yet this notorious old man stood
there before a committee of the highest legislative body of his
country and made oath that he was an honest man and unself-
ish citizen.

One of the best sustained polemics in the whole campaign, that
paragraph showcases Bierce's masterful blending of his old inclination to wage personal war with his newfound ability to reduce complex policy issues to readily comprehensible terms—and the joke
about Nevada adds just the right zinger to ensure that the piece
will be quoted and remembered. Want still more? Bierce sums up
Huntington's day's work as an example of promoting "plunder by
perjury."

Hearst Gives Himself a Pat on the Back

Maestro Hearst now jumped back into the limelight, playing his old
trick of reminding *Examiner* readers what an illustrious artifact they
held in their hands. On February 16—a Sunday and thus a slow
news day—the paper ran a feature, complete with respectfully drawn
portraits, on its panoply of far-flung correspondents. The piece leads
off with a smarmy disclaimer:

People who read "The Examiner" are so used to getting the
best, the quickest and brainiest service of news and special articles from all the world over that they expect it and take it as a
matter of course. "The Examiner" has no need to cry its wares
and no desire to make floral presentations to itself. Let there be
no misunderstanding on that point.

Having said which, the writer (almost surely Hearst himself) hands "itself" a floral presentation: "But these happen to be stirring times, and as one of the most striking of end-of-the-century developments it is interesting to take a glance at the men and women whose brains and pens are busy in the four quarters of the earth at the service of the readers of 'The Examiner.'"

Pride of place goes to Bierce because "there is no question in which Californians are so vitally interested at this time as the fight raging in Washington over the funding proposition." In his next breath, Hearst gives his special Washington correspondent a good stroking: "Perhaps [Bierce's name] should stand [at the head] of the list anyway, for all the distinguished company in which it finds itself." That "distinguished company" includes the *Examiner*'s London correspondent, Julian Ralph; its man in Cuba, Murat Halstead; and two scribes based in El Paso to cover Mexico and the border, W. W. Naughton and Annie Laurie (the pen name of Winifred Bonfils). With the possible exception of Annie Laurie, a "sob sister" who specialized in going undercover to pose as a vulnerable soul (a divorce-seeking wife, a downtrodden woman taken ill on the street, a Salvation Army worker, etc.) and chronicling the rude treatment she received in each guise, everyone else in this lineup has fallen into oblivion. Bierce was the clear front-runner, then and now.

Telegramgate enjoyed a reprise on February 18, thanks to a letter, reproduced in full on the front page, from S. O. Houghton, a former California congressman named as a signer of a pro-funding-bill wire. "My name . . . has been used without any authority from me and without my knowledge," Houghton thundered from Los Angeles. Bierce's accompanying article heaped praise on Senator John Tyler Morgan, Democrat of Alabama, who had taken up the cudgels against the funding bill. By grilling Huntington on the connections between the Central Pacific and the Contract & Finance Company, Morgan had left the old tycoon "supremely distressed"—it was the first time, in Bierce's recollection, that Huntington had seemed truly nonplussed by questioning. Morgan even forced some damaging concessions out of the witness: the directorates of the Central Pacific and the Contract & Finance Company were "the same men. He admitted that [the Southern Pacific] obtained the assets of the Central Pacific of whatever kind, the value of securities alone amounting to $116,000,000. But he held that it cost $7,000,000 or $8,000,000 to build the road." When asked about the Contract & Finance Company's books, Huntington said he "believed" they had been destroyed.

All this Morgan had managed to worm out of Huntington despite repeated attempts to defend him by such allies as Senator William Stewart, the Nevada Republican whose favor had been bought by the railroad. And a hard blow it was. By connecting the dots between the Contract & Finance Company, the Central Pacific, and the Southern Pacific, Morgan gave lawmakers a glimpse of how the Big Four had euchred the federal government out of roughly $100 million. "Of our modern Forty Thieves," Bierce cracked, "Mr. Huntington is the surviving thirty-six." Bierce closed with an encomium to the persistent gentleman from Alabama: "If there is in Washington one person who merits the respect and gratitude of the people of California, it is he. It is impossible to overstate the magnitude of the services done to our State by that able and courageous man." (Bierce did not speculate in print as to why Morgan so strenuously opposed bailing out the Central Pacific. For all we know, it may have been simply on the merits—after the fight was over, Morgan claimed to have had "no selfish interest in the matter nor have the people of my state.")

The following day brought more of the same, with Bierce professing to be amazed by Huntington's equivocations: "It was absolutely impossible to get a direct, intelligible statement from the witness in answer to any question whatever." More time was spent inquiring into the fate of those missing Contract & Finance Company ledgers, about which Huntington told a shifting story, being "quite sure that he had never seen [them], but whose destruction he had first advised, then suggested and finally was not quite sure he had anything to do with. Mr. Huntington's caution grew with reflection, and it is probable that eventually he will sturdily have opposed the destruction of those books." Huntington's evasions were less embarrassing than they might have been, however, because many of them were made to Senator Morgan alone. "There was not another member of the committee present," Bierce observed of one exchange, "and during the afternoon not more than two or three dropped in, even for a moment." So operated then—as it often does now—the world's greatest deliberative body.

Every Man Has His Price

One of the most famous stories about Bierce occurred—or, as I will argue, was inserted in garbled form—at roughly this point in the battle. He and Huntington had a personal exchange, though exactly what form it took is uncertain. According to biographer Carey McWilliams, the two men ran into each other on the Capitol steps. Huntington buttonholed Bierce and asked what it would take to get him to back off. Bierce demurred, but Huntington kept at him, demanding, "Well, name your price; every man has his price." Bierce is said to have replied that his price was $75 million, payable to his friend the secretary of the treasury—in other words, the full amount of the Central Pacific's debt. When Huntington was questioned about the incident later, he supposedly said, "Oh, I just wanted to see how big he was. I know now." In a footnote to his biography of Bierce, McWilliams cites the *Examiner* of February 22, 1896, as his source for this anecdote.

Something is amiss here, however. Bierce's February 22 dispatch makes no mention of the encounter; nor does any other article of his from the period. We have to jump to 1899 to find him referring to such a matter, in a "Prattle" column. Reminiscing, Bierce addresses his old foe directly:

Mr. Collis P. Huntington, do you remember that on a certain morning, when you sat in the reading room of a Washington hotel, a gentleman apprised you of my arrival in town as a representative of this paper? Do you recollect that you had the exceeding civility to ask him my price? Possibly, sir, you may not have forgotten that he returned to you later, telling you that he was authorized to say that my price was the amount of your company's indebtedness to the Government, and that as I might be out of town when you were ready to "fix" me, the sum might be handed to my friend the Treasurer of the United States. Thank you, Mr. Huntington; it is a real pleasure to blackmail a gentleman so "dead easy" as you.

McWilliams—and the numerous other biographers who have followed his lead—must have gotten the story wrong. Only three years had gone by, and Bierce could hardly have forgotten or wanted to skip over the staging of this drama as a face-to-face colloquy—if that was how it happened. The indirect approach, then, with messages carried back and forth between Bierce and Huntington by intermediaries, is likelier to be the true version. Although Bierce's comeback was classy—and went a long way toward giving the speaker that sense of "moral superiority" that he sought in newspaper controversies—it wasn't the quip heard 'round the world that it has been made out to be. Huntington had misjudged his enemy, but the notion that a fast-on-his-feet Bierce had squelched him on the spot, in public, against the symbolic background of the Capitol, appears to be wishful thinking.

Inevitably, Huntington and Bierce crossed paths from time to time—we know this from Bierce's boast that he had refused to shake hands with Huntington on two occasions, "once in presence of three members of the press in the corridor of the Capitol, and again in the room of the Senate Committee on Pacific Railroads in the presence of the committee and many gentlemen attending one of its meetings." But their most telling encounter may have come during the February 14th session of the Senate Committee on Pacific Railroads. As Bierce reported in the following day's *Examiner*, at one point Huntington skipped several pages of his prepared testimony, explaining that he would spare the committee his responses to certain personal attacks. Bierce goes on: "'If I did [read this material],' he said with a significant look at a critic for whom I have the highest respect, 'I might become personal myself.' So the portentous spectacle of Mr. Huntington becoming personal is one that must belong forever to the domain of imagination." The "critic for whom I have the highest respect" is, of course, Bierce, and so far as we know Huntington's "significant look" was the most intimate moment in their mutual histories.

"We Are Making Progress"

In the meantime, a new voice had joined the *Examiner*'s: the *Washington Star*, whose editor interviewed Bierce and wrote a sympathetic piece about the antirailroad fight, concluding with this salvo: "Ambrose Bierce—who has to write with a specially prepared pencil because pens become red hot and ink boils—is in charge of the Washington end of the Examiner's campaign. Mr. Bierce will not be remembered in Mr. Huntington's will." Being interviewed seemed to energize Bierce, who in his next report put a number on the Big Four's unjust enrichment: $15 million to $30 million apiece—figures, he said, that sound like something from "a grand larceny trial." In a cartoon, Swinnerton drew Huntington as a rotund parrot, weeping and molting after being roughed up by a bulldog with Morgan's features; and Bierce indulged in a flight of optimism: "With such an intellectual giant as Senator Morgan of Alabama doing battle for us in the Capitol, and so powerful and honorable a journal as the 'Star' standing up for us outside, it begins to look as if we should win."

The *Star*'s attention underscores what Bierce had accomplished so far: making the funding bill newsworthy. "Now the Washington newspapers publish full reports of each day's proceedings of the

Congressional committee on Pacific roads," he was soon able to declare, "as do several New York and Philadelphia papers, which did not before." The increased interest was making it harder for members of Congress to cherish the comforting notion that the funding bill was strictly a West Coast phenomenon, which they need not study carefully. Bierce continued to score points, notably against the hapless Grove Johnson, the railroad's lone friend in the California delegation. After a Louisiana congressman wondered aloud about the company's unpopularity—except with Johnson—in its state of origin, Bierce claimed that Johnson "modestly bent his goatlike head and emitted a faint odor of violets." Bierce summed up the positive developments by saying, "On the whole we are making progress."

Huntington fell ill at this point. Not much happened while he convalesced, although Bierce did coin a memorable epithet for handsome Congressman H. Henry Powers, he of the pro-railroad Powers Bill. Admiring Powers's beaming countenance, Bierce mused that "as Chairman of the Committee on the Visible Virtues he would be appropriately satisfactory."

On February 29, Bierce took the occasion of Huntington's continued absence to step back and analyze where things stood. He expressed his disappointment with most members of the House and Senate committees, who either knew too little of the funding-bill issue to ask good questions or, in the case of "the ever-superserviceable Grove Johnson," chose to play stooge for the railroad. Bierce went on to suggest a likely scenario for putting the controversy to rest:

> It is almost a foregone conclusion that the battle against the Funding bill will have to be made on the floors of the two houses, against nearly unanimous reports of their committees. Happily the judgment of the Senate Committee will be more than outweighed by the dissent of Senator Morgan, and that of the House committee discredited by the concurrence of Grove Johnson.

Huntington Is Caught Lying

At length Huntington returned to wrap up his Senate testimony. While recuperating, he had complied with a request by Senator Morgan that he read the report of the 1887 Pacific Railroad Commission—a chore he had not previously deigned to perform, despite Bierce's judgment that it was "one of the most elaborate, important and famous public documents ever published by order of Congress." Bierce had gotten in a nice dig after Morgan secured Huntington's agreement to do this homework:

> It is to be hoped that he will not only read it, but return the book in which it is contained. But two sets of these volumes are known to be extant. At one time there were many, but from time to time they have disappeared as mysteriously as the account books of the famous Contract and Finance Company.

Now, newly versed in the report's contents, Huntington "sat there in the presence of Senators, attorneys and members of the press and calmly asserted on his oath that the book was false and made up of idle gossip." As Huntington continued to tough it out, Bierce noted the impression he left: "I cannot help feeling that this wicked old man has a vein of madness in him."

The following day was little short of disastrous for Huntington. Questioning him relentlessly—and refusing to let the robber baron's senatorial friends intercede on his behalf—Morgan scored at least two damning points. First, he pressed Huntington on one of the main charges that were to figure in Frank Norris's *Octopus*. Had not merchants complained about the scandal of "goods from New York and elsewhere [being] carried through their towns to San Francisco and then brought back, paying the double charge"? Initially, the witness would admit no more than that he'd heard rumors of such a thing but assumed it had been stopped long ago. But "by dint of patience and persistence," Bierce wrote, "Senator Morgan made him virtually confess at last that he knew the practice had existed and did not know that it had ceased to exist."

Morgan's other coup was to insist that Huntington come clean about how little he had invested in the Central Pacific—far too little, it would seem to any disinterested observer, to justify the huge fortune he had made from building and running the railroad. Morgan had laid his groundwork the day before, as Bierce explained in his dramatic account of the two-day sparring match:

> Nothing could be got out of [Huntington] definitely, but he affirmed that his private fortune was very large, and that most of it had gone in. Indeed, the longer he was questioned, the more his investment grew. It grew into the hundreds of thousands, and there was a distinct presumption (enfeebled only by the incredibility of the witness) that it amounted to millions, for Mr. Huntington in those days was very rich. The examination was so tedious that several members of the committee uneasily inquired as to the relevancy of it, and demanded assurance that it would be connected with matters more obviously legitimate. They got no satisfaction. Mr. Morgan went his way regardless and explanationless.
>
> To-day threw upon yesterday a great white light. With no particular preliminaries Mr. Morgan handed Mr. Huntington a paper, explaining that it was that gentleman's Sacramento assessment list for the year 1861 and the three years following. The effect was dramatic exceedingly. Huntington perused the paper in absolute silence.
>
> Everybody bent forward as if to read it over his shoulder or through the paper. All were silent as he. This continued until it became painful even to those of us who do not love him as well as we should.
>
> Finally he spoke. His voice had so changed that one would hardly have known it; his manner—it is impossible to describe the subtle but profound change in his manner, as he said:

"I don't remember anything about this. It may be right."

This he repeated a number of times. Then he added feebly: "My property was mostly in New York. It was in money."

"How much?"

"I can't say: enough to pay my debts."

"Anything over?"

"Not much."

"Was your money in New York assessed?"

"I think not."

The figures of that paper were not made known.

Nobody seemed to want that done. It was obvious that the man had been caught in rank perjury, and that was enough for the time being. But that paper will be heard from again, and it may some day be marked "People's exhibit A."

After this drubbing in the Senate, Huntington fled to friendlier confines. He agreed to testify before the House Committee on Pacific Railroads, and Bierce thought he knew why: "to get his story on record in a coherent and connected form. Nobody there has the will to interrupt its continuity, or enfeeble its force by awkward and unfriendly questions." As reported by Bierce a day later, that is exactly what happened—though not *all* that happened. Once Huntington had read his prepared statement straight through, a few members dared quiz him about his proposal that the Central Pacific's repayment schedule be stretched out far into the next century, with a rock-bottom low rate of interest being charged on the balance. "One would have thought they wanted to know something," Bierce cracked.

And, finally, someone other than Bierce made a sardonic joke.

A member of the committee asked the "witness" if at the expiration of fifty or a hundred years under his "plan," the Central Pacific would not still be as deeply in debt as ever.

"Certainly," was his candid reply, "and that prosperous road, the New York Central, was never so heavily mortgaged as now."

"Nor its managers," said the sad-eyed member, "so rich," and silence fell upon the scene.

As quoted in an accompanying piece (not by Bierce), Huntington elaborated upon his ludicrous claim of robust home-state support: "There are perhaps a hundred men in California against us; smart fellows, too, because they have always got a living without working. They have a grievance because they were dismissed from the pay-rolls at my suggestion, and they want to get back, but they won't." One begins to see Bierce's point about the parlous state of the magnate's mind.

A Gloved Right Hand

Huntington struck back a few days later, as revealed in a flurry of correspondence printed along with Bierce's latest article. According to these letters, Huntington had thrown up a smoke screen by reviving the old charge that Hearst and the *Examiner* had accepted a handout from the Southern Pacific starting in 1892: $1,000 a month for kid-glove treatment in the newspaper. The implication was that the railroad's cancellation of the agreement in 1894 explained why Hearst was now hounding Huntington so mercilessly. The charge smacks of frustration, however, for in making it wasn't Huntington in effect implicating his railroad as a briber?

For that matter, "charge" may be too strong a word. "Insinuation" is more like it, given some initial doubt as to when and to whom Huntington had spoken. In one of those published letters, the *Examiner*'s editors urged Bierce to pin down whether or not Huntington had attacked the paper while under oath (for if he had, a charge of perjury might be brought against him). In another letter, a Democratic congressman confirmed the substance of Huntington's remark but made clear that it had been uttered after the committee was gaveled out of session. A subhead to Bierce's article put an unflattering spin on this timing: "Afraid to Testify to the Falsehood, [Huntington] Whispered It Outside."

Other papers were indeed on the Southern Pacific's payroll—the $125-a-month stipend discovered by Fremont Older when he joined the *San Francisco Bulletin* has already been mentioned. Five days later, however, in a front-page letter to his readers, Hearst argued that the *Examiner* had never been a kept sheet. "Any statement that 'The Examiner' ever received any money from the railroad for anything but legitimate advertising is an outrageous lie," he wrote from New York, "and is obviously enough an effort on the part of the railroad to discredit 'The Examiner' and weaken the effect of its fight against the Funding bill." He went on to describe an encounter in which a railroad "emissary" stopped by and complained of not receiving the deference due a generous client. "After some heated discussion," Hearst reported, "I told the railroad people that if they had thought to control 'The Examiner' by an advertising bribe they could keep their money and go to the devil." The publisher concluded by citing the strongest evidence in his favor: "the record of our columns."

A related article (not by Bierce) buttressed Hearst's defense by laying out the transaction in full, with the advertising contract and other related documents as addenda. Following that came another reprinted letter, this one from Bierce to the editor of the *Washington Star*, in which he threw out a challenge:

I have reason to think that Huntington will be given an opportunity to prove in court his accusation that "The Examiner" was once on the payroll of his company. In the mean time, if he will prove it to the satisfaction of three gentlemen— one to be named by him, one by me, and one by the two others—I hereby pledge myself to retire permanently from the service of "The Examiner." As he has frequently signified his earnest disapproval of my work on that paper, he should think my retirement desirable and advantageous.

I promise, moreover, that if he makes his accusation good I will take him by the hand, which recently I have twice refused when he offered it—once in presence of three members of the press in the corridor of the Capitol, and again in the room of the Senate Committee on Pacific Railroads in the presence of the committee and many gentlemen attending one of its meetings. As to this latter promise, I exact but one condition: Mr. Huntington is not to object to my glove.

Wisely, Huntington did not take Bierce's bait (or his gloved hand, either). But for once Huntington had put his opponents on the defensive. (This flurry of charges and defenses should have put an end to the matter, but didn't. As we shall see at the end of this chapter, several months later a certain malcontent dredged up the Southern Pacific-*Examiner* contract yet again, this time in scurrilous terms.)

In a Bit of a Shindy

Another stretch of dead time now ensued, with Bierce confessing in print that "Pacific railroad matters are deadly dull." That dullness may not have been wholly unwelcome, however—the *Examiner*'s special correspondent had been on fire of late, filing a dozen stories in one period of just over two weeks. He didn't share his boss's inclination to make a public fuss about how he did what he did or the amount of effort it required. But Bierce did take time out to convey the flavor of his hectic workday in a private note to a writer friend:

It is true that I have had to stop writing personal letters, for mere lack of time. The life of a newspaper correspondent here has only one advantage—brevity. It is a little longer than that of a car-horse, but not much. Here is an outline of what I have been trying to do. Be at the Capitol by 10 a.m. Attend committee meeting and keep an eye on both Houses at the same time. Talk with dozens of men of my specialty. When both Houses have adjourned go home to dinner—no time for luncheon. Between 7 and 10 telegraph to N.Y. "Journal" an editorial on Cuba, and the substance of my latest dispatch to "Examiner." Then rewrite and amplify (and fortify) for "Examiner"—enabled to do so by the three hours difference in time. Home to bed at, say, 2 a.m., to be routed out probably once or oftener by telegrams. No Sundays.

O wouldn't you like to be in this business? 'Fore God, I don't know how I have taken time to relate it. . . .

You say I "ought to be happy": Well, I'm in a bit of a shindy; that's all that makes it endurable; and I'm having rather the better of it. And I'm (as yet) well.

The mills of Congress ground slowly on, and occasionally a Bierce dispatch was bumped off the *Examiner*'s front page by hotter news: "TORTURED BY THE FIERCE APACHES," screamed the headline for one such story. The day before—under the headlines "THIS IS THE FUNDING BILL . . . Entirely Satisfactory to Huntington and the Union Pacific Representatives"—Bierce had devoted nearly the whole of a long piece to summarizing the latest version of the bill to embody the railroads' wishes—a dutiful chore that he enlivened only by taking occasional swipes at the California delegation. What worried him was that the Californians had thus far contented themselves with carping at the other side's plans, of which there were many: "'the Hubbard plan,' 'the Huntington plan,' 'the Frye plan,' 'the Satan plan,' and so forth." It was high time for them to offer an alternative of their own. "It will be observed that this is distinctly a Huntington bill," he wrote at the end of his précis. "I wish I could add that it will be opposed by a distinctly Californian bill." Otherwise, he predicted direly, "If there is no Pacific railroad legislation this session that gratifying result will apparently be due to a direct intervention of Divine providence." At this point, he made a lukewarm assessment of his side's prospects: "There is now a reasonable hope that we shall accomplish at least a respectable defeat."

He sounded the you-can't-beat-something-with-nothing note again the next day, although in the meantime the home-state delegation had begun to stir. Good thing, too, Bierce declared, because he disagreed with the view that House Speaker Reed was unlikely to bring a funding bill to a floor vote this session, for fear of loosening the Republicans' hold on power in the Pacific states. To Bierce the amount of effort Huntington was pouring into his cause—the "small army of high-priced attorneys" at his command, "the hundreds of thousands of dollars" at his fingertips—suggested that he expected action; and, of course, he ought to know.

It wasn't long, however, before Bierce indulged himself in a time-is-on-our-side burst of optimism. A new rumor had it that Congressional leaders wanted to adjourn by June 1, a schedule that would go hard on such nonessential business as the funding bill. He cautioned, however, against merely playing a waiting game: "We are still a long way from the edge of the woods. . . . Happily we are now better prepared, or soon shall be, to make an aggressive fight."

Of Rivers, Harbors, and Divine Intervention

On April 7, Bierce reported that Morgan was about to deliver a major speech spelling out his opposition to the latest pro-railroad Senate bill and offering his alternative. The special correspondent then mentioned an action taken in the House the day before. The river and harbor bill had emerged from committee with a surprising last-minute addition: an appropriation to improve the harbor at Santa Monica, California. Retreating from the ebullience of just two days earlier, Bierce expressed his fear that similar stealth might be employed to pass the funding bill. "The observer who pats himself on the back and murmurs into his own ears, 'the old, old story' of the impossibility of Pacific Railroads' legislation this session is living in a fool's paradise."

In warning readers about Congress's tendency to erupt unexpectedly, Bierce may seem to have digressed from the funding-bill fight. But he had good instincts as a newsman. Although he could not have foreseen exactly where this new controversy would lead, it was smart of him to bring it up, if only to give a sense of how far Huntington's greedy reach extended, for Huntington and the Southern Pacific had a keen interest in the harbor appropriation. Unlike San Francisco, Southern California lacked a natural deepwater harbor. Huntington and associates were pushing Santa Monica as the best site for improving upon what Nature had bestowed because they controlled the rail line serving the town. Also eyeing Santa Monica avidly was a buddy of Huntington's, the Comstock multimillionaire John P. Jones. Jones represented Nevada in the U.S. Senate but used the bulk of his political power to look tenderly after his own holdings, including some 25,000 acres of land he owned in and around Santa Monica, a town he'd virtually put on the map. Huntington and Jones had no stake, however, in a rival harbor site favored by both California senators and every congressman from the state except (naturally) Johnson: the one at San Pedro, which Bierce called "the natural port of Los Angeles." If enacted, then, the appropriation would have increased the value of Huntington's and Jones's portfolios and allowed the Southern Pacific to expand its transportation monopoly in California. The House committee later reversed itself, striking out the item, only to have the Senate restore it. The harbor squabble was to prove more important—and more helpful—than Bierce and his readers could have guessed.

First, however, the Hearst-Bierce cause met with another check: Senator Morgan fell ill and couldn't deliver his big speech. Early reports had him in a very bad way, but by the end of the day Bierce was happy to say that "hopes of his recovery [were] more freely entertained." Bierce could also take solace in evidence that his own attacks on Representative Johnson were rattling that gentleman, who petulantly announced his refusal to enter any committee room in which an employee of the *Examiner* could be found. While he was at it, Bierce took another potshot at Representative Powers, describing him as "a faultlessly respectable person, dignified in his demeanor, devout in his religion, pure in his personal life and addicted to the duty of cutting his country's throat."

The Santa Monica harbor affair continued to brew, and Bierce noticed that it was having an unintended effect. The stakes were big (this was the first installment of a projected $3-million cost), and the underlying issues were not opaque: no bonds, no mortgage liens or sinking funds, no stretched-out period of repayment, no heroics by hard-driven construction crews—just a naked attempt to grab a cushy preference from Uncle Sam. As Bierce noted on April 12:

> It is clear now that one of the hardest blows that the funding scheme has incurred was delivered by the awkward arm of Mr. Huntington when he invented the Santa Monica theft. His failure to get that appropriation has done more than merely deprive him of the immediate profit that would have accrued to him—it has directed attention to him and his larger plans in a way that is distinctly injurious to his hopes. . . . Several members of Congress have recently come to "The Examiner" headquarters seeking light upon it, and have expressed for the Huntington people a new and wholesome disesteem. I am told that the members of the California delegation have been sought in the same way. So it seems probable that in attempting to break into the United States Treasury in the daytime this too candid plunderer has merely caused it to be better guarded against his more stealthy incursion by night.

Again, as with those trumped-up telegrams, Huntington was in essence doing Bierce's job for him.

As for Morgan, he remained bedridden, but one of his aides slipped Bierce a copy of the senator's anti–funding bill speech, now slated to be offered as a minority report dissenting from the committee's expected approval of a pro-railroad bill. Long and scathing, the document sharpened Bierce's regret that Morgan couldn't be on hand to deliver it in person. Bierce had to content himself with re-printing most of it, with commentary by himself, in the *Examiner* of April 21. As the following excerpt shows, Morgan was a fine pur-veyor of vitriol in his own right (although, to be sure, he had prob-ably benefited by a thorough briefing from Bierce himself):

> Congress was probably moved by the grandeur of this enter-prise and an overestimate of its cost to yield to the importuni-ties of these companies for the enactment of this peculiar law. With a lobby that cost more than $2,000,000 on the Pacific end of the line that is yet in active eruption, vomiting frauds and falsehood with shameless effrontery, and with the Credit Mo-bilier at the other end of the line that has stained the records of Congress, nothing has been omitted that could be done to make the Government build these roads at its own cost, and then at the end of thirty years to abandon its interest in them to the contrivers of this plot, rather than pay the principal of the bonds, doubled in amount by the still stranger act which, for the first time in our history, gave priority to a private debt over the debt due to the Government.

At this point, Bierce probably had no idea how the fight would turn out. In an article published in anticipation of House action on the Powers Bill, he noted that someone had counted Huntington's lobbyists as they roamed the halls of Congress: twenty-six of them. Yet Bierce allowed himself to sound a note of cautious optimism. "The opposition to the railroad bill is taking heart," he reported, a development he considered "fairly attributable to the circumstance that every member of Congress, every head of a Government de-partment and every distinguished man in the service here is in daily receipt of 'The Examiner.'" An odd postscript followed. "As a single example, Speaker Reed, who has a tenderness for the gentle art of caricature (which also had a leaning toward him) has the walls of one of his rooms profusely decorated with 'Examiner' cartoons, and in their silent influence grows unconsciously a wiser and a better man." One would like to know more about these cartoons and what Reed thought of them, but Bierce said no more about the speaker's decorating philosophy.

Insulting the Speaker

The headline for the story of April 25 went so far as to assert that a corner had been turned: "HUNTINGTON HAS A LOSING FIGHT." It's doubtful that Bierce penned this cheery message, however, because his text failed to bear it out. Some observers were saying that the funding bill might not come up for debate this session, but Bierce was less sanguine. He suspected that the source of this rumor might be Huntington himself, trying to put his enemies off their guard. For, after all, "Huntington is a snake whom it is unsafe to grasp with a bare hand when he is vanishing under a rock; one may be very sure he is doubling in, and that his head is guarding his tail." Bierce went on to traduce the speaker of the House, who seemed not to have made up his mind about the wisdom of moving the bill: "My own opinion of Speaker Reed is that if he had been Judas Iscariot he would not have betrayed the Son of Man with a kiss. He has a larger ambition than that; he would have kissed the entire Jewish nation and charged sixty pieces of silver per capita."

This seems foolhardy. It was one thing to write off Chairman Powers as Huntington's marionette: Having repeatedly and publicly sided with the railroad, Powers was a lost cause. But why speak so nastily of Reed? Why offend a potentate who hadn't taken a hard line on the bill and who could still do your cause a lot of harm? It was, in my view, Bierce's only mistake of the campaign.

Ironically, in other circumstances, Bierce would probably have taken a shine to the speaker. Renowned for his quick wit and ace debating skills, the three-hundred-pound gentleman from Maine was the sort of lawmaker for whom others dropped what they were doing to gather 'round and listen when he took the floor. His definition of a statesman as a politician who is dead was redolent of *The Devil's Dictionary*, and Reed once disparaged a pair of bumbling colleagues with a quip that Bierce might have envied: "They never open their mouths without subtracting from the sum of human knowledge." Reed had the charming ability to exult in his own virtuosity and make you like it. Once, after delivering a reply so adroit that it left his opponent speechless, Reed purred, "Having embedded that fly in the liquid amber of my remarks, I will proceed." More to the point, he is one of the few politicians on record as having refused to take money from Huntington. (Told of the rejection, Huntington had expressed shock: "The others have taken it.") Wisely, someone cut the Judas comparison from the version of Bierce's piece reprinted in Hearst's *New York Journal* on April 29.

Bierce continued to complain good-naturedly about a duty he probably hadn't foreseen when he took the job—serving as a reference desk. "Open-minded members, frankly confessing the ignorance of inattention, are diligently seeking light," he wrote. "Some of them are always applying to your correspondent for information; and there are not enough hours in the day in which to impart it." If his most important task was simply to call attention to the funding bill (because the more you knew about it, the more likely you were to oppose it), then perhaps a corner had indeed been turned.

The Death Blow Falls

Then again, maybe not. Another spell of inaction now set in. Both the Senate and House committees had reported out a pro-railroad bill, but as April gave way to May, the controversy was in limbo. On May 6, Bierce captured the fluid state of affairs in a dispatch—consisting of a single, perplexed paragraph—to the *New York Journal*:

The mystery continues, and all predictions fail. The Pacific Railroad's funding bill does not "come up." It was to "come up" yesterday, and again it was to "come up" to-day. A week ago it was to have been "up." It's "coming up" is marked by the same delays that characterized its secret progress toward the distinction of being "reported." Your correspondent could fill a column every day with emphatic assertions about the time fixed for it by those "close" to Speaker Reed, "close" to Mr. Huntington, "close" to the House Committee on Rules— close to everything but the truth. As to speculation and conjecture by the "longheads" (with ears to match), the entire paper would hardly suffice to hold all that. The total result of my observation is that the time when the Funding bill is to come up for debate in either House is unknown to any soul in Washington. That, however, is not saying that it is unknown to Mr. Huntington, who has no soul.

Suddenly, the next day, the logjam worked free. Through bluster and bribery, Huntington had thus far managed to finesse the fact that the heavily Republican California congressional delegation contained only a single member, Grove Johnson, who was on the railroad's side. But now betrayal came from an unexpected source: the state Republican Party. The headline for Bierce's dispatch read "FUNDING DEALT ITS DEATH BLOW," and for once the text that followed was in full agreement. Meeting in Sacramento, the party had passed a resolution opposing the funding bill. As an alert congressman pointed out, the action "[controverted] the effect of the repeated assertions of Mr. Huntington that there were not more than a hundred people in California opposed to a funding bill." Another lawmaker reacted to the news more succinctly: "That's bully."

The party that Huntington had served faithfully for decades had just made a fool and a liar out of him, and Bierce linked the treachery to the fall elections: "The resolution distinctly foreshadows the loss of California's electoral vote for the Republican candidate [for president] if a Republican Congress ventures to pass that bill—and California's electoral vote is thought by the party to be a precious possession which they hold in fee simple." Although he modestly refrained from saying so, Bierce's printed tutorials had surely helped alert the party bosses to the danger posed by the funding bill to the fortunes of their entire ticket in November. Huntington, who had been closeted with Senator Jones when word came, was said to have found the news "very unwelcome." A related story cited *The Wall Street Journal* to the effect that Huntington had "about given up hope of securing action at the present session."

Aftershocks from this upheaval were felt for days. Huntington reacted as was his wont, by trying to peddle influence. According to Bierce, Huntington's spear-carriers sought to curry favor with one congressman by suggesting that he take his family on a California vacation, all expenses paid. Another member was said to have received unsolicited railroad passes in the mail, which he indignantly returned.

Yet the "Battle of the Harbor Saints"—Monica versus Pedro—was still being fought, and perhaps Huntington could salvage a victory there. To that end, he deployed his forces. Bierce reported seeing "Tapeworm Boyd [squirming] on one of the back benches" while "down on the floor Grove Johnson glided about from Senator to Senator, whispering counsel and then vanishing like the glimmer of firelight on a window pane." Senator Stephen White of California and others pushed for a solution that was hard to argue against: Given the complexity of the issues, let's appoint a commission of experts—preferably engineers—and entrust the decision to them. "COLLIS DREADS A COMMISSION," asserted the headline of Bierce's next dispatch. Nonetheless, this exit route gained favor, partly because, as Bierce noted, "Senator Jones was not in evidence to-day. Perhaps some good angel had come to him in a dream and told him that his activity in a matter in which he had a direct pecuniary interest was a piece of indecency of which the meanest country magistrate would blush to be guilty and for which he would be publicly disgraced."

By May 13, the deal was done—a commission was the way to go. "To-day," Bierce's dispatch began, "Mr. Huntington saw the dishonest work of years come suddenly to naught." Huntington backers tried to save face by calling the commission a "compromise," but Bierce was having none of that. "The commission was thrust upon Huntington," he wrote; "he had to take that or nothing." Bierce singled out White for his fine work on the Senate floor—this appears to be one of those relatively rare cases when a senator's eloquence changed enough minds to affect the outcome of a vote.

But Bierce hastened to issue a warning: Look for the wily Huntington to try to corrupt the commission. At least, however, Bierce added, "the country has been shown that he can no longer count with confidence upon his own way of having it. To have absolute security from him we should have to kill him—to which I can see no objection."

Bierce was right about Huntington's intention to skew the commission, and the old tycoon acted sooner than expected. The question of who should name the five commissioners had yet to be decided, and Huntington lobbied to have it done by Congress, rather than by President Cleveland, as White had intended. But White beat back this threat, too, and a conference committee reported the bill out in a form to that senator's liking—"CLEVELAND WILL NAME THE BOARD," the *Examiner* confirmed on May 23. (On March 2, 1897, the commission rendered its verdict: San Pedro was the better choice for a deepwater port for Los Angeles. Congress abided by the decision.)

In essence, that was it. The great monopoly had been beaten at every turn. Oh, one couldn't rule out the possibility that the funding bill would be revived in the lame-duck session after the fall election, but even if so, its enactment in a pro-Huntington form looked doubtful. On May 27, a worn-out but elated Bierce declared victory in a diatribe that is worth quoting in full:

> The close of the session is in sight, and, in all probability, Huntington will be unable to get his Funding bill up in either house, even if he had the hardihood to attempt it. His hundreds

of thousands of dollars paid to half-a-hundred high-priced lobbyists has been absolutely wasted. These conscienceless malefactors have fed him fully of false hopes to the last moment, being naturally reluctant to let go their hold upon him as long as he could be made to believe in their power to gather figs from thistles and grapes from thorns. But the end of their power to derive otherwise than by telling the truth—than which they would rather fall—has come at last. The scales have fallen from the eyes of their wretched master; he has retired to the Cave of Adullam to gnaw his gold-worn fingers in impotent rage and curse mankind. He "drags at each remove a lengthening chain" of bitter memories.

In all that he has attempted during the session he has been beaten; and if he renew the struggle next winter, he must do so with broken prestige, his pretensions discredited, himself despised by those who once sought his alliance, entreated his favor and ran with glad feet in the pathway of his will. He could not now secure consideration for his villain bill if he dared. If he could and did, it would not pass the House. If it passed the House a half-dozen men could talk it to death in the Senate. If it passed both houses it would incur the Presidential veto. Mr. Cleveland has his vices, but a forgiving disposition is not among them, and I happen to know that the treacherous attempt to take out of his hands the power to appoint the board of engineers in the San Pedro–Santa Monica matter has incensed him. Huntington is now as powerless at the White House as at the Capitol.

What new combinations and alliances he may make during the recess, none can conjecture, but this meanest of all mean men in life or history—this indefatigable seeker for unfair advantage—this promoted peasant with a low love of labor and an unslackable [sic] thirst for gain, being already so rich that he stinks—this Huntington person is dead until December.

Step lightly, stranger, where so'er you tread;
All spots are sacred, save where he lies dead.

My work here is at an end. To friends, co-workers, well-wishers and readers, greeeting and benediction.

In San Francisco, a celebratory bash took place on May 29. Citizens turned out in force, lighting a bonfire at Fifth and Market streets and filling adjacent Metropolitan Hall for an evening of speeches and cheers. "It was remarkable," crowed the *Examiner*, "that a meeting called on so short notice, and completely ignored by some leading papers of the city, should have had so large an attendance. The great hall was packed to the doors and hundreds had to be turned away disappointed." James D. Phelan, soon to succeed Sutro as mayor of San Francisco, pointed out in his speech that "our newspapers were almost a unit in opposition" to the funding bill, but the *Examiner* larded its account of the festivities with tributes sent to itself and its special correspondent.

Representative Bell of Colorado declared that "when a great journal like 'The Examiner' takes a decided stand upon any question its influence must necessarily be great, but when it conducts such a campaign as that newspaper has against the Pacific Railroads Funding bill it would be difficult to overstate its power." Barham of California stated that "the fitting, burning, liquid, lightning sarcasm and treatment of the subject by Ambrose Bierce caused many a lobbyist to wince and Congressman to think. I am of the opinion that 'The Examiner' is entitled to great credit for its treatment of the case." For Hillborn of Connecticut,

The history of the contest about the funding bill would be incomplete without some mention of Ambrose Bierce, the special correspondent of 'The Examiner.' Aside from what he has written to 'The Examiner,' New York 'Journal' and Washington 'Star,' which produced a profound impression, his personal efforts in furnishing information to committeemen and members were almost invaluable.

The *Examiner* rounded out its coverage of the gala with a sentence that harked back to the earliest days of the battle. "For the first time in its career of lawlessness and oppression the Southern Pacific has been checked and placed on the defensive. It is now fighting in its last ditch. . . ."

Those "personal efforts" by Bierce had taken their toll. He decamped to Englewood, New Jersey, where he spent a month recovering from the strain of overwork. Not until November did he return to San Francisco and pick up "Prattle" where he'd left it.

Early in the new year, at long last, Speaker Reed appeared ready to "move" the funding bill, and Bierce sounded a wistful note in his column of January 10, 1897: "I feel rather like a fool sitting here three thousand miles away while my co-workers of last session set their breasts against this giant iniquity. Faith, it were good to be there again in the thick of it." A few days later, the House rejected the bill by a vote of 168 to 102. Hearst and Bierce's victory was complete.

"Our Willie"

Almost lopsided, the Southern Pacific's January 10 defeat might have piled up that kind of margin if not for an event that had taken place two days earlier: a defeated congressman had stood up and made a venomous speech. This was the inimitable Grove Johnson, who had lost his seat in the November elections. For William Herrin, the Southern Pacific's chief counsel, Johnson's defeat was the worst blow of all. It will, he predicted, "naturally cause other friends to be extremely reluctant to acknowledge their friendship to railroad instincts." But Johnson was entitled to wear the cloak of congressional immunity for a few more weeks, and in his bitterness he decided to stretch it to the fraying point by giving new life to a weather-beaten charge.

The *Examiner* has a very large circulation. . . . It has done great good in California. It has exposed corruption, denounced villainy, unearthed wickedness, pursued criminals, and rewarded virtue.

At first, we Californians were suspicious of "Our Willie," as Hearst is called on the Pacific Coast. We did not know what he meant. But we came to believe in him and his oft-repeated boasts of independence and honesty. Daily editorials, written by "Our Willie," hired men praising his motives and proclaiming his honesty, had their effect. Besides, "Our Willie" through his paper was doing some good.

We knew him to be a debauchee, a dude in dress, an Anglomaniac in language and manners, but we thought he was honest.

We knew him to be licentious in his tastes, regal in his dissipations, unfit to associate with pure women or decent men, but we thought "Our Willie" was honest.

We knew he was erotic in his tastes, erratic in his moods, of small understanding and smaller views of men and measures, but we thought "Our Willie," with his English plaids, his cockney accent, and his middle-parted hair, was honest.

We knew he had sought on the banks of the Nile relief from loathsome disease contracted only by contagion in the haunts of vice, and had rivalled the Khedive in the gorgeousness of his harem in the joy of restored health, but we still believed him honest, though low and depraved.

We knew he was debarred from society in San Francisco because of his delight in flaunting his wickedness, but we believed him honest, though tattooed in sin.

We knew he was ungrateful to his friends, unkind to his employees, unfaithful to his business associates, but we believed he was trying to publish an honest paper . . . .

When William R. Hearst commenced his abusive tirades against C. P. Huntington and the Southern Pacific Compan and the Central Pacific Railroad Company and all who were friendly to them, and to denounce the funding bill and all who favored it as thieves and robbers, we thought his course was wrong, his methods bad, and his attacks brutal, but we believed "Our Willie" to be honest.

When C. P. Huntington told the truth about "Our Willie" and showed that he was simply fighting the railroad funding bill because he could get no more blackmail from the Southern Pacific Company, we were dazed with the charge, and as Californians we were humiliated.

We looked eagerly for "Our Willie's" denial, but it came not. On the contrary he admitted that he had blackmailed the Southern Pacific into a contract whereby they were to pay him $30,000 to let them alone, and that he had received $22,000 of his blackmail, and that C. P. Huntington had cut it off as soon as he knew of it, and that he was getting even now on Huntington and the railroad company because he had not received the other $8,000 of his bribe. He admitted by silence that the Southern Pacific Company was financially responsible, but that he dared not sue it for the $8,000 he claimed to be due because of fear that his blackmail would be exposed in court.

With brazen effrontery only equalled by the lowest denizen in the haunts of vice "Our Willie" knows so well in every city of the globe, he unblushingly admitted he had blackmailed the railroad company, but pleaded in extenuation that he did not keep his contract, but swindled them out of their money. . . .

To learn "Our Willie" was nothing but a common, ordinary, everyday blackmailer—a low highwayman of the newspaper world—grieved the people of California, myself included. . . .

To which the only sensible reply is "What's so bad about middle-parted hair?"

In his biography *Citizen Hearst* (1961), W. A. Swanberg denied that Hearst was suffering from a venereal (or any other) disease.

With commendable diligence, Swanberg went on to test the charge that the advertising contract with the Southern Pacific had colored the *Examiner*'s coverage of that corporation. After combing through editions of the paper from April–May 1892 (two months before the contract went into effect) to August–September 1894 (two months after the contract was cancelled), he found "no evidence that [Hearst's] news treatment was affected in the slightest by the advertising deal." However "erotic" or "erratic" he might have been, Hearst "was entirely innocent of selling out to the S.P."

A Settlement at Last

After delivering his diatribe, Johnson slunk off into oblivion. But in a political development that almost beggars belief, his son, Hiram Johnson, was not only elected governor of California in 1910 for his populist convictions; Johnson the younger went on to make good on them by pushing through a law that subjected the Southern Pacific to stringent regulation.

The funding-bill issues lingered on, however. Government officials were reluctant to take the logical step of forcing the railroad out of business and selling off its assets because, as Congressman Powers pointed out, "These very men whom you are now scolding about, the very men who own the terminals and own these connecting lines are the only ones who can safely bid on the property, and probably they will be the only bidders." What a terrible irony that would have been: putting Huntington and his minions right back in charge of the Central Pacific, with no more assurance than before that its obligations would be met. But Huntington and the other Southern Pacific owners ran a risk, too. If they gave up control of the Central Pacific, they would probably also spoil a perfectly good monopoly. For both sides, the incentive to reach a settlement was great.

Congress managed to placate everyone by handing off the funding shortfall to another commission, this one composed of three agency heads from the Cabinet of the new president, Republican

William McKinley. This body rendered its decision in February of 1899. The Central Pacific was ordered to pay its debt over a ten-year period, in twenty installments of roughly $3 million apiece, with the Southern Pacific standing behind its sister road as a guarantor. (In return for this concession, the Southern Pacific was allowed to consolidate its hold on the Central Pacific.) Although ten years was a far cry from the half-century or longer extensions that Huntington had sought so assiduously, out in California Bierce said he approved the deal only "with difficulty." On another occasion, however, he acknowledged that the bill's defeat had been "an enormously long stride toward the open."

As for the grandee whom the steadfast Grove Johnson had served so well (and so foolishly), some critics suggest that Huntington shrugged the loss off and carried on exactly as before. Carey McWilliams, however, saw things differently, as the beginning of the end:

> [The defeat] marked the doom of Southern Pacific dominance in California, for in the mayoralty campaign of 1896, Fremont Older managed to get his candidate, James D. Phelan, a liberal, elected mayor of San Francisco. The tide had turned and it did not cease rolling on to victory until Hiram Johnson had been elected Governor. Then, after he had framed the famous act creating the Railway Commission and amending the State Constitution so as to give the newly created commission sweeping powers of regulation and control, the Southern Pacific episode was closed once and for all.

Huntington had died in the summer of 1900, however, so he wasn't around to feel the lash of Hiram Johnson's reforms. But Daniel Lindley points out that in the three-plus years of life that remained to him after the 1896–97 defeat, Huntington had seemed as recalcitrant as ever. In a long letter to his man on Wall Street, he had taken a tough valedictory line:

As far as my part in the inception, construction, and operation of the Southern and Central Pacific Railroads is concerned, I am satisfied with what I have done. No man is perfect and the man does not live who can look back and say that he has made no mistakes, but the motives back of my actions have been honest ones and the results have redounded far more to the benefit of California than they have to my own.

Still, it is instructive to compare Huntington's reactions on the two occasions when he and the railroad took a beating. After losing the Thurman Act battle in 1878, he had yowled for both public and private consumption: the antiboodle climate of that period had worked against him, and he'd felt victimized by circumstances. In 1897, he accepted his loss quietly, perhaps because he had no one to blame for it but himself.

Post-Mortem

Huntington and his advisers had indeed made three errors. In ascribing pro-funding-bill views to California notables who did not hold them, they had given Bierce an early windfall—an easy first round at a time when he was still getting in shape for the contest. Huntington's attempt to corrupt Bierce (whatever form it may have taken) had bolstered Bierce's self-confidence by helping him achieve one of his personal goals in fighting a journalistic duel: Demonstrate your own moral superiority. And Huntington's carelessness in allowing the funding controversy to get mixed up with the Santa Monica vs. San Pedro harbor decision had been his biggest miscalculation. The slowest-witted member of Congress could hardly fail to note the crassness of trying to sneak into law an appropriation favoring the maritime aspirations of a town where a well-known robber baron and a prominent U.S. senator owned a railroad and other properties. The harbor mess had slopped over onto the funding-bill controversy, causing lawmakers who had previously stayed aloof to seek out Bierce for enlightenment.

One last miscalculation by Huntington is more forgivable. The days when a big corporation could keep a whole state in line by stuffing money into the pockets of its officials and opinion makers were coming to an end, but an old-school partisan like Huntington either hadn't noticed the change or didn't know what to make of it. As Pulitzer and Hearst had demonstrated, a rambunctious publisher could outflank the moneyed establishment by appealing directly to the populace. The resulting upticks in circulation and advertising revenues would more than offset the bribes foregone. Grove Johnson, who took handouts from the Southern Pacific, couldn't hang on to his House seat because the *Examiner*, which didn't, was free to expose him as the hireling of a nefarious corporation. In looking back over the *annus horribilis* in which a sure thing had turned into a botch, Huntington might well have concluded that he was losing his touch—and decided to keep this alarming news to himself.

Bierce, on the other hand, had played an expert game, marred only by a single intemperate outburst: that comparison of Speaker Reed to Judas, which, fortunately, seems to have done little harm. Besides working overtime, mastering financial issues with which he'd had little previous experience, making himself available to legislators seeking enlightenment, and sitting through hour after hour of committee hearings and floor debate, Bierce had also done what he was best at: inflicting damage by calling upon his singular talent for verbal assault. More than a decade after the fact, Charles Edward Russell wrote a series of pieces on the nation's railroads for *Hampton's Magazine*. In the one dated September 1910, he reminded readers how effectively Bierce had carried out his assignment from Hearst.

These articles were extraordinary examples of invective and bitter sarcasm. They were addressed to the dishonest nature of the bill and to the real reasons why the machine had slated it for passage. When Mr. Bierce began his campaign, few persons imagined that the bill could be stopped. After a time the skill and steady persistence of the attack began to draw wide attention. With six months of incessant firing, Mr. Bierce had the railroad forces frightened and wavering; and before the end of the year, he had them whipped.

(Russell might have noted yet another contribution made by Bierce's "incessant firing": its influence on the equally powerful work of another, younger California writer, Frank Norris.)

One last aspect of Bierce's campaign deserves mention. He had never been better at—or, probably, taken so much pleasure in—his work. As Hannah Arendt points out in her book *On Revolution*, few human endeavors give more satisfaction than influencing the course of civic events. "Americans knew that public freedom consisted in having a share in public business," she wrote, "and that the activities connected with this business by no means constituted a burden but gave those who discharged them in public a feeling of happiness they could acquire nowhere else." Bierce's happiness would have been magnified by what was at stake. He hadn't just participated expertly in public debate, he had won a costly victory in the big leagues of the nation's capital.

Something else might have buoyed him up, too—a feature of the campaign that Bierce might not have fully recognized at the time (because, after all, he still had years of writing ahead of him) but that he might well have suspected. Those sixty-some articles supply what is otherwise missing from his dossier. He may have been incapable of producing a novel or of assembling his firsthand impressions of the Civil War into a unified treatment, but in 1896 he threw himself into a great cause, whose ingredients he probed and mastered and whose dramatis personae he satirized with elan over a five-month span. Whether he knew it or not, Bierce's articles in opposition to the funding bill add up to the masterpiece he was otherwise unable to write.

Theodore Judah

(Courtesy of California State Railroad Museum)

Collis Huntington

(Courtesy of California State Railroad Museum)

Leland Stanford

(Courtesy of California State Railroad Museum)

Mark Hopkins

(Courtesy of California State Railroad Museum)

Charles Crocker

(Courtesy of California State Railroad Museum)

Tunnel interior in the
Sierra Nevada
*(Courtesy of California State
Railroad Museum)*

Locomotive in
Bloomer Cut on
western slope of
the Sierra Nevada.
*(Courtesy of California
State Railroad Museum)*

Portrait of Ambrose Bierce
(Courtesy of Library of Congress)

Snow shed under construction
in the Sierra Nevada
*(Courtesy of California
State Railroad Museum)*

Frank Norris

(Courtesy of Library of Congress)

Cartoon by James Swinnerton
in the *San Francisco Examiner*
of December 14, 1896

(Courtesy of Library of Congress)

seven

The Beast Emerges from Within Frank Norris

The other great writer preoccupied with the Southern Pacific in the late 1890s was a prince and a paragon. Benjamin Franklin Norris Jr. came from old New World stock, with a *Mayflower* passenger among his forebears. Norris's daddy was rich, his ma was good-looking, and their boy grew up with servants in the house and, as schoolmates, the offspring of George M. Pullman (inventor of the Pullman car), Marshall Field (department stores), and Philip D. Armour (meat-packing). After trying his hand at drawing and painting, young Norris decided that his true calling was literature. He was right. In the short time given him, he wrote seven novels, two of them now regarded as American classics. His hair turned prematurely gray, and he suffered from skin problems, but the blemishes don't show up in photographs taken of him, in which his lanky frame and regular features complement his elegant attire. He married a beautiful woman, and they seem to have been happy together. His contemporaries had nothing but good to say of him. His co-biographers, who tracked their quarry for over thirty years, concluded that he "appears to have modeled human nature at its best."

Norris's artistic achievement is all the more remarkable considering what he wrote about, and how. Unlike other well-born novelists of his era, he did not stick to familiar subjects from the milieu in which he'd grown up. Take Henry James and Edith Wharton, for example. In book after book, they scrutinized the moral dilemmas faced by refined characters much like themselves. In contrast, Norris's best work is about the hand-to-mouth lives of people with whom he had little in common: an unschooled and unwholesome dentist in an urban slum and struggling farmers in California's arid Central Valley. In addition—and this was perhaps Norris's governing impulse—he harbored outsized ambitions. As a writer, he wanted to measure up to the scope and excitement of nineteenth-century America, to capture the throb of its cities and the sweep of its prairies, to produce not just single novels but a trilogy about a pervasive and fundamental commodity: wheat. (His urge to paint on a broad canvas couldn't have been further removed from Bierce's miniaturist leanings.) Norris's breadth of vision and his tendency to look outside his own background for fictional material worked together to make him the writer he wanted to be.

Few of those who knew Norris as a young man, however, would have picked him as most likely to succeed. He puckishly signed one of his first journalistic pieces "Dilettante," and he lived up to the label. By then he had not only studied painting in California and France but also taken a drifter's approach to American higher education.

As early as his application letter to the University of California, Norris had made no secret of his maverick tendencies. "I am willing to forego the diploma," he wrote, "so thoroughly am I persuaded that the course which leads up to it . . . would be more detrimental to me than otherwise." In the end, he might have graduated all the same if it hadn't been for his disaffection with mathematics; he needed a course in that subject to fill out his undergraduate requirements but couldn't be bothered to take it. He did study with one of the university's big names, however: Joseph LeConte, who taught geology and zoology so as to meld Darwinian evolution with a belief that the physical world manifests the mind of God. In his book *Evolution: Its Nature, Its Evidences, and Its Relation to Religious Thought*, published in 1891, the year before Norris entered Cal, the scientist-philosopher asked a rhetorical question that was to find an echo in the last lines of his famous pupil's longest and best novel, *The Octopus*, almost a decade later. The LeConte version went: "May we not say that all physical evil is good in its general effect— that every law of Nature is beneficent in its general operation, and if sometimes evil in its specific operation, is so only through our ignorance [of God's ways]?"

Norris dropped out in the second semester of his senior year, content with what he called an "honorable dismissal." That fall (of 1894), at the advanced age of twenty-four, he moved to Cambridge, Massachusetts, with his mother and his brother Charles, seeking at Harvard what he hadn't found at Cal: a good course in fiction writing. He got what he wanted from a professor named Lewis E. Gates, who, in the words of Norris scholar James D. Hart, "emphasized the need to bring romanticism into association with common life so as to create a 'renovating imaginative realism.'" Gates taught the same class at Radcliffe College that semester, where his students included another Californian, Gertrude Stein (she got a C, Norris an A). The young man's status as a Special Student did not put him on track for a Harvard degree, but that wasn't what he'd come for. A few years later, he recycled some of the sketches he wrote for that class in his first great novel, *McTeague*, which he dedicated to Gates. For all its desultoriness, then, Norris's academic career seems to have given him just what he wanted.

His freedom to sample colleges and their courses like a man at a buffet supper was made possible in part by his father's financial success. The Michigan-born B. F. Norris, as he was known, had waged his own rebellion against prescribed education. When his father took him to Grand Rapids at age fifteen to be enrolled in a boarding school, B. F. made a detour to a jewelry store, which hired him as an apprentice. His rise to prosperity was rapid. After being promoted to traveling salesman, he went into business for himself. By 1860, in his mid-twenties, B. F. had a wife and daughter and was listed on the census rolls as a watchmaker living in Lockport, Illinois, outside Chicago. Ten years later, he held a half-interest in a wholesale jewelry business, a bankroll estimated at $20,000, and real estate investments valued at $50,000.

In the interim, he had divorced and remarried. His second wife was Gertrude Doggett, a Chicago schoolteacher turned actress. Acting was a suspect profession for a woman then, and Gertrude's appearance, as captured in a surviving photo, would have given little comfort to prudes. With heavy-lidded eyes, a sensuous curl to her lips, and plenty of makeup on, she looks like a precursor to the sultry Mae West. But it was Gertrude who contributed *Mayflower* ancestry to the marriage, along with a strong work ethic as a social climber. The couple had five children, three boys and two girls; Frank, their second child, came along in 1870. Gertrude quit performing in public and channeled her frustrated-actress syndrome into dramatic readings for her children. B. F. immersed himself in his work and battled ailments exacerbated by the harsh Chicago winters. In 1885, he sought relief by moving the family to San Francisco, forcing Frank to leave the tony private school in which he had rubbed shoulders with the scions of Midwestern plutocracy.

B. F.'s health stabilized, and he hit the road. He had good reason to visit Illinois, where his business was still based, but he also wandered farther afield, and the marriage began to crack under the strain of his frequent and prolonged absences. Meanwhile, Gertrude's thespian past proved less of a handicap in the freewheeling West than it had in Chicago, and mentions of her in newspaper society pages indicate that she had maneuvered the family into San Francisco's elite circles—a well-connectedness that got Frank admitted to the Bohemian Club, to which Collis Huntington (and, briefly, Ambrose Bierce) also belonged. Nonetheless, the marriage reached the end toward which it had been trending. In 1893, B. F. drifted away for good, and the following year Gertrude obtained a divorce. B. F.'s real-estate portfolio had grown fatter over the years, and in lieu of alimony Gertrude received title to property worth a million dollars in today's money.

The rupture may have done Frank a favor—as a writer, if not as a son. His parents had formed a pattern soon to be made much of by the German novelist Thomas Mann: stiff-backed, bourgeois father and dreamy, artistic mother. According to Norris's brother Charles, B. F. dismissed Frank's writing as "thimble-headed bobbism," and there might have been trouble if the father had maintained financial control over his aesthetical son. But with Gertrude now at the apex of both the family and a real-estate empire, Frank was free to go his own way. The disdain of such a father—both imperious and negligent—is likely to have instilled an "I'll-show-him" attitude in his talented son.

While his parents' marriage deteriorated, Frank had studied art at the California School of Design in San Francisco and the Académie Julian in Paris. We know little about how he fared at the School of Design, other than that none of his paintings was chosen for exhibition. As for the Académie, it upheld the ossified tradition of assigning its students mythological subjects, to be rendered as convincingly as the lurid stories and semidivine (and often entirely nude) characters would allow. The Julian was no dead end, however: Alphonse Mucha, soon to be a renowned designer of Art Nouveau posters, was a classmate of Norris's, and Henri Matisse studied there a couple of years later. None of Norris's work from the Julian has survived, but it's safe to assume it didn't measure up to his own standards—back in the States in 1890, he set his sights on that literary career.

His first book, published while he was a student at Cal, was the sort of thing one might expect from a romantic Francophile: *Yvernelle: A Legend of Feudal France*. He was a sophomore when it came out, published by J. B. Lippincott and subsidized by Gertrude;

the work—a narrative poem about a knight, a curse, two maidens, and the last-minute "rescue" of one, Yvernelle herself, before she can pronounce her vows as a nun—sounds sophomoric indeed. While in France, however, Norris had fallen under the sway of a writer who would have given Yvernelle a kick in her feudal French pants: Émile Zola.

A few years later, Norris raved about some of Zola's most striking qualities in a review of a new novel:

> As is the rule with this author's works, *Rome* leaves one with an impression of immensity, of vast illimitable forces, of a breadth of view and an enormity of imagination almost too great to be realized. You lay the book down, breathless; for the moment all other books, even all other *things*, seem small and trivial.

Here is another source of the mightiness that imbues Norris's best fiction: a literary model who set an example of addressing big topics in grand style. Norris's infatuation prompted him to sign his letters, half-jokingly, as "the Boy-Zola," and a look at the French writer's life and times is called for.

As the nineteenth century came to a close, many of the cherished customs and eternal verities that had prevailed at its start lay in ruins. A spate of inventions—the railroad, the telegraph, electrical lighting, the telephone, and the automobile—had shortened distances, facilitated communication, and sped up a pace of existence that had hardly changed in centuries. More than that, the whole configuration of economic and civic life was in flux, with people flocking from the countryside into cities, small firms amalgamating into large corporations and corporations into trusts, labor unions springing up to assert workers' rights, and government wondering how to keep all these new behemoths in check. Money and power flowed to industrial firms, banks, and labor unions in such quantities that state budgets looked paltry in comparison. Historian Richard Hofstadter pointed out that in 1888 "a certain railroad with offices in Boston employed 18,000 persons, had gross receipts of about $40,000,000 a year, and paid its highest-salaried officer $35,000," whereas the Commonwealth of Massachusetts "employed only 6,000 persons, had gross receipts of about $7,000,000 and paid no salary higher than $6,500." Signs of prosperity were everywhere—except among the working class; as the American political economist Henry George observed, "[the] association of poverty with progress is the great enigma of our times." There were epic cases of graft and corruption, attempts to corner markets in commodities, financial panics, runs on banks, and strikes that ended in violence. There was also an urge to exalt influential or highly visible personages, ranging from inventor Thomas Edison and banker J. P. Morgan to entertainers Buffalo Bill Cody and Sarah Bernhardt, as the media gained the ability to anoint and sustain mass-market celebrities. Seldom had the ordinary citizen felt more at the mercy of forces beyond his or her control. Writers such as Zola felt called upon to expand the range of fiction and confront genteel readers with the tribulations of urban outsiders, who despite their great numbers were surprisingly easy to ignore.

Victorian-era men and women also experienced jolts to received wisdom. An educated person in the year 1800 could have maintained an unruffled belief in the creation story as spelled out in the Book of Genesis, even subscribing to Anglican Archbishop James Ussher's calculation of 4004 B.C. as the universal starting date. By century's end, however, new geological discoveries and improved accuracy in the dating of fossils had shredded Ussher's timeline and reduced Genesis to an elaborate metaphor, leaving the literalism of a six-day creation tenable only for those who refused to look at the evidence around them. At the same time, Darwin's theory of natural selection, which explained so much about how the animal kingdom is organized, suggested that humans have far more in common with lower forms of life than we would like to admit—some of those forces beyond our control, it turned out, welled up from within us. Social philosophers adapted Darwinism to explain and justify the rigors of laissez-faire capitalism. The phrase "survival of the fittest"—coined not by Darwin but by one of his more astute readers, the English philosopher Herbert Spencer—captured what was thought to be an iron law of the marketplace: In business, as in physiological evolution, the strong and the well-adapted win out, and any damage done to individuals is a natural by-product of the surge toward overall betterment.

Creative writers took note of these developments by curbing their inclinations to idealize heroes and reward perseverance with happy endings. Novelists lowered their sights from the heroic deeds of the well-born and the temporary setbacks of the upwardly mobile to the ordeals of ordinary folk who might never overcome their innate limitations or the socioeconomic conditions holding them back. Behavior once considered unsavory—adultery, for example—was depicted and analyzed with almost surgical precision, as in Gustave Flaubert's *Madame Bovary*. Sacred cows were slain, as when Mark Twain had Huck Finn declare he would rather go to hell than betray his boon companion, the runaway slave Jim. (The twentieth-century critic Leslie Fiedler suggested a handy way to tell romantic and realistic fiction apart: Compare Mark Twain's affable portrait of his childhood in *The Adventures of Tom Sawyer* with his bleak version of the same material in *The Adventures of Huckleberry Finn*.) Instead of expressing lofty sentiments in well-turned phrases, characters in fiction started talking as they would in real life, voicing their mundane concerns in regional accents and unorthodox diction, which authors captured in phonetic spelling and imperfect grammar. The most consistent American exponent of literary realism was William Dean Howells—influential critic, former editor of the *Atlantic Monthly*, and author of several novels on American social problems—who befriended and mentored Frank Norris.

The young Norris had praised Howells's work, especially *A Modern Instance* (1882), his novel of divorce. But ultimately Norris judged Howells's kind of realism too tame, too apt to dwell on what Norris derided as "the drama of a broken teacup, the tragedy of a walk down the block, the excitement of an afternoon call, the adventure of an invitation to dinner." (Realism was utterly at odds with the neo-Gothic imagination of Ambrose Bierce, who heaped scorn on the movement in his *Devil's Dictionary*: "REALISM, *n*: The art of depicting nature as it is seen by toads." More to his liking was romance, or "fiction that owes no allegiance to the God of Things as They Are." Concerning Howells, Bierce harrumphed that "he can tell nothing but something like what he has seen or heard, and in his personal progress through the rectangular streets and between the trim hedges of Philistia, with the lettered old maids of his acquaintance curtseying from the doorways, he has seen and heard nothing worth telling.")

In his essay "A Plea for Romantic Fiction," Norris called for realism to give way to a reinvigorated romanticism, which he defined as "the kind of fiction that takes cognizance of variations from the type of normal life. . . . Romance may even treat of the sordid, the unlovely—as, for instance, the novels of M. Zola. (Zola has been dubbed a Realist, but he is, on the contrary, the very head of the Romanticists.)" Elsewhere Norris fell in with the majority by calling the new approach "naturalism." In a full-dress essay on Zola, Norris laid out what was in store for "naturalistic characters." "They must be twisted from the ordinary, wrenched out from the quiet, uneventful round of every-day life and flung into the throes of a vast and terrible drama that works itself out in unleashed passions, in blood, and in sudden death." In Norris's canon, then, Zola's fortissimo novels—with their vivid, sometimes grotesque characters, the clash of tremendous social forces, and ample doses of brutality, murder, and madness—had elbowed Howell's quieter ones aside.

Zola's method was to apply to his characters insights he had picked up from the new scientific learning and practice. A person's behavior, he believed, could be explained by carefully documenting his heredity and environment as they combined to influence his actions. This wasn't to be done in a mechanistic way—Zola made allowances for the exercise of free will; as he once asked, "But where can the man be found who, in the stress of strife, does not exceed what is necessary?" Zola also employed humor and flights of invention to provide relief from his characters' steady unraveling, as in a set piece from *L'Assommoir* (1877) where the lowlife characters throw a wedding banquet and get chaotically drunk. A few of his novels— *Au Bonheur des dames* and *Germinal* come to mind—end happily, or at least with the protagonist still alive and holding up his head. (Like some of his disciples, Zola sometimes talked a rougher game than he played.) Still, it's not unusual to finish a Zola novel feeling as though you'd just watched a drawn-out autopsy.

The prolific author put his theories to work in his Rougon-Macquart series (named after the interrelated French families to which many of its characters belong): twenty novels, written between 1871 and 1893, in which he traces down through the generations the effects of such genetic flaws as susceptibility to drink and a craving for violent sex, in the context of such socioeconomic shifts as the mechanization of farming and the influx of the poor into big cities. Among the best of these novels—and one of several that Norris read and commented upon—is *La Bête humaine* (1890), sometimes translated as "The Beast Within," a story of trains, the engineers who drive them, and the women who put up with them both. Writing to a friend, Zola explained his aim in *La Bête humaine* in terms that encapsulated naturalism as he saw it. He wanted, he said, to evoke "the passage of progress on its way towards the twentieth century, and in the midst of a dreadful and mysterious drama to which all are blind—the human beast within civilization."

To accentuate the near helplessness of many of his characters, Zola often personified the forces, institutions, and contraptions that assail and crush them. In *Germinal* (1885), when a subsidence of the earth destroys the mighty pump of a coal mine whose owners hellishly exploit their workers, Zola remarks that "the evil beast, crouching in its hollow, sated with human flesh, had drawn its last long heavy breath." In *Au Bonheur des dames* (1883, translated as "The Ladies' Delight"), a Parisian department store makes an unlikely candidate for the come-to-life treatment. Constantly expanding at the expense of its workers and the nearby shops that it forces out of business, the store is compared to a gigantic steam engine and then to a "monster," against which everyone but its customers must struggle for economic survival. One of the trains in *La Bête humaine* is similarly depicted as ogrelike, with a "flaming eye" that changes into "the ravenous mouth of a furnace" as it closes in on an observer. When Norris came to write his own novel about trains, *The Octopus*, he sounded the note of railroad-as-monster with almost feverish insistence.

Zola attracted disciples in France, notably Guy de Maupassant and the Goncourt brothers. But the movement he fathered enjoyed even greater success in the United States, where its practitioners included Hamlin Garland, Stephen Crane, Jack London, and Theodore Dreiser. Of all the Yankee acolytes, however, none followed the Zola blueprint more closely than Norris.

After leaving Harvard in 1895, Norris returned to San Francisco and began freelancing for local newspapers. He thereby submitted himself to what was considered the best possible discipline for a beginning writer: sampling and reporting on the world's endless variety. Norris's early work met with enough enthusiasm that he was inspired to emulate the dashing journalist Richard Harding Davis by jaunting off as a foreign correspondent. For his destination, Norris chose South Africa, where he could observe the Boer uprising and send "letters" reporting what he saw to the *San Francisco Chronicle*. An excerpt from one of these dispatches indicates how much progress he'd already made as a stylist: "Upon the equator [the ship] had slid through still, oily waters, blue as indigo, level as a cathedral floor, broken only by the quick flash and flight of hundreds of flying fish, flocks of them flushed by the great hull." That sentence may have an f-word too many, but even so it's a lovely, evocative piece of work.

During his two-and-a-half months in South Africa, Norris came down with what was probably either dengue fever or malaria (he was to be susceptible to fevers for the rest of his life). Back home, he landed his first regular job, as a writer for and associate editor of *The Wave*, a weekly San Francisco magazine by which he was linked to both Huntington and Bierce. The magazine had been founded in 1890 to drum up interest in the snazzy Hotel del Monte near Monterey, a property of Huntington's Southern Pacific Railroad. That tie had loosened over the years, but *The Wave* was still conservative in its politics. Otherwise, it sounds rather like *The New Yorker* in its mid-twentieth-century heyday, combining, as noted by California historian Kevin Starr, "the high spirits of an undergraduate humor magazine with the chatty nonchalance of a town-and-topics review." Among the writers drawn to this showcase was Bierce, who occasionally contributed short stories. Norris's tenure with *The Wave*, 1896–97, puts him in San Francisco during Bierce's sustained attack on Huntington's funding bill. Norris would surely have followed this campaign as it unfolded in the *Examiner*; a few years later he refreshed himself with its contents before starting to write *The Octopus*.

As an editor, Norris was less than ideal—being shaky on spelling and punctuation, he couldn't very well impose them on others. But as a writer he excelled at turning out the kind of aren't-we-interesting? feature to be found in the Style or Living sections of today's newspapers: e.g., a piece on what became of the five hundred tons of garbage generated by San Franciscans each day; one on the route taken by a message sent from the city to South Africa; one on the food and drink produced by the Italian Swiss Colony in the nearby Sonoma Valley; one on how a fifty-ton gun—a "monster," a "leviathan"—was moved from the iron works to a fort overlooking the Golden Gate, where it went on duty guarding the bay.

To *The Wave* for May 22, 1897, Norris contributed a rousing list of fetching local subjects available to aspiring writers:

Kearney street, Montgomery street, Nob Hill, Telegraph Hill, of course Chinatown, Lone Mountain, the Poodle Dog, the Palace Hotel and the What Cheer House, the Barbary Coast, the Crow's Nest, the Mission, the Bay, the Bohemian Club, the Presidio, Spanish town, Fisherman's wharf. There is an indefinable air about all these places that is suggestive of stories at once. You fancy the names would look well on a book's page. The people who frequent them could walk right into a novel or short story and be at home.

Some of those people walked right into Norris's own fiction, notably *McTeague*, subtitled *A Story of San Francisco* and offering an invaluable portrait of the city's grittier side. Norris also stored up experiences that came his way as a reporter; one of these, a visit to a "great whaleback steamer taking on grain for famine-stricken India," became a source of inspiration for his wheat trilogy.

Norris's approach to journalism was to insinuate himself into the action, occasionally by narrating in the second person. "You got off the train feeling vaguely intrusive," begins a piece on the Santa Cruz Venetian Carnival of 1896. Once he had sized up a scene and captured its details, he was ready to step back and look for a larger meaning, a sweeping confluence of phenomena which less-attentive reporters might miss. Here he is again at that carnival, late at night, after it has shut down and everyone else has gone home:

And then, in that immense silence, when all the shrill, staccato, trivial noises of the day were dumb, you heard again the prolonged long hum that rose from the city, even in its sleep, the voice of something individual, living a huge, strange life apart, raising a virile diapason of protest against shame and tinsels and things transient in that other strange carnival, that revel of masks and painted faces, the huge grim joke that runs its fourscore years and ten.

If this sounds Zolaesque, it should: Norris wrote it while at the height of his infatuation with the French novelist. *The Wave* had recently published Norris's review of *Rome* (quoted from above), and his essay "Zola as a Romantic Writer" ran in the same issue (June 27, 1896) as the Santa Cruz carnival piece.

The Wave also published ten short stories by Norris, but as his stay at the magazine lengthened, he became restless. He'd let himself get sucked into a group of arch local litterateurs called Les Jeunes, only to decide that bantering and carousing with them was taking a toll on his work. He broke with the group, but early in 1897 his professional stagnation plunged him into a nervous crisis. He recovered by bearing down on his short story writing. The tales became more pessimistic and fatalistic. In one of them, McTeague and his wife, Trina, made their debut in print. On the whole, however, Norris's short stories are mediocre, and he probably sensed that he had no gift for the form. All the more reason, then, to concentrate on the novel—the longer, perhaps the better—as the genre in which to make his mark. By the fall of that year, he was hard at work on the book in which Mac and Trina perform their dance of death.

Norris finished *McTeague* in a ninety-day burst of creativity but didn't immediately try to sell it. Instead, he went to work on something pedestrian, *Moran of the Lady Letty*, an adventure novel about a meek fellow who gets in touch with his inner he-man after being shanghaied to toil on a pirate boat. (A generation after Norris's death, *Moran* gave a plum role to a new movie star named Rudolph Valentino.) Not only was the story serialized in *The Wave*; it was syndicated by *McClure's Magazine* and then published in book form by Doubleday and McClure Company. Derivative though it was, *Moran* brought Norris attention and made it easier for the daring *McTeague* to get into print.

By then, Norris was on the *McClure's* staff. He had not only vaulted from the West Coast to the East and from a regional magazine to a national one—a monthly that was carving out a niche by taking aim at political corruption and corporate bullying—but had also quit taking money from his mother. The job offer had come after he moved to New York in 1898 and stopped by the magazine's offices; the starting salary was a modest $50 a month. According to friends, Norris went through a rough patch on arriving in Manhattan late that winter: a period of living in humble digs and having to watch his expenses. He did manage to hobnob with his betters, however, including Howells, whom he met on March 7 and approved of for being "especially fond of a good joke."

Norris's income may have been on the low side, but on the strength of his South African trip he could claim to be a seasoned war correspondent. When the Spanish-American War broke out in the spring of 1898 (thanks in large part to drumbeating and saber rattling by the Hearst papers), *McClure's* sent its new staff writer south to cover it. Among his fellow reporters were Richard Harding Davis himself, representing the *New York Herald*, and Stephen Crane, with Hearst's *New York Journal*.

Owing to *McClure's* monthly schedule, Norris wasn't expected to file up-to-the-minute dispatches; instead he wrote think pieces that went behind the scenes to explain such mysteries as how news is gathered in a war zone. He left an irreverent portrait of his fellow scribe Crane, though it came out not in *McClure's* but—more than a decade after Norris's death—in *The New York Evening Post* of April 11, 1914. The piece is not only amusing but perhaps also revelatory. It has been taken as evidence that Norris, like Bierce, envied the *Red Badge* hotshot—although, as Norris's biographers point out, Crane's heavy drinking left him open to a more severe roughing-up than the tongue-in-cheek one administered by Norris. This, at any rate, is how one of American literature's two brightest young lights of the 1890s saw the other as they whiled away the hours on a vessel steaming toward war:

The Young Personage was wearing a pair of duck trousers grimed and fouled with all manner of pitch and grease and oil.

His shirt was guiltless of collar or scarf and was unbuttoned at the throat. His hair hung in ragged fringes over his eyes. His dress-suit case was across his lap and answered him for a desk. Between his heels he held a bottle of beer against the rolling of the boat, and when he drank was royally independent of a glass. While he was composing his descriptive dispatches which some ten thousand people would read in the morning from the bulletins in New York I wondered what the fifty thousand who have read his war novel and have held him, no doubt rightly, to be a great genius, would have seen and thought could they have seen him at the moment.

One yearns to read more of this encounter, and of relations generally between these two prodigies, both of whom were to die within the next few years.

At first, the war proceeded with almost farcical bathos, as Bierce was quick to note from his perch in San Francisco. Comparing a recent skirmish in Cuba with an earlier one, he wrote in the *Examiner*: "It was a trivial affair, hardly superior in dignity to our glorious victory at Matanzas, where several of our big cruisers and a monitor pot-shotted a Spanish mule." At length, however, the fighting heated up, giving Norris his dose of what U.S. Secretary of State John Hay called a "splendid little war." For Norris the fun included meeting William Randolph Hearst in the flesh and playing at war, in which capacity Norris accepted at gunpoint the surrender of some Spanish soldiers.

The war also allowed him to display his knack for hearing and describing sounds not picked up by ordinary ears:

The firing of rifles on the battlefield is not loud; it is not even sharp when heard at a distance. The rifles sputter, as hot grease sputters, the shots leaping after one another in straggling sequence, sometimes in one-two-three order, like the ticking of

a clock, sometimes rushing confusedly together, and sometimes dropping squarely in the midst of an interval of silence,
always threatening to stop, yet never quite stopping; or again
coming off in isolated rolls when volley firing is the order. But
little by little the sputtering on our left gathered strength and
settled down at length to steady hammer-and-tongs work.

Yet he experienced disillusionment, too. Whatever else it might
be, war was perverse, dealing out undeserved cruelty to women and
children and engendering a near total breakdown of sanitation.
He also grew disenchanted with the Cuban insurgents, who struck
him and other correspondents as no less brutal than the authorities
against whom they were rebelling. And he came down with a stubborn case of malaria.

Finally, Cuba brought to the surface one of Norris's few flaws.
After the war ended with Spanish capitulation, he watched a "superior" race take its victory lap through Santiago:

Even though not a soldier, it was impossible not to know their
feeling, glorifying, arrogant, the fine brutal arrogance of the
Anglo-Saxon, and we rode on . . . at a gallop through the
crowded streets of the fallen city, heads high, sabres clattering,
a thousand iron hoofs beating out a long roll, triumphant,
arrogant, conquerors.

By the third appearance of "arrogant" or "arrogance," one wonders if the word doesn't suit the writer himself as well as the men he
is observing. Yet it would be unfair to close the book on Norris's
three-month stint as a war correspondent without noting the brilliant detail he dropped into his eyewitness account of how an American general, his aides, and some reporters reacted to news of the
war's end. Dumbstruck, they all stared "at a little green parrot who
lives in the premises [as it] trundled gravely across the brick floor."

From his experience as a domestic feature writer and foreign correspondent, Norris had gained an enviable skill for a novelist: He was a great noticer.

Among the people he noticed was Jeannette Black, a San Francisco belle whom he'd met at a society affair before shipping out to Cuba. On returning to California to recuperate from his fevers, he squired her on hikes above the bay and applauded her decision not to come out as a debutante. He also began writing a novel, *Blix*, whose title character has Jeannette's sturdy good looks and high spirits. Norris's biographers suggest that *Blix* was written partly to win over his mother, who considered Jeannette inferior to the Norrises. Whether or not this ploy worked is unclear, but the novel was bought for serialization by a monthly magazine called, of all things, *Puritan*, and eventually published in hardcover by Doubleday and McClure.

Out West, Norris started yet another novel, a trendy story of Arctic exploration called *A Man's Woman*. Eventually it, too, was published, but almost everyone, the author included, considered it a step backward. Back in New York and missing Jeannette in late 1898, he resumed his duties at *McClure's*, nursed *A Man's Woman* to its feeble fruition, suffered malarial relapses, and endured an unusually harsh winter. By early 1899, however, everything was looking up. *Moran of the Lady Letty* came out, to praise from Howells. *McTeague* was about to be published, *Blix* was being serialized, and Norris had an idea "so big that it frightens me at times but I have about made up my mind to have a try at it": a trilogy of novels about wheat.

Once he got going, the ex-dilettante accomplished so much, in such a brief span of time, that it can be hard for us—as it may have been for him—to sort out the timing and impacts of all his jammed-together projects. But one *fin-de-siècle* endeavor stands out from the rest: *McTeague*. With a conventional success or two now under his belt, Norris was ready to spring this harrowing manuscript on an unsuspecting world.

As the critic V. S. Pritchett noted, one of Zola's literary traits was "the idealisation of the ugly." Norris had announced his readiness to explore the new fictional territory staked out by the naturalistic school: "the unplumbed depths of the human heart, and the mystery of sex, and the problems of life, and the black, unsearched penetralia of the soul of man." In *McTeague*, Norris's Zolaesque interest in ugliness and his fascination with the sex drive gave birth to an unflinching candor that, more than a century later, can still disturb the reader.

Norris based the novel on a real-life case he'd read about in the newspaper: a working-class man had murdered his estranged wife, who worked as a janitor in a kindergarten, in order to get hold of her bankroll. In Norris's version, the killer is the hulking McTeague, Mac for short, whose "mind was as his body, heavy, slow to act, sluggish. Yet there was nothing vicious about the man. Altogether he suggested the draft horse, immensely strong, stupid, docile, obedient." Working as a dentist, he meets Trina, his future wife, when she comes to him as a patient.

In the first half of the book, Norris recounts their awkward courtship in a slightly amused tone, giving Trina a German-American martinet of a father who in a funny accent insists that his wife and children always be crisp and on time. Amid the comedy, however, Norris foreshadows the novel's dark second half—the story of the couple's degeneration—by repeatedly making the same point about Mac. Deep down, he is an animal whose base instincts are roused by his binge drinking. "It was the old battle," Norris writes,

old as the world, wide as the world—the sudden panther leap of the animal, lips drawn, fangs aflash, hideous, monstrous, not to be resisted, and the simultaneous arousing of the other man, the better self that cries, "Down, down," without knowing why; that grips the monster; that fights to strangle it, to thrust it down and back.

This tug-of-war between Mac's good and bad natures becomes the novel's main business.

The McTeagues are content at first, and their future looks plush after Trina wins $5,000 in a lottery. But Mac has been practicing without a license (there was no certification of dentists when he took his on-the-job training in a Sierra Nevada mining camp, and his bewilderment when the state dental board shuts him down is touching). Trina has problems of her own. Far from making her feel secure, the lottery winnings cause her endless anxiety. She invests the sum, insisting that none of it be spent. Assuming control of the household funds, she becomes such a tightwad as to refuse Mac carfare when he goes out looking for work. Whenever he is away, she runs to the chest in which she stores the money she earns by whittling toy animals, takes out the coins, and fondles them as another woman might her silks or furs. (In *Greed*, the 1924 film version of the novel, the gold-tinted coins give off such a luscious sparkle that the viewer sees why Trina—played by ZaSu Pitts—is so enamored of them.) Her obduracy first annoys Mac, then enrages him, and he takes out his anger in a lurid way:

> The people about the [boarding] house and the clerks at the provision stores often remarked that Trina's fingertips were swollen and the nails purple as though they had been shut in a door. Indeed, this was the explanation she gave. The fact of the matter was that McTeague, when he had been drinking, used to bite them, crunching and grinding them with his immense teeth, always ingenious enough to remember which were the sorest. Sometimes he extorted money from her by this means, but as often as not he did it for his own satisfaction.

Tina's reaction to this abuse, however, is not what one might have expected.

And in some strange, inexplicable way this brutality made Trina all the more affectionate; aroused in her a morbid, unwholesome love of submission, a strange, unnatural pleasure in yielding, in surrendering herself to the will of an irresistible, virile power.

The Boy-Zola had grown up. In that frank depiction of sadomasochism, he had outdone the master.

At length, in a drunken frenzy, Mac kills Trina and flees to Death Valley, where he is hunted down by an old friend-turned-enemy. In the end, Mac kills his nemesis, but not before they end up handcuffed to each other without a key. Miles from water, latched to a corpse, Mac is doomed by the valley's unbearable heat.

Howells praised *McTeague*, and the young Willa Cather, reviewing it for a Pittsburgh newspaper, noted how artfully Norris had employed "the only truthful literary method of dealing with that part of society which environment and society hedge about like the walls of a prison," giving readers "a true story of people, courageous, dramatic, full of matter, and warm with life." Other reviewers, however, found the novel obscene and repulsive. It didn't sell well, not even in the bowdlerized edition that soon crowded out the original. It's not a book likely to appeal to readers who insist on being fond of or identifying with the main characters, but it *is* the kind that can become an obsession. As each detail of the McTeagues' downfalls clicks into place like a tile in a mosaic, the reader can easily find himself reaching the same verdict as Norris had when he read Zola's *Rome*: "all other books, even all other *things*, seem small and trivial."

This is true of *McTeague* even though it's not an overly long book (it takes up about three hundred pages in the Library of America's Norris volume). The novel not only does justice to Mac and Trina's unhealthy relationship while also painting an unforgettable series of street scenes. It also points to a cruelty found in any big city: how it betrays its weakest residents by inviting them in and then not looking out for them when they stumble and lose heart. In writing *McTeague*, Norris confirmed his hunch that observing and depicting the animal impulses in the denizens of an urban slum was a formidable, almost heroic assignment—and one to which he was equal. He'd followed the rules of naturalism—and given his own ambitious nature a workout—by sketching the "vast, illimitable forces" that trapped his lowly protagonists in their sordid surroundings.

The greatest tribute to *McTeague* may have come a quarter-century later, when another creative soul responded to the book's largeness, so much so that when he set out to adapt it, he went slightly mad. This was Erich von Stroheim, a Hollywood director who read *McTeague* circa 1920, with mounting excitement. As an actor, Stroheim was known as The Man You Love to Hate. As a director, he might have been called The Man Who Sought to Film *McTeague*—Every Word of It. The story of Stroheim's obsession with transferring the whole of the novel (and then some) to film shows what a jolt Norris's feverish writing could give to a kindred spirit. *McTeague*, I think, is one of those rare works of art that can't be fully understood without looking at what was made of it in another medium.

Born Erich Oswald Stroheim in 1885, he grew up in Vienna, where his father owned a hat store. Although young Erich relished the polyglot, cosmopolitan atmosphere of the imperial capital, he failed to make good on his ambition to have a military career, and his Jewishness and limited education dampened his prospects in civilian Austria. In 1909, he emigrated to the United States, where he draped his name with the noble particle "von." He made his way to California and caught on as an extra in movies. To stand out from the crowd, he adopted a striking persona—cropped hair, white gloves, a monocle, the continental habits of clicking his heels and kissing women's hands—and this colorful pose led to steady work. He supplemented his acting roles (butler, martinet, villain) by advising his directors on the niceties of military garb and European mores. In the early years of World War I, as Germany was flexing its military might and filmgoers took an interest in all things Prussian, Stroheim's Teutonic expertise made him a valuable man to have around.

While continuing to act, he became a set decorator, then an assistant director. In 1919 he talked Carl Laemmle, head of Universal Pictures, into letting him direct *Blind Husbands*, about a love triangle in the Tyrol, from a script by Stroheim himself. *Blind Husbands*, however, was not the title Stroheim had wanted; that was *Pinnacle*, which Laemmle nixed because the public might confuse it with the card game pinochle. Laemmle was being inane, but Stroheim's reaction to the substitution was wildly disproportionate to the harm done. The film, he asserted in a full-page ad he took out in *Motion Picture News*,

> was the child of my brain—and heart. I had created it—I loved it. The *title* was just as much a part of the picture as any scene in it. A beautiful title, a meaningful title, a title that meant everything to the man who created it, a title that represented months and years of creative effort in producing this picture— all tossed away in a moment for a name which is the *absolute essence of commercialism*. A name in which there is no beauty—no sense of the artistic. A name which I would have rejected in disgust had it been submitted to me. I would, in fact, have been ashamed of myself had I even thought of it.

Such a to-do from a rookie who had been granted the privilege of bringing his own brainchild to the screen in his first try at directing! Not to mention that he was wrong on the merits. "Pinnacle" is a vague, all-purpose word, signifying little by itself, while the suggestive *Blind Husbands* ably describes what the movie is about. Stroheim's tantrum was a preview of excesses to come.

On the set, Stroheim fussed over minutiae because he was convinced that nuances of dress and behavior could make all the difference in verisimilitude. The point seems incontestable until you examine the lengths to which he took it. For a casino scene in one of his continental movies, he ordered fake bills modeled so closely on French francs that they slipped into circulation, with banks exchanging them for U.S. dollars; he had to appear in federal court to answer to a counterfeiting charge. For the soldiers in *Merry-Go-Round* (1923), he commissioned underwear embroidered with their country's royal coat of arms. Not surprisingly, these skivvies didn't appear on screen—nor were they meant to. "The public, of course, will not see the underwear," Stroheim admitted, "but the actors *must* know they are wearing authentic undergarments." Again not surprisingly, he was fired from *Merry-Go-Round*, which was finished by another director.

In grin-and-bear-it mode, Universal turned Stroheim's spendthrift ways into publicity. As the cost of his next completed film, *Foolish Wives* (1922), mounted, the studio put up a billboard on Broadway by which the public could check the latest eye-popping figures. He might have gotten away with his extravagance if it hadn't been for another foible—the cinematic equivalent of logorrhea. This was an auteur who left almost nothing out. His camera lingers while his players act out scenes that most other directors would have abbreviated or skipped altogether.

Biographer Arthur Lenning observes that "the history of each Stroheim film is a nightmare," and *Greed*—as Stroheim retitled *Mc-Teague* for the cinema—was the biggest bad dream of all. He was not just seduced by the material, which departed sharply from his Continental specialties—this was a roughnecked American story, with no place in it for monocles or embroidered underpants. In Norris, Stroheim also recognized a fellow stickler for artistic integrity. In the foreword to the finished film, Stroheim put up on the screen a defiant passage from a Norris essay, which lionizes the novelist who can stand up and say: "'I never truckled, I never took off the hat to Fashion and held it out for pennies. By God, I told them the truth. They liked it or they didn't like it. What had that to do with me? I told them the truth; I knew it for the truth then, and I know it for the truth now.'" It's a stirring boast, if not a terribly accurate one for the man who originally made it. Norris did truckle—by writing the pot-boiler *A Man's Woman* to earn extra money. And although such a declaration of independence might roll easily off the tongue of a novelist, who has to please only an editor or two to get a manuscript into print, it's less believable when repeated by someone caught up in the collaborative and costly art of filmmaking. But Norris's ringing words confirmed Stroheim's self-serving view of the director as titan, a Beethoven behind the camera, responsible to no one or no thing except the integrity of his own artistic vision.

By the time Stroheim read *McTeague*, it had already been filmed once, as *Life's Whirlpool* (1916), but he had in mind a version that would eclipse any other conceivable *McTeague*. Determined to convey the novel's relentless brio in full, he worked from his own shooting script, which ran to three hundred pages, almost as long as the book itself; in some places he even added to the story, filling in more background than Norris himself had deemed necessary. Lenning counted up: "It has taken Stroheim 67 pages of script, approximately one-fifth of the scenario's length, to bring us to the point where Mac meets Trina on page 104. It took Norris only thirteen pages, one twenty-fifth of the novel!"

For the sake of authenticity, Stroheim and his cast and crew went on location, not only to San Francisco but also to Death Valley. In August! His studio—not Universal this time, but Goldwyn—tried to talk him out of subjecting movie people to such a punishing climate, but Stroheim insisted, his only concession being to tote along a shortwave radio so that the studio could keep in touch. During six weeks of filming in the desert, the temperature reached 132 degrees in the shade; Jean Hersholt, the actor playing McTeague's nemesis, lost twenty-seven pounds and ended up in the hospital. When he and

Gibson Gowland, as McTeague, failed to bring the desired fury to their climactic battle, the director urged them, "Fight! Fight! Try to hate each other as you both hate me!"

Stroheim handed in forty-two reels of film, which translates into nine hours of viewing—triple the running time of D. W. Griffith's three-hour epic, *The Birth of a Nation*. Stroheim's plan was to screen the movie in two parts, with an intermission for dinner. Like Wagnerites at Bayreuth, those in attendance would be not so much spectators as pilgrims. The studio, which in the interim had merged with another into Metro-Goldwyn, was having none of this. They took *Greed* away from the director and started cutting. When they got word from the New York Censorship Board that "all scenes of McTeague biting Trina's fingers" should be eliminated, they happily picked up the scissors again. Finally, in 1925, they released a 140-minute version of the film. In this butchered form, *Greed* failed at the box office, with *Variety* calling it "morbid and senseless . . . a decisive and distinct flop."

Stroheim failed to keep a copy of his director's cut, and the studio recycled the excised scraps of film, thus ensuring that *Greed* would never again be seen in its entirety. After directing a few more films, Stroheim had to fall back on his acting; his most memorable later appearances were in Jean Renoir's *La Grande illusion* and Billy Wilder's *Sunset Blvd*. Toward the end of his life, Stroheim lamented that he had "made only one real picture in my life and nobody ever saw that. The poor, mangled, mutilated remains were shown as *Greed*." Yet the movie finally came into its own. In 1958, a year after Stroheim's death, *Greed* was named one of the ten greatest films of all time in a poll of experts at the Brussels World's Fair. In 1999, scholars restored *Greed* to 242 minutes, with the lost footage represented by some six hundred still photos, originally taken for publicity purposes.

Stroheim's temperament was such that he might have run into similar trouble if he'd undertaken to film other early-twentieth-century naturalistic novels: Dreiser's *Sister Carrie*, for example, or Crane's *Maggie: A Girl of the Streets*. But the inexorable dynamism of *McTeague*, the unremitting concentration with which Norris notes each whorl of Mac and Trina's downward spirals, is almost unparalleled in American fiction. You can see why Stroheim became so mesmerized by the book, how it tempted him to indulge his near maniacal inclusiveness as never before. And you have to admire an artist who could legitimately boast of never having "truckled."

At the same time, however, you can't help shuddering to think of a nightmare that Stroheim might have had after the wrecking of *Greed*. In the dream, he writes a treatment of Norris's other, longer, more complex masterpiece, *The Octopus: A Story of California*. He takes it to a studio, which gives the green light. Stroheim attacks the project with his customary gusto and thoroughness, and the end result is a fifteen-hour rough cut. Stroheim realizes it's too long, but after screening it for himself and friends he also knows it's stupendous, a work of art without parallel in cinematic history. Hoping against hope that the studio bosses will see the blazing rightness of what he's accomplished, he submits his film. And then the horror begins.

eight

Norris Picks Up a Rake

McTeague the character is an *echt* naturalistic hero-victim, betrayed by inheritance (his susceptibility to drink and his bestiality, especially as exhibited in his sexual behavior) and cramped by his environment (a neurotic spouse, a shabby neighborhood in a crowded and indifferent city, the movement to professionalize the healing arts). Along with Crane's *Maggie*, *McTeague* the novel set a new American standard for the unflinching depiction of human deterioration. But for all its strength and comprehensiveness, *McTeague* didn't fully satisfy its ambitious author. Norris had written a concerto, but he thought he had it in him to compose a vast symphony.

The projected wheat trilogy gave him the chance to stretch himself, marshaling forces worthy of Zola. Norris got underway by following the Frenchman's road map, as it were. In preparing for a new novel, Zola might spend six months or more visiting locations and gathering information on social conditions, industrial processes, and the kinds of people to be found in their midst; his notes for *La Bête humaine*, by no means his longest novel, ran to 677 pages. In like manner, Norris set out to learn all he could about the production of wheat. In April of 1899, he informed a friend of his intention "to study the whole question as faithfully as I can and then write a hair lifting story . . . . I mean to do it thoroughly.—Get at it from every point of view, the social, agricultural, political.—Just say the last word [on] the R.R. [i.e., railroad] question in California."

He planned the trilogy so that each volume would correspond to a stage in the grain's progress from field to table. The first book, *The Octopus*, would address wheat as it was grown in California—with special emphasis, as that "R.R." reference implies, on the crop's entry into the stream of commerce. *The Pit* would pick up the saga as wheat pooled in Chicago as an item to be bought, sold, and speculated upon in the commodities market. *The Wolf* (which Norris did not live to write) would follow the grain overseas, where it would be used to alleviate a European famine.

Samuel S. McClure, owner of the eponymous magazine, was co-owner of Doubleday and McClure, which published Norris's books, a cross-relationship that made the novelist's task easier. In the spring of 1899, Norris wangled a paid leave of absence. "Go back to California. . . .," Frank Doubleday told him. "Plot out a series of novels about the people there. Put in plenty of blood and bowels. Keep 'em up to the *McTeague* standard, and write, write, write."

First, however, Norris went to the library and read, read, read. Only two years had gone by since Hearst and Bierce's defeat of the Southern Pacific, and Norris reacquainted himself with that campaign by perusing back issues of the *San Francisco Examiner*. As his biographers note in an understatement, "Whatever degree of animus Norris held against the Southern Pacific when he came [back] to California, the *Examiner* did not lessen it." Depending on how much digging he did, Norris might also have unearthed some of the insults Bierce had flung at the "railrogues" before ever setting foot in Washington, D.C. (There is no record, by the way, of Norris and Bierce ever having met.)

Once Norris had his fill of archival work, he drew upon family connections to obtain an interview with Collis Huntington. As mentioned, the two men belonged to the same club, and in fact their paths had crossed at least once before. Back in 1887, when the Norris family was still functional, they had traveled to Europe, staying in Paris at the same deluxe Left Bank hotel where Huntington was registered. Whether the two parties socialized then is unknown, but the coincidence points to an overlap of their circles. Twelve years later, in a letter to a friend, Norris enthused over his imminent meeting with the last surviving member of the Big Four: "The Wheat affair is building up *Big* and I am getting the stuff pretty well in hand and hope to have an interview with C. P. Huntington before the end of the week."

The session with Huntington helped Norris make good on his vow to consider "every point of view." If we can judge the real thing by its counterpart in *The Octopus*—the meaty conversation between the railroad magnate Shelgrim (read Huntington) and the poet Presley (more or less a surrogate for Norris)—Huntington held up well under Norris's questioning, and may even have contributed something to the novel's plot. We'll examine Shelgrim's defense of the railroad's tactics later in this chapter, but for now Norris deserves credit for seeking out and listening to the real-life tycoon and for being enough of an artist to let Huntington's fictional doppelgänger speak intelligently for himself and his corporate brethren rather than simply bare his fangs and snarl.

Before returning to New York, Norris interviewed Huntington a second time, and according to Norris's widow the two became "good friends." But neither the friendship nor Huntington's vaunted persuasiveness brought Norris around to the tycoon's point of view. That fall, Norris received a letter from a fellow employee at Doubleday who had sniffed out the subject matter of his novel in progress. She urged him to strike a blow for big business and its efficiencies by portraying the trust as a useful innovation to which Americans might as well reconcile themselves. (Similarly, the robber barons themselves tried selling the trust to lawmakers and the public as an antidote to what they invariably called "ruinous competition.")

Norris wrote back that he was already "enlisted upon the other side"—that is, against the corporations and in favor of those upon whom they trod.

Even if he'd wanted to, however, it's not easy to see how Norris could have acted upon his colleague's recommendation. A novel celebrating the brave new world of monopolies sounds, in this case, like a book that takes the reader inside the corporate realm, showing how the railroad is managed and how its hierarchy holds up against the pressures of dealing with customers and bankers. Norris would have been hard put to make such a tale dramatic, and in any case, once he'd chosen the book's title, there was no turning back. It was suggested to him by Keller's famous "Octopus" cartoon, which drew upon the popular image of the "devil-fish" as a ravenous killer. (In letters to friends, Norris jauntily called his work in progress "the Squid.")

Viewed in one way, Norris's approach to his material may seem a betrayal of his class—or at least of the one to which his mother aspired. Yet the atmosphere of his workplace alone might have been enough to steer him away from the capitalists' corner. Under its owner's ambitious leadership, *McClure's* was responding to the nationwide disgust with monopolies by restyling itself as *the* forum for antitrust journalists. Two of its three soon-to-be-famous investigative reporters were already on staff during Norris's tenure: Ray Stannard Baker, whose beat was labor relations, and Ida Tarbell, who was homing in on Standard Oil (the third paladin, Lincoln Steffens, a specialist in uncovering urban graft, joined the magazine a few years after Norris left). *McClure's* would have been a poor fit for a defender of the laissez-faire status quo. Indeed, in attacking an obvious stand-in for the Southern Pacific in *The Octopus*, Norris has been seen by many as a fellow "muckraker" (the term came courtesy of President Theodore Roosevelt, who adapted it from John Bunyan's *Pilgrim's Progress* in 1906), using the techniques of fiction to expose the machinations of the closest Western equivalent to the Eastern oil and steel trusts.

But *The Octopus* is not just another variation on a theme by Zola. Norris neither traces the bloodlines of his ranchers and railroad men nor makes much effort to analyze their behavior scientifically. (This neglect may be partly a matter of scope: Norris may have been thinking big, but measuring the effects of heredity and environment on the choices made by even a handful of the many characters in the novel would have stretched an already long book to immense proportions.) Whether consciously or not, he was departing from Zola's recipe for how a naturalistic novel should be cooked to seek a rather different flavor—what might be called "extreme realism." The result is a novel that comes close to the spirit of Greek tragedy.

There *was* something Zolaesque about *The Octopus*, however: Norris's identification with the underdog. Just as Zola would not have dreamed of praising the directors of the mining company in *Germinal*, so Norris was unlikely to frame *The Octopus* as a tribute to the Southern Pacific's efficiency and power. Another mentor of Norris's may have helped deepen his animus toward corporate executives. Norris read Howells as closely as he did Zola, and a passage in *A Hazard of New Fortunes* (1890), Howell's novel of strife between capital and labor, suggests where the loyalties of men like himself and Norris would instinctively lie. As Lindau, a social scientist, explains to March, a magazine editor:

> Not the most gifted man that ever lived, in the practice of any art or science, and paid at the highest rate that exceptional genius could justly demand from those who have worked for their money, could ever earn a million dollars. It is the landlords and the merchant princes, the railroad kings and the coal barons (the oppressors to whom you instinctively give the title of tyrants)—it is these that *make* the millions, but no man *earns* them. What artist, what physician, what scientist, what poet was ever a millionaire?

This was written long before J. K. Rowling's Harry Potter royalties made her a billionaire, but the point was valid in its day. Norris identified most strongly with people for whom a man like Huntington had little use: hardworking but not very well paid artists and scholars. On the other hand, Norris's responsibility was not to vent his personal sympathies but to tell his story as best he could. Fortunately for readers, in his view that entailed giving each side its due, fashioning well-rounded, imperfect characters rather than grievances made flesh, and putting into play an insight later summed up by a line from Jean Renoir's great film *The Rules of the Game*: "The awful thing about life is this: everyone has his reasons." Norris was an artist, not a polemicist, and to write him off as merely a muckraker with imagination is to do *The Octopus* an injustice.

Norris extended his research by traveling to the Central Valley and elsewhere to tour wheat fields and talk with growers. Again, his membership in the Bohemian Club stood him in good stead: He spent several weeks on the ranch of another club member, Gaston Ashe, in San Benito County. It so happens that San Benito is closer to the Monterey Coast than to the Central Valley, but to suit his artistic purposes Norris dragged the Ashe spread east, over a mountain range or two, and borrowed freely from its daily life. Norris stayed with the Ashes long enough to watch the harvest and rounded out his homework by riding on a combine as it cut and threshed wheat.

Norris also bestowed an old Spanish mission on the Central Valley, when in fact all of California's missions line up along the coast. His willingness to make free with the state's geography was one of the few traits he shared with the Big Four, but this wasn't to be the only instance of narrative sleight of hand in *The Octopus*. At some point in his research, Norris came across the Mussel Slough Tragedy, the gunfight that took place in the Central Valley in the spring of 1880. On reading newspaper accounts of the incident, he must have had a eureka! moment. Here was raw material for just the kind of dramatic showdown between the railroad and farmers that his story needed. If he moved the event forward to the mid-1890s, when the novel seems to be set, he would have a fulcrum on which the whole book could turn: the occasion when his railroad emerges from the mist of respectability it likes to surround itself with and stands exposed as the heartless bully it has been all along. In a letter to a friend, Norris said he wanted *The Octopus* to speed up "all of a sudden to a great big crushing END, something that will slam you right between your eyes and knock you off your feet." He found his slam at Mussel Slough.

Norris took time out that summer of 1899 to court Jeannette Black, whom he found so bewitching that he confessed to a friend, "It's a wonder I don't forget me own name these days." He made a success of that project, too: Before returning to New York, he proposed, and she said yes.

As Norris worked on the new novel in New York, some of his ships came in: *Blix* was published in September of 1899, *A Man's Woman* in February of 1900. At the same time, he was getting antsy at *McClure's*. He knew he wasn't much of a copy editor. He *was* good at talent spotting, however, and when an opportunity came to put that skill to use, he took it. Frank Doubleday had switched book publishing partners, replacing McClure with Walter Page; Norris came over to the new firm as an acquisitions editor. The deal was sweetened by a reduced schedule; he was now free to devote half of each workday to fiction writing, with a portion of his salary counted as an advance on royalties. How right he was for the new job can be seen in what happened when a promising manuscript landed on his desk: Theodore Dreiser's *Sister Carrie*, about an urban working girl who quits her humdrum job to become a kept woman—and makes a go of it. Norris urged the firm to publish the novel, and they agreed to do so. He continued to push hard even after they had second thoughts owing to Dreiser's failure to make Carrie pay for her sins in the end. They brought out *Sister Carrie* begrudgingly and only because Dreiser refused to let them back out of the deal. Though initially a failure, the book, of course, ultimately vindicated Norris's judgment.

Another milestone in Norris's life came on February 12, 1900, when he and Jeannette were married in an Episcopal ceremony. Gertrude Norris must have made her peace with Jeannette by then, for she accompanied the bride-to-be from California to New York and attended as one of the two witnesses. The newlyweds moved to Roselle, New Jersey, a suburb of Manhattan, and the husband finagled an even better work schedule. Now required to be in the office only three days a week, he had bigger chunks of time in which to write *The Octopus* at home. He submitted the manuscript in the fall of 1900.

Renamed the Pacific and Southwestern, the railroad makes its presence felt in the novel's first sentence, when Presley, through whose point of view most of the story will be told, hears a noon whistle blowing from the railroad shops down by the Bonneville depot. He's riding his bicycle at the time—a low-tech contrast to the mighty engines and long chains of freight cars that will roll across the landscape throughout the novel. On reaching that depot, Presley stops to chat with Dyke, a train engineer. Dyke tells Presley that, rather than accept a proposed company-wide pay cut, he has decided to resign. He had lodged a protest, citing his loyalty to the company during a recent strike as reason to be spared the reduction, only to be told it wouldn't be fair to single him out. "Fair!" he shouts at Presley. "Hear the P. and S. W. talking about fairness and discrimination. That's good, that is." We're not halfway through the first chapter, and already, in having the railroad vilified by one of its own, Norris has set the tone in which it will be portrayed.

Soon Presley runs into Vanamee, a mystically inclined shepherd who is tending his flock. Moved by the encounter, Presley has an epiphany: the life force throbbing all around him would make an ideal subject for the epic poem of the West he feels destined to write. But after dark that same day, his idyll is shattered when a train passes through and mows down several of Vanamee's sheep, which have strayed onto the track. As Presley grieves over the slaughter, the first chapter closes with this stem-winder of an indictment:

> Presley saw again, in his imagination, the galloping monster, the terror of steal and steam, with its single eye, cyclopean, red, shooting from horizon to horizon; but saw it now as the symbol of a vast power, huge, terrible, flinging the echo of its thunder over all the reaches of the valley, leaving blood and destruction in its path; the leviathan, with tentacles of steel clutching into the soil, the soulless Force, the iron-hearted Power, the monster, the Colossus, the Octopus.

The sheep-kill was an accident, but Norris wastes no time in introducing one of the railroad's purposeful outrages. With the rainy season due any day, the region's most prominent ranchers, the father-and-son team of Magnus and Harran Derrick, are champing to get hold of the new ploughs they've ordered from the East. One day they find themselves at the depot just after those ploughs have arrived, plainly visible on a flatbed car. Naturally, they expect to take their new possessions directly home, but S. Behrman, the railroad's odious agent, warns them off. Westbound freight must first go to the hub in San Francisco, from where it will be redirected. What he doesn't add, but the Derricks know, is that a higher short-haul rate will apply to that reshipment. Shouting at Behrman, Harran Derrick spells out what this means:

> "Think of it! Here's a load of stuff for Bonneville that can't stop at Bonneville, where it is consigned, but has got to go up to San Francisco first *by way of* Bonneville, at forty cents per ton and then be reshipped from San Francisco back to Bonneville again at *fifty-one* cents per ton, the short-haul rate. And we have to pay it all or go without. Here are the ploughs right here, in sight of the land they have got to be used on, the sea-

son just ready for them, and we can't touch them. Oh," he exclaimed in deep disgust, "isn't it a pretty mess! Isn't it a farce! the whole dirty business!"

Behrman's by-the-book reply is hardly calculated to win the railroad friends: "I can't change the freight regulation of the road."

The reshipment and corresponding rate hike are mere irritants, however, compared to a goad that the railroad is about to inflict. As the ranchers explain during a gathering at the Derricks', some years earlier the Pacific and Southwestern had distributed flyers encouraging settlement along its right of way, on federal land set aside for the railroad company as an incentive to build the road. The flyers contained this come-on: "*The Company invites settlers to go upon its lands before patents are issued or the road is completed, and intends in such cases to sell to them in preference to any other applicants and at a price based on the value of the land without improvements.*" Later in the same text, the railroad had repeated the no-increase-owing-to-improvements language, mentioning $2.50 an acre as a suitable price for most tracts. Lured by these terms, many ranchers in the vicinity of Bonneville have in essence become squatters, their land secured to them only by the railroad's word.

Now it appears that the railroad will renege on the promise implied in those circulars, offering the land for sale at prices reflecting the value added by farmers who took the bait, moved in, acquired livestock, put up fences, built houses, dug irrigation canals, and planted crops. This rumor infuriates the farmers, who calculate that their handiwork has increased the land's value to about $20 per acre—although Norris now introduces some complications. Also on hand at the Derricks' is Genslinger, editor of the local paper, who raises an interesting point: "The presence of the railroad has helped increase the value of your ranches quite as much as your improvements. Why should you get all the benefit of the rise in value and the railroad nothing? The fair way would be to share it between you." This reasoning is lost on the ranchers. "They agreed to charge but

two-fifty," one of them replies, "and they've got to stick to it."
(Later Genslinger and his paper will be accused of being the railroad's hired mouthpiece—a matter that Norris never quite re-
solves.) Another mark against the ranchers is that some of them
nurture speculative greed in their hearts: As one confesses, "I'll bet
I could sell [my land] to-morrow for fifteen dollars an acre, and if I
buy of the railroad for two and a half an acre, there's boodle in the
game." Elsewhere Norris implies that, for many of the farmers
(Dyke among them), a jump in the railroad's selling price will cause
real hardship, not just a loss of "boodle." But notice has been served:
the issue is less clear-cut than the growers would like to pretend.

The ranchers' animosity toward the railroad is due above all to
the company's invincible political control. No matter which way the
ranchers turn, the railroad—which pays off the state legislature and
makes sure that the state railroad commission is controlled by its
handpicked flunkeys—manages to block them. So demoralized are
the ranchers that when one of them suggests stooping to the Pacific
and Southwestern's level by furtively stacking the railroad commission with pro-farming men, the idea catches on. As the meeting at his
house ends, the righteous Magnus Derrick has rejected this scheme,
but not unequivocally, and the others have formed an entity called
the League.

Norris assembles the growers and their families for a grand barn
dance, which plays out as a comedy redolent of the marriage feast in
L'Assommoir—until a messenger shows up with envelopes for several of those in attendance. The railroad has picked this highly in-
appropriate moment to formally announce its intention of offering
the long-cultivated and -inhabited plots for sale at prices ranging
from $22 to $30 per acre. Even those who, like Magnus Derrick,
had been reluctant to join the antirailroad conspiracy are now furious with "the implacable, iron monster with whom they had to deal,
and again and again the sense of outrage and oppression lashed them
to their feet, their mouths wide with curses, their fists clenched tight,

their throats hoarse with shouting." A remark by Harran Derrick foreshadows what is likely to happen: "Matters are just romping right along to a crisis these days."

When the growers refuse to pay the inflated prices for the land, the railroad sells it to parties who are presumed to be dummies, acting on behalf of the company itself, which allegedly plans to turn around and resell the land at even higher markups. The growers refuse to give up their ranches, and the railroad sues to eject them.

As the lawsuit wends its way to the U.S. Supreme Court, the growers scheme to effectuate their plan to take over the railroad commission. Two votes will do it, and they obtain one the old-fashioned way: by bribing state legislators to appoint a pliable Southern Californian. The second vacancy goes to a consensus candidate: Lyman Derrick, Magnus's other son, who walked away from ranching to become a San Francisco lawyer. Magnus has finally agreed to be the League's spokesman, and the League considers his son a sure pro-farm vote on the commission—only to be foiled once again when Lyman turns out to have been secretly bought off by the railroad.

In the afterword to the Signet Classic edition of *The Octopus*, Oscar Cargill suggests that the source for the fixing-the-commission story was none other than Huntington, who told Norris that California ranchers had attempted such a takeover in real life. According to Cargill, Norris then turned to a politically savvy friend for help in fleshing out this part of the story. If Cargill's theory is true—and it sounds likely—Huntington's tattling inspired one of the novel's finest set pieces: the scene in which Lyman Derrick is called to account for voting against the interest of the ranchers, who had backed him for the commission thinking he was one of their own. As for being corrupted by the railroad, as we've seen, that was a widespread condition in California—so much so that Ambrose Bierce had downplayed the chances of finding anyone not so tarnished in the opening lines of an 1885 poem: "'We want a man the

Railroad can't control!'/ The humor tickled every little soul; / Assenting giggles ran through all the land/ And idiots approved what rascals planned."

Lyman's treachery radicalizes Presley, who shelves his Western epic and instead writes a socialistic poem called "The Toilers" (a fictional equivalent to Edwin Markham's famous polemic "The Man with the Hoe"); it becomes a sensation.

Of all the railroad's sins, perhaps the cruelest is its treatment of Dyke, the engineer who quit his job rather than accept a pay cut. Afterwards, he had a brainstorm. Hops were the next big thing! On the strength of the railroad's quote of two cents a mile per ton for hauling the crop, he planted his entire acreage in hops. But months later, when it's time to harvest the hops and send them to market, Dyke learns that the railroad has doubled the rate for hops—behind his back and without telling him. His protests that he relied on the lower rate and that the increase will ruin him fall on deaf ears, and he goes berserk, robbing a train at gunpoint and becoming a fugitive from justice.

Norris now assembles the growers for another joint effort, a hunt of the jackrabbits that help themselves to growing crops. Although the hunt is bound to end bloodily, with the cornered rabbits being slaughtered, the farmers, their wives, and their children treat it as a lark, to be capped off by a feast. By this point the reader has gotten used to seeing trouble invade carefree celebrations, and a cloud of foreboding hangs over the jackrabbit kill. Sure enough, before the meal can be served, word comes that Behrman (the railroad's agent) and various lawmen are out in force, "serving writs in ejectment and putting the dummy buyers in possession" of the growers' land, going so insultingly far as to strip houses of furniture and pile it up along the right of way. The Leaguers arm themselves and take up positions in a ditch beside the road down which the railroad bunch is expected to come.

A close look at the gunfight—along with a comparison with what historians now think actually happened at Mussel Slough—will be taken in the following chapter. For now, suffice it to say that in Norris's telling the battle is a tragedy of misunderstandings, fear, and hotheadedness which leaves eight men needlessly dead, Harran Derrick among them. Afterwards, the railroad temporarily abandons its campaign to oust the ranchers but seals off the region for several hours, thereby hoping to make its version of the gunfight the one remembered outside the valley.

From time to time the growers have fingered the railroad's president, Shelgrim (as with several of the novel's characters, no first name given), as the ultimate source of all their woes. An excitable member of the League had raved about the man's apparent omnipotence:

> Shelgrim owns the courts. He's got men like [Judge] Ulsteen in his pocket. He's got the Railroad Commission in his pocket. He's got the Governor of the State in his pocket. He keeps a million-dollar lobby at Sacramento every minute of the time the legislature is in session; he's got his own men on the floor of the United States Senate. He has the whole thing organised like an army corps. What *are* you going to do? He sits in his office in San Francisco and pulls the strings and we've got to dance.

Now, in the aftermath of the killings and with the Supreme Court having ruled against the ranchers, Presley stops by the railroad's headquarters in San Francisco on a whim. Shelgrim gives in to a whim of his own: curious to have a look at the author of "The Toilers," he grants Presley an audience. Like Huntington in real life, Shelgrim is a big, broad-shouldered septuagenarian who wears a silk skullcap—perhaps to hide his baldness (during the funding-bill controversy, Bierce had teased Huntington about his "infertile pate") or perhaps simply because that's the fashion among corporate kings these days (the frontispiece to Ida Tarbell's *History of the Standard Oil Company*, published a few years later, shows John D. Rockefeller wearing a similar cap).

To Presley, Shelgrim is a revelation. He doesn't breathe fire. In fact, before the interview starts, he surprises the poet with the kindly way in which he disposes of a personnel matter—by granting a hard-up employee a raise. As their conversation begins, Presley is struck by the tycoon's keen mind and human frailties, among them "the faintest suggestion of a lisp." More important, in answer to Presley's suggestion that he could remake the railroad into a model corporate citizen if he chose, Shelgrim forces the poet to reexamine his preconceptions:

> Control the road! Can I stop it? I can go into bankruptcy if you like. But otherwise if I run my road, as a business proposition, I can do nothing. I can *not* control it. It is a force born out of certain conditions, and I—no man—can stop it or control it. Can your Mr. Derrick stop the Wheat growing? He can burn his crop, or he can give it away, or sell it for a cent a bushel— just as I could go into bankruptcy—but otherwise his Wheat must grow. Can any one stop the Wheat? Well, no more then can I stop the Road.

Presley comes away bemused. If Shelgrim is right, it's not so much the railroad that is to blame for the growers' plight as the exigencies of competition in the marketplace, and even Nature itself, with its "colossal indifference . . . a gigantic engine, a vast cyclopean power, huge, terrible, a leviathan with a heart of steel, knowing no compunction, no forgiveness, no tolerance, crushing out the human atom standing in its way, with nirvanic calm. . . ." Shelgrim may be guilty of protesting too much—after all, we just saw him, with a lift of his finger, override the railroad's customary indifference to human suffering—but there is no easy answer to his claim of ultimate helplessness. In fact, the picture he paints of economic forces beyond the ability of any one man or firm to master on its own can be viewed as an unwitting plea for the government to step in, passing laws that condemn predatory business dealings and create regulatory commissions with enough integrity, staff, and enforcement powers to protect the public from confiscatory rates, and the railroads from each other.

Whatever it may lead to, Shelgrim's articulate self-defense marks an advance on the treatment of similar characters by Zola. Especially in *Germinal*, his novel of bloody conflicts between coal miners and the owners who squeeze them dry, Zola portrays the corporate hierarchy as a squad of pasteboard villains—obtuse, condescending, and willfully blind to the poverty and poor health that are their workers' lot. Probably as a result of his interview with Huntington, Norris recognized that the lords of industry and finance are wedded to their own agendas and needs, and may be prisoners of implacable forces much like the workers and settlers they exploit.

At the same time that Norris was raising naturalistic fiction to new heights of sophistication, Zola himself—perhaps because his involvement in the Dreyfus affair had gone to his head—was writing more like a prophet than an artist, as Norris himself was quick to point out. Here he is, dismissing a new Zola novel, *Fécondité* (part of a tetralogy unrelated to the Rougon-Macquart series), when it came out in 1899:

> The purpose for which Zola wrote the book ran away with him. He really did care more for the depopulation of France than he did for his novel. Result—sermons on the fruitfulness of women, special pleading, a farrago of dry, dull incidents, overburdened and collapsing under the weight of a theme that should have intruded only indirectly.

The difference between late Zola and Norris of *The Octopus* is that, although the American cared deeply about the damage inflicted on

Californians by the Southern Pacific, he really did care for his novel more.

The spell cast by Shelgrim loses some of its magic as Presley surveys the shoot-out's aftereffects, including the death by starvation of a widowed farm woman, the descent of another woman into prostitution, and the humiliation of Magnus Derrick, last seen teetering on the brink of madness. Ultimately, there is no doubt where Presley's (and Norris's) sympathies lie. Over dinner at the swanky home of a railroad baron, the poet reduces the case to its bare bones: "because the farmers of the valley were poor, these men were rich." The corporate leaders go unpunished, but fate catches up with their representative, the egregious S. Behrman. After accidentally falling into the hold of a ship, he is killed by its incoming cargo: a crushing, smothering flood of wheat.

The novel ends with Presley on board that same ship, bound for India, where the wheat will feed hungry people and where the encounter with a radically different culture may nourish his hungry soul. Inspired once again by the mystical Vanamee, Presley reflects on the everlastingness of wheat, of the human race, of life itself: "The larger view, always and through all shams, all wickednesses, discovers the Truth that will, in the end, prevail, and all things surely, inevitably, resistlessly work together for the good."

Presley sounds a bit like Dr. Pangloss here, and some critics have accused his creator of being unduly influenced by the prevailing American optimism of the time, which he may have picked up from his Cal professor LeConte. Norris's biographers point out, however, that he hinted at Presley's naiveté more than once in the novel, thus putting some distance between himself and his character's bromides.

As a whole—and especially considering its patient teasing out of the motives of each main character—*The Octopus* may be the most artful rabble-rousing novel ever written. As literary historian Robert Spiller pointed out, it was also "the most ambitious of American novels up to its time (with the exception of *Moby-Dick*)."

It sold well—33,000 copies—and got good notices, including this one from a reviewer at the original *Washington Times*: "There is something like Zola about Mr. Norris, as many of his critics have remarked; but it is Zola with all the Gallicism taken out of him, purified, strengthened, set in the clean, fresh air of the West."

Much of the novel's power derives from Norris's use of the showdown at Mussel Slough to effect a traumatic but aesthetically satisfying release of tensions that have built up over hundreds of pages. Indeed, it's no exaggeration to say that Mussel Slough made *The Octopus* the masterpiece that it is. How accurately Norris's treatment of Mussel Slough reflects the truth as historians have reconstructed it, however, is another matter.

nine

Mussel Slough Under
a Microscope

In undertaking *The Octopus*, Norris set out to write the best novel he could, not necessarily to catalogue the Southern Pacific's misdeeds or harp on the official neglect that let the railroad get away with them. Yet why bother to invent outrages when the reality of an unfettered and much-scorned railroad can serve as ready-made material? The temptation to borrow from what was widely considered historical fact would have been all the stronger because, as Norris surely knew, readers would enjoy seeing a favorite villain (decked out in the thinnest of disguises) indicted once again on familiar charges. Especially when it came to the rates charged and the paths taken by shipments, Norris relied on widely heard complaints about the Southern Pacific to fill in his portrait of the Pacific and Southwestern as a voracious outfit that, in the absence of competition, becomes a heartless, heedless exploiter of the growers who depend on it to move their crops.

Norris was aware of how the regulatory framework of Gilded Age America reflected the dominant economic philosophy. By today's standards, much of the Pacific and Southwestern's business would be considered interstate commerce, but circa 1900, when the novel's action takes place, lawyers and judges gave that term a narrow meaning. Despite the certainty that at least some of the wheat grown in the Central Valley would find its way to Europe, the California leg of its travels was considered intrastate commerce. That left regulation up to the state commission, which Norris accurately depicted as stacked with pro-railroad hacks. Even if, by some act of legal legerdemain, the Interstate Commerce Commission could have been persuaded to step in, it was pretty timorous itself, and in any event pro-business federal courts were in the habit of second-guessing its decisions. In the novel, the mere mention of the agency's name elicits this jibe from a grower: "Hoh, yes, the Interstate Commerce Commission . . . that's great, ain't it? The greatest Punch and Judy show on earth."

In setting rates, then, the Pacific and Southwestern is essentially on its own. Its spokesmen justify their high and seemingly capricious charges on the basis that the firm deserves a "fair return" on its investment, but that term seems to have been extraordinarily elastic. Nor was it easy for outsiders to discern the cost basis used for a particular railroad's "fair" rate of return. The real-life Southern Pacific was suspected of overstating the cost of building the road, or of padding the amount by using lavishly expensive materiel and rolling stock, or both. According to railroad economist Stuart Daggett, the belief that the railroad charged high rates wasn't just based on folklore. In his history of the Southern Pacific, he draws a comparison: In the early 1890s "the average receipts on the entire Southern Pacific system were exactly twice the average receipts per ton per mile on the Illinois Central, and materially greater than those of most roads in other parts of the country."

The Derricks' frustration at seeing their newly purchased ploughs exposed on a flatbed car and not being allowed to take delivery until the items have gone to San Francisco and back, racking up a higher short-haul charge in the process—that, too, was based on actuality. As pointed out by a legal scholar in an informative article on railroad rates in *The Octopus*, "Perhaps nothing engendered more hostility against the railway industry in the Gilded Age than the railroads' discriminatory imposition of far higher rates on short hauls than on long hauls over the same routes." In fact, however, such differentials might not have been as unconscionable as they sound. Long hauls were usually interstate trips, and competition from other railroads could have a depressing effect on prices. In charging for short hauls within California, on the other hand, the railroad could flex its monopoly. A firm in this position would not be irrational to want to make up for losses it might incur on long hauls by charging more for short ones, and some of the short routes might carry so little traffic as to justify a higher rate. None of this reasoning, however, was likely to appease outsiders, assuming they could even follow it. Nor, in *The Octopus*, does the Pacific and Southwestern try to enlighten its customers. Pressed repeatedly to explain the "rule" for calculating his company's rates, S. N. Behrman gives an imperious and patronizing reply: "[He] emphasized each word . . . with a tap of one forefinger on the counter before him: 'All—the—traffic-will—bear.'" What the Derricks find most infuriating is that they can't speed up delivery of their plough by the simple method of specifying what path it should follow; not until a decade later did a new federal law go into effect by which customers were allowed to designate the routes taken by their shipments—and that change applied to interstate traffic only.

While testifying before the Senate Pacific Railroad Committee in 1896, Huntington vouched (very reluctantly) for the accuracy of the charge that the railroad inflicted doubling-back on its customers. As related by Bierce,

Mr. Huntington was asked if any complaints had been made by merchants at places east or south of San Francisco that their goods from New York and elsewhere were carried through their towns to San Francisco and then brought back, paying the double charge.

The surprise of the witness had a good deal of resemblance to a genuine emotion. He doubted that he had ever heard of such a thing. However that may be, it was evident he had not expected to hear of such a thing to-day, as his surprise was perhaps not entirely unfeigned. Being closely pressed, he admitted that he had a dim recollection of such a complaint in the early days of the road, but he had supposed the matter had been corrected. Nor could any amount of pressure squeeze out of him a direct admission that the practice had been in vogue later. He did, though, explain that the freight charges to a way town might be enough greater than that to San Francisco, through the way town, to equal the regular charge back to the way town. At least that was what he seemed to be trying to say in defense of his oath and trying to make unintelligible in defense to his nature.

By dint of patience and persistence Senator Morgan made him virtually confess at last that he knew the practice had existed and did not know that it had ceased to exist.

Huntington's defensiveness about double-backing suggests that even he found it hard to take.

On the other hand, the blow suffered in the novel by Dyke—the former Pacific and Southwestern employee who planted his fields with hops thinking he had a low transportation rate locked in, only to have the railroad raise it unilaterally without telling him—rings less true. The railroad would have been likelier to sit down with Dyke and work out a pay-what-you-can deal than to insist on driving him to ruin (a ruined customer is almost by definition a customer no more). Yet this much should be acknowledged: Nothing stopped carriers from raising rates without prior notice until federal law was amended in 1910, and that change had no bearing on intrastate commerce. In real life as in *The Octopus*, a man in Dyke's boots would have had little recourse if the railroad suddenly hiked the rate on hops or any other commodity.

To sum up: In his dramatization of the lesser practices and incidents that combine to enrage the railroad's customers and lower its standing in the fictional counterpart to the Mussel Slough region, Norris gave a mostly accurate picture of the discouraging—and often incomprehensible—reality. But what of the novel's climactic event, the shoot-out and multiple killings that clinch the case for the railroad as a monster? Here the weight of evidence is against Norris, suggesting that the fatal exchange of shots at Mussel Slough was no massacre, and that in the settlers the railroad faced a surprisingly tough and shrewd foe. As illuminated by Richard J. Orsi and other historians, the true story of Mussel Slough is far more complex than the morality play presented in *The Octopus* and the similar reenactments in the novels *Blood-Money*, *Driven from Sea to Sea*, and *The Feud of Oakfield Creek*. Indeed, it's not unfair to say that the episode has been misunderstood and distorted in the retelling by virtually every writer who has made imaginative use of it.

Mussel Slough was Southern Pacific territory, and, strictly speaking, the disputed land there had nothing to do with the Central Pacific or the building of a transcontinental line. But similar considerations affected the management and disposal of land grants for both railroads, which of course had the same owners—the Big Four—after they in effect merged. Although Norris freely combined aspects of the Central Pacific and Southern Pacific for his portrait of the fictional Pacific and Southwestern, when necessary in this historical account of Mussel Slough I will distinguish between the two real-life railroads.

For the Central Pacific, the portion of its subsidies which consisted of federal land had been a sore point from the 1860s on. Geography had not been kind to the western road. Crocker griped that most of the California acreage it received was wasteland, and another Central Pacific official rephrased the complaint in covetous terms: "The grant to the Union Pacific was of a garden; that to the Central Pacific of a desert." No wonder that sales of Central

Pacific land lagged far behind the amount unloaded by the Union Pacific.

Not that the Big Four weren't trying. It would have been short-sighted of the Central Pacific (and later of the Southern Pacific) to hang on to its grant lands or offer them for sale at exorbitant prices. The smart move would be to convey the land expeditiously, at reasonable prices, to buyers who would make productive use of it. Why? Because the firm's income stream depended on filling its boxcars with local produce and its passenger cars with local people. This was precisely the strategy favored by Huntington, not in a statement written for public posturing but in a letter sent within the firm: "What we get by the sale of the lands is not the object; but it is that we may have a title to convey to others, so that they can put on the necessary improvements and cultivate the same so as to give the railroad something to transport, which of course is what it wants." That letter was written in 1892, but its reasoning would have been just as sound decades earlier, when (in 1875) the chief of the Southern Pacific's land department had advised its San Joaquin Valley agent to the same effect:

> We want the country settled because it does not pay to run Railroads to places where there are no people. The company . . . desires to hold out the strongest inducements to actual settlers to go upon unencumbered land, to use it and occupy it, and to give such persons who do so, the preference over all others, under all circumstances.

One more factor complicated the railroad's attempts to put its land grants to productive use: delays in the conveyance of title. The Interior Department's General Land Office was understaffed and poorly managed; it could take years for a promised parcel of land to wend its way through the cumbersome process, and clouds on the railroad's title gave hope to those who quarreled with the notion of giving it so much land to begin with.

It so happened that the Southern Pacific's holdings in the vicinity of Mussel Slough—an area about twenty miles long and ten miles wide, south of Fresno in what was then part of Tulare County and is now in Kings County—were among its best. But here another obstacle presented itself. The company's right to the land was under challenge by speculators and settlers who were acting on a kind of bet. One of them admitted as much in a much-quoted letter to the editor of the *Visalia Delta* shortly after the shoot-out, in which her brother was among the slain. In an impassioned bid for support, Mary E. Chambers recollected how she and her husband came to the area in the first place:

> In the fall of 1869 we were living in Placer county; my husband at the time being in the employ of the Central Pacific railroad company. Being away from home all the time I was anxious that he should get land somewhere and settle down, and make us a home. At the time we heard of this land in Tulare being forfeited by the [Southern Pacific] railroad company . . . and that it was to be thrown open for homestead and preemption settlement. I therefore persuaded Mr. Chambers to go and locate, and in November 1869, he came here and located on railroad lands; then came back, bought an outfit, and moved his family . . . arriving in Tulare January 7, 1870.

For people like the Chamberses, the railroad's rumored surrender of lands to the United States, followed by their disposal to the public under the homestead or preemption laws, was a consummation devoutly to be wished (under preemption law, a party already settled on a tract of land had the first right to buy it). If the reversion came to pass, settlers would be able to pick up land at the bargain federal price of $2.50 per acre, rather than at the higher prices (reflecting the local real-estate market) that the railroad would have been free to ask. The Chamberses and other hopefuls had jumped the gun by squatting on some of the contested land.

Their hope rested on a tenuous series of assumptions. An 1866 federal law (not to be confused with the various laws governing the Central Pacific's building of the transcontinental line) had promised federal land to the fledgling Southern Pacific as a subsidy. That land fell into the typical alternating pattern (odd-numbered sections, each encompassing six hundred and forty acres, would go to the railroad while the even-numbered ones stayed in federal hands), along a path from the San Francisco Bay area south to the Colorado River—but with the specification of that path left to the railroad itself. The Southern Pacific's original management first favored a coastal route, only to reconsider in 1867. On second thought, an inland route through the Central Valley looked preferable, not least because of the valley's good soil and favorable prospects for irrigation. The Interior Department accepted the new route, which crossed the Tulare Basin, a natural sink through which flowed an arm of the Kings River called Mussel Slough, and withdrew land from the public domain for eventual transfer to the railroad.

A year later, Interior reversed itself, ruling that the route change was at variance with the railroad's charter from the state, thereby voiding the federal land grant. In making this decision, Secretary of the Interior Orville Browning seems to have bowed to pressure from disappointed coastal boosters and William S. Chapman, a well-known land speculator who had long had his eye on federal land in the valley. In the interim, the Southern Pacific had come under new ownership: the Big Four, fresh from their triumph at Promontory Summit and eager to expand their presence in California. Sold on the inland route, they, too, began applying pressure—a game at which, of course, they had few peers. Their man in the East, Huntington, went to work. Browning overturned his own ruling, and the Southern Pacific had its land grants again—at least for a while. When the Grant administration took over, the new interior secretary, Jacob Cox, reinstated the cancellation of those grants. This time Huntington bypassed Interior, appealing to the California legislature and the U.S. Congress. Both bodies complied with his wishes, the California lawmakers by special act and Congress via a joint resolution; by the end of June 1870, the Southern Pacific had secured the route it preferred, along with the right to the corresponding land grants, in the Central Valley.

Regardless of the flip-flops, the result seems right: to believe that the railroad had aced itself out of its land subsidy by changing a decision that was its to make in the first place requires a "gotcha" mentality that pounces on loopholes. True, the frontier was closing, and arable land was in short supply. Granted, Mary Chambers had reason to be proud of the hard work she, her husband, her brother, and other settlers had undertaken—including the digging of irrigation ditches—to transform barren ground into productive farm country, to make the wilderness "blossom and bear," as she put it. But in pouring so much effort into land to which their claim was dubious, the Chamberses had taken an awful chance.

Nor does the Chamberses' situation as homesteaders who actually settled on and improved a tract seem to have been typical. According to Orsi, "Few of the squatters, despite their rhetorical defenses of their actions, were defending their 'homes.'" In a letter to the *San Francisco Argonaut* published in 1881, a disgruntled valley resident gave it as his opinion that the Mussel Slough settlers

> have entered on the railroad land with a full knowledge that it was railroad land. They were told so, time and again, by the officers in the land office at Visalia. They did not go on those lands through a mistake, but have gone on for speculation, determined, if they cannot whip the railroad company out of the land, to have the use of it for eight or ten years free of rent and taxes. In a large number of cases this land has changed hands from one to three, and even four times. . . . This railroad land has been the principal stock in trade in the Mussel Slough

country. And the [settlers' organization] and the railroad land together have been the source of a great deal of trouble and bad feeling in this part of the country.

The timing of events is not kind to the settlers' position either. Only a few would-be owners had arrived in the Tulare Basin before the late 1860s, when rumors of the possible forfeiture began to circulate. One who hearkened to these rumors and passed them along was John J. Doyle, a former miner, schoolteacher, and farmer who in 1871 occupied land earmarked for the railroad near the town of Grangeville and recast himself as a lawyer, apparently by the simple expedient of hanging out a shingle. In his new role, he lent credence to the forfeiture talk, setting off a rush to Mussel Slough. As the region began to fill up, Doyle stood to gain not only as a squatter but also as a wheeler-dealer. According to Orsi, he "secretly contracted with several hundred neighbors to defeat the railroad's title in exchange for twenty-five cents per acre in gold."

As mentioned, the Southern Pacific hoped to nurture a region that would flourish and feed cargo and passengers to its trains. One step it took toward that end was to draw up the brochures that figure so prominently in *The Octopus* and other novels—as promises relied upon by the farmers and then treacherously broken. Yet the railroad didn't distribute the first brochure until 1876, several years after opportunists had begun streaming into the region, so it's questionable whether many newcomers relied on the wording to their disadvantage.

The circumstances pleaded by Mary Chambers were emotionally appealing (making her an ideal spokesperson for the settlers' cause) but probably exceptional. In her letter to the *Delta*, she mentions an occasion when she and her husband paused before undertaking further improvements because they felt "uneasy about the land." Accordingly, she says, "we wrote . . . to the railroad land office, and received a circular stating the land would be [priced at] $2.50 per acre for plain land, and from $5 to $7 for timber land.

This put us at ease." Chambers skipped a "from," which came be-fore the circular's $2.50 figure, and an "upwards," which came after it, but even so she may have had a case. A good lawyer might argue that, in going ahead with new projects, the Chamberses relied to their detriment on prices quoted in a document sent them by the railroad itself. (In rebuttal, however, the railroad might point to the brochure's penultimate section, which contains this catchall state-ment: "There is but one price—that fixed by the Company. . . .") How many others might have been similarly misled is impossible to say, but, again, the time line is not helpful to the settlers' cause.

In a 1976 law-review note on the settlers' arguments, the writer summed them up as being "of questionable legal validity." But Mary Chambers's letter had a dramatic effect in the court of public opin-ion. Her cri de coeur seems to have been the chief source of the weight placed on those railroad flyers in book after book. She, and not that canny speculator Doyle, became the "public face" of the Mussel Slough squatters.

Back in the late 1870s, the Southern Pacific was in a tough spot. As the wheels of the General Land Office continued to turn slowly, the settlers and speculators banded together to contest the rail-road's right to take title if and when it should be proffered. Under-standably, the railroad mounted a stout legal defense—a corporation that failed to protect what it considers its own property would be derelict in duty. "Spare no pains, or any reasonable expense, to win this land for the company," the Southern Pacific's land department instructed one of its agents, and the railroad went to court seeking to eject unauthorized settlers (who, in its eyes, were mere interlopers). In this way, the railroad's get-the-community-up-and-going policy was trumped by the felt necessity to vindicate its property rights.

As for the Settlers' League, as the six-hundred-member organi-zation was called, historians today tend to view it in the context of the many vigilante groups, some of them led by Confederate veter-ans, that popped up in the West in the decades after the Civil War. In his book *No Duty to Retreat*, historian Richard Maxwell Brown broadened the vista further, interpreting the Mussel Slough shoot-out as a manifestation of two nineteenth-century phenomena. The first was what he called "the Western Civil War of Incorporation," in which small farmers and would-be settlers resisted large farmers (often cattlemen) in their attempts to enclose property, and corporations (often railroads) in their attempts to seize large swathes of choice federal land. The second phenomenon studied by Brown was the inclination to stand your ground—using force, if need be—against attempts to take away your life or property. In his account of Mussel Slough, Brown portrays the settlers more sympathetically than Orsi does. But even Brown makes the Settlers League sound like a scary bunch:

> Such were the mounting tensions inflamed by the settlers' fears of being made homeless by the railroad . . . that in less than a year the daytime, legal activities of the Settlers' League were eclipsed by the night-riding of league members garbed in masks and gowns to hide their identities.

In November of 1878, the League burned down the house of a pro-railroad farmer; this and other acts of violence alienated potential allies.

If Doyle was the brains behind the League, Major Thomas Jefferson McQuiddy, a former Confederate cavalryman who headed the new organization's militia, supplied the brawn. The anti-Leaguers had belligerents of their own, including Walter J. Crow, a well-to-do farmer and crack shot who at one point threatened to kill a squatter if he didn't abandon land that Crow wanted. The anti-Leaguers introduced a crude note of class-consciousness by calling the squatters "sandlappers," roughly equivalent to today's "rednecks." In Brown's words, the population of Mussel Slough had split "into two hostile, violence-prone factions, each imbued with the social doctrine of no duty to retreat."

For all their menacing aspect, the settlers drew support from various quarters, including the *San Francisco Chronicle*, which sounded a note that resonates down through the years by comparing the squatters to patriots at the Boston Tea Party. The paper went on to warn the railroad that if it maintained its policy of oppression, the farmers "would strike the first blow against land monopoly and corporate greed."

The settlers' worst fears were confirmed when a case testing the railroad's position came before a federal judge in 1879. His Honor was Lorenzo Sawyer, known to be not only a stalwart defender of corporate prerogatives in general, but also a friend of Stanford and Crocker in particular, going all the way back to their Gold Rush days. More troubling, Sawyer owed the inception of his judicial career to Stanford, who as governor had appointed him to the state bench in 1862. The notion of a judge recusing himself to avoid a conflict of interest was still in the larval stage in the nineteenth-century West. Even so, by accepting a case with so much built-in bias, Sawyer had tainted the proceedings in advance. His ruling came as no surprise to the settlers. He decided every issue in favor of the Southern Pacific: Its change of route had been legal, the secretary of interior lacked authority to overturn a congressional land grant, and Congress and the state of California had approved the switch anyway.

Whatever one might think of Sawyer's rulings on the merits, coming from a man with his strong ties to one side they begat cynicism—and prompted an appeal. The Southern Pacific, however, was not slow to capitalize on the decision. In the spring of 1880, it filed twenty-three suits to eject settlers from land now confirmed as its own. The decision and the railroad's follow-up enraged the Leaguers, who posted signs warning people not to purchase lands from the railroad and, in a show of strength, paraded nightly through the town of Hanford. The vigilantes went so far as to order selected railroad employees and sympathizers to leave the area, and some of them obeyed. Almost simultaneously, however, the League was passing off its membership as the salt of the earth. In a petition to President Rutherford B. Hayes, who visited San Francisco in 1880, the signers described themselves as the founders of "an American community, in which peace and order, honesty and decency, industry and economy, plenty and comfort prevailed." The petition made no mention of donning masks and gowns, riding around that American community at night, and committing arson.

The Southern Pacific was now selling land, at prices that mostly ranged from $10 to $20 an acre, offering it first to those already occupying it. These figures were higher than what the railroad charged for its holdings elsewhere in the Central Valley, but according to Orsi "the railroad's [Mussel Slough] prices . . . coincided with those on unimproved lands changing hands on the even-numbered government sections, even among the squatters themselves. . . . Everyone recognized that Mussel Slough land was exceptionally valuable." If this is so, the settlers' belief that they were being penalized for having made improvements to "their" land appears groundless. Rather, it looks as if the Southern Pacific was simply keeping an eye on the local real-estate market.

At this point, what might be called the Crocker Factor came into play. The Big Three (as they now were) had divvied up offices in their two main corporations as follows: Stanford was president of the Central Pacific, Huntington vice president of the Central Pacific, and Crocker president of the Southern Pacific. This gave Crocker primary responsibility for handling the Mussel Slough dispute. As suggested in a petty way by his spite fence, and in a grand way by his relentless driving of his Central Pacific work crews, he was a man who couldn't stand to lose at anything.

Huntington and Stanford urged caution and compromise. The unrest in Mussel Slough was taking up a lot of the company's time and underscoring its reputation for hard-heartedness, and Huntington and Stanford recommended that any settler willing to recognize the company's title be given the chance to buy "his" land at a reduced rate. Stanford even condescended to visit Mussel Slough in March of 1880, touring the area with Doyle and other Leaguers. This summit meeting ended with a promise by Stanford that the railroad would lower its land prices, discounting any increase in value that might be thought attributable to the settlers' irrigation system, and the settlers took this to mean prices in the neighborhood of $5 per acre. But Crocker balked. Arguing that these malcontents had trifled with the Southern Pacific long enough, he insisted on upholding the railroad's rights, by means of forced evictions if necessary. And he refused to agree to the $5-per-acre figure or anything like it because he couldn't stomach what he considered a willful misreading of the brochures.

The railroad finally committed itself on paper in late April, sending out letters that lowered prices by $1 to $4 per acre. The settlers scoffed at such "slight reductions," demanding 50 percent off instead. After replying that the company had made its last, best offer, Stanford dashed off to visit Huntington in New York, leaving the dispute to the only partner still in California, the obdurate Crocker. Stanford deserves much blame here—not only for washing his hands of the matter but also for not knowing Crocker as well as he should have.

Yet even Crocker had second thoughts about the collision toward which the railroad and the settlers were heading. On May 7, he wrote his two partners in New York, seeking their counsel and promising to do as they advised. By the time the letter reached them, however, it was too late.

Not without reason, the League felt betrayed by the judicial system. They decided to rally at a picnic on May 11, and their nearness to the boiling point can be gauged by their choice of a speaker for the occasion: their new lawyer, Judge David S. Terry. In the end, Terry couldn't make it, but the League knew what they would have gotten in him—a friend of the working man who was also a notorious hothead. In 1859, he had resigned as California chief justice in order to fight a duel with one of the state's U.S. senators, David Broderick, whom Terry shot dead.

In the not-too-distant future, Terry was to be shot dead himself. After being hired as a lawyer for Sarah Althea Hill, a beautiful adventuress seeking alimony from the Comstock Lode multimillionaire William Sharon, Terry wed his client in 1886 (Sharon had died in 1885). The case, which turned on whether or not Hill had once been Sharon's lawfully wedded wife or merely his mistress, came before a three-judge federal court. One member of the panel was U.S. Supreme Court Justice Stephen J. Field, considered by Hill and Terry to be a puppet of the Sharon family; another member was Sawyer. When the decision went against the Terrys, they blew up in court. Hill accused Field of being bought, and when a federal marshal tried to remove her from the courtroom, Terry knocked him down. Hill was sentenced to a month in jail for her outburst, Terry to six months for his. In August of 1889, an unexpected encounter between the Terrys and Field in Stockton, California, ended with David Terry being killed by Field's bodyguard, David Neagle. (Neagle was brought to trial for the killing, but when you learn to which judge the case was assigned—the inescapable Lorenzo Sawyer—you'll be able to guess the outcome. Neagle wasn't just acquitted, he was commended.) So died the man deemed a fitting inspiration for members of the Settlers' League on May 11, 1880.

As it turned out, Terry's hell-raising skills would have been superfluous. Whether by chance or design, a federal marshal named Alonzo W. Poole and the railroad's land grader (a "grader," in this usage, was someone who classified land for possible sale), William Clark, chose that morning to serve writs of ejection on a number of settlers. Poole's sympathies lay with the Leaguers, many of whom were his friends, but he felt duty bound to enforce the law. En route in a buggy, the two were joined by Crow and another anti-League firebrand, Mills Hartt, both of whom hoped to take over relinquished tracts. (Crow and Hartt appear to have been acting for themselves and not as stooges fronting for the Southern Pacific. Crow in particular had been vocal about wanting to buy selected tracts from the railroad for quite some time.) Poole and Clark carried revolvers, while Hartt and Crow had brought along a small arsenal of pistols, rifles, and shotguns. They first called upon a man named Braden, who was not at home. They lugged his belongings out into the road, and one of them ill-advisedly left a kind of calling card on the Braden doorstep: four cartridges, which afterwards the settlers cited as symbolic intimidation.

Word of the marshal's progress reached the picnickers. As Poole and company drove onto the spread of a man named Brewer, at about ten thirty in the morning, they were met by forty or fifty settlers, on horseback and armed with rifles. Hartt and Crow reached for their guns, but Poole told them not to shoot first. Saying "I think I had better go and meet them," Poole got down from his buggy and advanced on foot. The settlers surrounded him, protesting the unfairness of carrying out evictions while court cases were still pending and demanding that he hand over his revolver. When he refused, one of them shouted, "On peril of your life, surrender your pistol!" (Fifty yards away, Clark heard this as "God damn you. Give up your arms!") Poole refused once more, and the Leaguers placed him under armed guard. A Leaguer named James Harris made the same demand of Hartt and Crow. Instead of complying, Hartt reached for the guns, which were under the wagon seat, only to be restrained by Crow.

The horses' movements had stirred up dust, impairing everyone's vision. In the confusion, a horse lurched and knocked Poole down. Orsi tells what happened next:

> Thinking the settlers had attacked the marshal, Hartt and Crow instinctively dove for their arms. In an instant, Harris, Hartt, and Crow all fired. Eyewitnesses disagreed over who shot first; Clark and most others said that it had been either Hartt or Crow. Hartt toppled over with a mortal wound; Harris and a settler named Iver Knutson, ironically a friend of

Crow's, fell dead on the spot. As his team bolted, Crow hit the ground running toward the fallen marshal, reeling off shots from his revolver and shotgun, with settlers in pursuit. Exchanging fire with Poole's guards, he killed both of them. Within a minute, twenty or thirty shots rang out, but Poole, Clark, and most settlers did not fire their weapons.

When the firing stopped, Hartt and five settlers lay dead. Poole, Clark, and Crow were unhurt. Poole and Clark urged Crow to run for it, which he did, making for his father-in-law's house, two miles away. McQuiddy, the League's military leader, advised Poole and Clark not to serve any more eviction notices. They agreed, and he escorted them to a town from which they caught a train to San Francisco. Crow was found dead later that day, a mile-and-a-half from the Brewer place; he'd been shot in the back.

In Norris's scenario, the numbers involved are rather different: only eleven settlers plus an onlooker, Presley, against the marshal and about a dozen deputies. The lawmen have been spotted serving eviction notices and carrying out furniture from the houses of targeted settlers. But the settlers agree to make one last appeal to the marshal in hopes of averting violence, and in any event not to fire first. They take up positions in a ditch that gives them protection, and when the marshal and company ride up, Magnus Derrick emerges for a parley. As he and the marshal talk, raising their voices and gesticulating, the other lawmen surround them. This threatening sight brings more settlers out of the ditch. A nervous horse accidentally knocks a settler to the ground, and one of his comrades, misinterpreting the cause, fires a retaliatory shot. "Instantly," Norris writes, "the revolvers and rifles seemed to go off of themselves. Both sides, deputies and Leaguers, opened fire simultaneously." Six men, all settlers, are killed (down one from the seven in reality, two of whom were on the marshal's "side"), and Presley is left both radicalized and despondent.

Norris now has the railroad seal off Mussel Slough from the outside world, letting out only such information as favors its cause.

In fact, however, early reactions from the press were mixed. Although most local papers blamed the Southern Pacific for the killings, the *Chronicle* departed from its pro-settler policy to observe that this time vigilantism had gone too far. Even Bierce, than whom the Southern Pacific had no greater journalistic enemy, criticized the League in the pages of the *San Francisco Post*, singling out Doyle as "the Mephistopheles who for his own aggrandizement has led these settlers into all the trouble in which they find themselves."

A year later, writing in *The Wasp*, Bierce nominated Crow as a worthy addition to the roster of the West's heroic gunmen. By then Bierce had reverted to antirailroad form—"It is not denied that the corporation evicting [the settlers] is a heartless, shameless and monstrous tyranny"—but he thought it only fair to recognize Crow for his "death struggle . . . the startling terrors of his departure from this life, baptized with the blood of men, saluted with the wails of widows and orphans—the grim nobility of this dead hero lying in state and no man daring to approach his body." Bierce had a point. Mussel Slough was one of the bloodiest episodes in Western history, and none of the region's famed gunslingers—not Wyatt Earp, not Wild Bill Hickok, not Billy the Kid—dropped as many men at one time as Crow did. He cut a striking figure, too. Brown describes him as "blond and quiet—almost a mute—but . . . one of the finest marksmen in all of California." That Crow and his dubious distinction have been forgotten while his inferiors and their exploits live on in books and movies and ballets may be largely due to the misapprehension that he was working for the railroad. (Bierce, incidentally, made no mention of the Mussel Slough affair in his 1896 campaign against the Southern Pacific, presumably because the funding bill centered on the doings and indebtedness of the firm's sister line, the Central Pacific.)

Regardless of the complexities, the Mussel Slough shoot-out boded ill for the Southern Pacific's public image. It wasn't long before the deceased settlers had become the pitied subjects of a martyr myth. Keller's octopus cartoon appeared in *The Wasp* in July of

1882—he depicted the whole state in the monster's clutches, with gravestones and empty boots and the words "Mussel Slough" off in one corner—and was followed by others in the same vein. Bierce went back to publishing anti–Southern Pacific squibs and poems. In California, fund drives raised money on the settlers' behalf. Back East, newspapers interpreted the settlers' resistance as a populist uprising against monopoly. In Europe, Karl Marx hailed the shootout as a foretaste of the coming anticapitalist revolution. In the realm of literature, Morrow and Post published their antirailroad novels in the early 1880s, with Mussel Slough serving as a pivotal incident in each; Royce weighed in a few years later. Nuances of the settlers' backgrounds and aspirations, of the long back-and-forth between railroad and squatters with its punctuating outbursts of violence, of the protracted legal battle and the polluting effect of apparent judicial favoritism—all these had been overlooked. What leapt out at onlookers instead was a familiar syndrome: a rapacious monopoly had stopped at nothing to cheat hardworking farmers of their share of the American dream.

The legend of the Mussel Slough massacre prevailed because it told people what they thought they already knew, because it corroborated stereotypes, because it fed the desire for easily recognizable good and bad guys. The League itself put its finger on the widespread readiness to believe the worst of the Southern Pacific in a pamphlet published shortly after the shootings:

> All good people sympathize with the right. Generous impulses and a desire that justice shall prevail are with them universal. Among them jealousy of railroad corporations does not exist simply because they *are* corporations, but because it is known to all men that they too often take advantage of their great power to annoy and oppress individuals.

It was "known to all men"—or at least strongly suspected—that, in a battle between the railroad and ordinary citizens, the railroad would invariably take the low road. To put it in journalistic terms, "TRAGEDY IN CENTRAL VALLEY: Confusing Battle Ensues After Railroad Loses Patience in Lengthy Feud with Risk-Taking Squatters" would have made an accurate but tepid headline. "RAILROAD GUNS DOWN FIVE IN CENTRAL VALLEY: Agents of Brutal Monopolist Massacre Farmers Whose Only Fault Is Trying to Hang on to What They Achieved by the Sweat of Their Brows"— now that would have sold papers!

Novelists, of course, have every right to borrow from and tinker with real-life incidents, and Norris et al. can hardly be blamed for writing so powerfully that their fictional treatments of Mussel Slough have obscured the reality. Historians and critics, however, have a duty to insist that not even the most striking passages in a novel should be allowed to obliterate the facts. In *Sunset Limited*, his history of the Southern Pacific, Orsi lists a dozen books that purvey false versions of Mussel Slough, among them Oscar Lewis's *The Big Four* (1938), a veritable fountainhead of errors about the episode from which many subsequent writers have drunk. Orsi might have added one more, Carey McWilliams's otherwise commendable biography of Ambrose Bierce. In enumerating the follies and outrages that fueled Bierce's satire in the 1880s, McWilliams gives this short but wildly inaccurate version of Mussel Slough: "The railroad sent armed thugs ... to oust settlers, and their pet gunman, Walter Crowe, slaughtered farmers from ten in the morning until the last hours of the afternoon, when he was shot dead." (On top of everything else, McWilliams misspelled Crow's name.)

Two twentieth-century novelists can be added to the group making use of Mussel Slough. In May Merrill Miller's *First the Blade* (1938), the saga of a family that takes up wheat farming in the Central Valley, the El Dorado Pacific Railroad is a formidable presence. "[It owns] more power than any company in the nation had ever owned before," the novel's heroine reflects—a claim that could not truthfully have been made of the Southern Pacific. The El Dorado charges inconsistent rates to growers, throws its weight around in asserting its rights to squatters' lands, and provokes a showdown (unnecessary because a lawsuit is still pending) in ranch country.

Somewhat to the reader's surprise, however, the heroine's husband emerges from that showdown unscathed; more than that, he and his family go on to prosper. At times Miller seemed to be suggesting that, in the rapidly filling West with its profusion of contested titles, land ownership is not the panacea it may be back East. Yet in the end the husband embarks on a new career as "proprietor of a real estate business." As for the El Dorado Pacific, after the shoot-out it drops out of the story. Although Mussel Slough and its aftermath take up two long chapters (and more than eighty pages) in the book, they make little difference in the main characters' lives.

In *Ambrose Bierce and the Queen of Spades* (1998), his first mystery featuring the writer as an amateur detective (there were to be four more), Oakley Hall stuck with the standard interpretation of the shoot-out: the railroad as precipitating fiend. The characters lodge several other familiar complaints against the railroad—the rate disparities between long and short hauls, the buying of politicians' votes and of judges' decisions, Crocker's spite fence—but it's the so-called "Mussel Slough Massacre" that galls the fictionalized Bierce and his young sidekick the most. Hall was a native Californian and a longtime director of the writing program at the University of California, Irvine; the uncritical acceptance of the received wisdom on Mussel Slough by a man in his position indicates how much work is in store for those who would set the record straight.

Among recent examples of a writer who accepts the legend as fact is Joan Didion, in her memoir *Where I Was From* (2003). "The stuff of the novel, the incidents on which the narrative turns," she writes of *The Octopus*, "came directly from actual events in what was then Tulare County." Not so—as we've seen, Norris swallowed the popular version of the incident and played fast and loose with "actual events." To characterize how the material was derived from fact, "loosely" would be a far more accurate adverb than "directly." On the other hand, Didion provides a useful analysis of the wording of the railroad's much-discussed brochures (which she mistakenly calls "lease agreements"), accusing the settlers of being "under [a] rather willful misapprehension" as to the price they would eventually pay for title to the land they claimed. The brochures said "from $2.50 upward per acre," and "upward," Didion observes, is "the word the ranchers preferred to miss."

Didion is also astute in noting Norris's ambiguity toward his ranchers. Singling out Magnus Derrick as their representative, she argues that Norris's growers "were of a type common enough in California . . . entrepreneurs in search of the shrewd venture, men who might themselves have been running the railroad had they seen the opportunity, held the right cards, been quicker players." Her observation applies perfectly to that self-appointed lawyer, Doyle, who later prospered as a real-estate developer. But Didion detects in Norris's portrait of the growers a "dissonance its author grasped but failed to resolve." For her, in other words, this is a bad thing, whereas to me the parceling out of authorial sympathies is one of the novel's strengths, making for a more evenhanded and interesting conflict than the ones in *Blood-Money* and other Mussel Slough novels, or in the typical Zola novel. For that matter, Didion exhibits a dissonance of her own in how she refers to Mussel Slough: At one point it's a "shootout," at another a "slaughter."

In her justly praised political writing, Didion is noted for being a grind, willing to pore over documents by the ream in order to trip up wrongdoers on their own words. Too bad that, in recalling her early years in California, she overlooked the ample scholarship that undercuts the myth of the Mussel Slough massacre.

At the railroad's insistence, the U.S. attorney indicted several League members, five of whom, Doyle included, were found guilty of obstructing justice (no need to mention who the trial judge was).

A permissive prison warden did much to assuage their pain. During their eight-month sentence, the five convicts were allowed to come and go at will, they were fêted in person at out-of-jail dinners, their wives were permitted to move in with them, and one prisoner got engaged to the jailer's daughter. After their release, they were welcomed home by a crowd of 3,000 supporters. McQuiddy had been indicted, too. But not only did he remain at large; he won the nominations of both the Anti-Monopoly League and the Greenback Party in the 1882 race for governor of California. He came in fourth, but in 1886 the charges against him were dropped.

The adverse publicity accruing to the Southern Pacific had rattled even Crocker. In late May of 1880, he agreed to a deal by which the asking prices for Mussel Slough land went down an additional 12.5 percent. Although some Leaguers declared it wasn't enough, many others rushed to take advantage of the offer. By June of the following year, nearly all of the railroad's Mussel Slough land had been sold or leased. In 1883, when the U.S. Supreme Court upheld Judge Sawyer's decision vindicating the railroad's title, the case was practically moot.

Despite McQuiddy's failure as a candidate, the League's politics lived on in the radical Workingmen's Party, which many settlers joined after it was founded in 1877. The new party's candidate won the San Francisco mayoral race of 1879, and the party went on to lead the movement that hatched a new California constitution with a number of antirailroad clauses. As noted earlier, however, the railroad found ways to dodge those provisions, and another thirty years were to go by before the Southern Pacific was ousted from its dominant position in state politics. (For more on these developments, see the following chapter.) Richard Maxwell Brown, however, believes that the settlers' agitation was of lasting benefit to Mussel Slough. The resulting pattern of small landholdings helped the region to preserve its rustic beauty and integrity at least until the early 1990s, when he wrote *No Duty to Retreat*. As Brown described it, that legacy could be seen in the contrast between, on the one hand, the well-preserved town of Hanford ("one of the loveliest cities of the Central Valley") and the nearby farms, on which grew a variety of crops; and, on the other hand, farther south in the valley,

> an austere monoculture featuring vast acreages devoid of human habitation. . . . Virtually deserted except for a small cadre of corporate employees, this land is owned and operated by some of the greatest agribusiness enterprises of California. The beauty, diversity, and human vitality of the small- and medium-farm Mussel Slough country to the north is entirely absent.

Strike Mussel Slough from the bill of particulars in *The Octopus* and you would still have a damning case against the railroad. Like the models from which it was drawn, the Pacific and Southwestern sets rates that seem perverse; buys the votes of legislators; stacks the deck of the commission tasked with regulating it; conducts itself with indifference to, if not contempt for, public opinion; and allows its top executives to enrich themselves, unjustly and on a vast scale, by exploiting the government's willingness to hand out subsidies without making sure they are fully needed, much less properly accounted for. But it's the Mussel Slough shoot-out—with its facts shaded to suit the purposes of fiction—that supplies the novel with fire and indignation. It's Mussel Slough that vividly confirms the widespread conviction that the Pacific and Southwestern's real-life counterparts used their unchecked power to defy the public interest. It's the vigor of the Mussel Slough story line that converts the book's title from merely an apt metaphor that appears to have been coined almost simultaneously by a tendentious novelist (Morrow) and a mischievous cartoonist (Keller) into an enduring symbol of corporate rapacity.

Unlike *McTeague*, so far *The Octopus* has not given rise to a memorable version in another form (the material might make a better opera than a film). But *The Octopus* naturally had particular resonance in California, feeding the popular uprising that led to the victory of reform candidate Hiram Johnson in the 1910 governor's race and the subsequent enactment of such Progressive measures as the initiative, referendum, and recall. Theodore Roosevelt had a strong reaction after reading *The Octopus* in 1901. Writing to his old friend Owen Wister, Roosevelt first dismissed Norris as a "reformer who is half charlatan and half fanatic, and ruins his own cause by overstatement" and then acknowledged the novel's power by scolding Norris for not reminding readers that his criticisms did not apply to the entire West. Roosevelt added that he was "inclined to think . . . that conditions were worse in California than elsewhere." A few weeks later, Roosevelt became president, and his strong anti-monopoly convictions led him to revitalize the stagnant Sherman Antitrust Act, making it a workable trust-busting mechanism. *The Octopus* belongs in the select company of Upton Sinclair's *The Jungle* and Harriet Beecher Stowe's *Uncle Tom's Cabin*: novels that have exerted a profound influence on American politics. Even more than with most fiction, however, it's important to remember that the story isn't the literal truth.

✥ ten ✥

Endings

Early in 1901, Frank and Jeannette Norris decamped to Chicago, home of the nation's largest grain market, which he wanted to see in action for the novel he was preparing to write: *The Pit*. That Norris was now a famous author only enhanced his innate appeal. After a few weeks of being peppered with invitations by sociable Chicagoans, he and Jeannette put out word that they were leaving town. In fact, however, they secretly stayed on, and Frank could now work in peace. As he had with *McTeague* and *The Octopus*, he combed through newspaper archives for background and inspiration; this time raw material came from the career of financier Joseph Leiter, who had managed to corner wheat in 1897, only to overreach and nearly go broke the following year. Norris's neglect of mathematics now came back to bite him, however. It took extensive coaching for him to understand the mechanics of futures trading—knowledge essential to his account of the scheming by his protagonist, specula-tor Curtis Jadwin, to corner the market in wheat.

On returning to New York, the Norrises moved from the suburbs into Manhattan, where on January 9, 1902, they became parents—it was a girl, Jeannette Williamson Norris, nicknamed Billy. *The Pit* 's gestation proved to be more troublesome. Norris had made Laura Jadwin his main fictional observer, but as she was connected to wheat through marriage only, this became a strained approach. Figuring out what's wrong with a work in progress is one thing, however, and fixing it another. Norris succeeded only at the former. The plot centers on the rehabilitation of the Jadwins' marriage— which Curtis had jeopardized by neglecting Laura to pursue his obsession with dictating the price of wheat—and large chunks of the book read like breezy popular magazine fiction (indeed, the novel was serialized in *The Saturday Evening Post*). The wheat-cornering maneuvers are well-done (in the end, Norris did master the intricacies of commodities trading), and when Jadwin explains why he can't drop his cornering campaign, he echoes Shelgrim in *The Octopus*: "Corner wheat! It's the wheat that has cornered me. It's like holding a wolf by the ears, bad to hold on, but worse to let go." On the whole, though, *The Pit* lacks the firebrand intensity, the depth of characterization, and the complex narrative mastery of its immediate predecessor.

Thanks to the popular and critical success of *The Octopus*, Norris was in demand by magazine and newspaper editors. Among several essays he wrote during these last months was "The Frontier Gone at Last," in which he seems to have thrown off his worship of all things Anglo-Saxon. "Will it not go on," the piece concludes, "this epic of civilization, this destiny of all races, until . . . we who now arrogantly boast ourselves as Americans . . . may realize that the true patriotism is the brotherhood of man and know that the whole world is our nation and simple humanity our countrymen?" (Note that whereas only a few years back Norris had used "arrogant" as a term of endearment for U.S. soldiers in Cuba, now he applies it pejoratively to his parochial fellow Americans.) In person, he remained his charming self. As one of his Doubleday colleagues recalled after his death, "Whenever [Frank] stopped at my desk for a chat, it always gave a new lift to my day. There was a sort of tonic quality about him, quiet and simple though he was, that stirred and warmed you."

On the strength of his freelance earnings, however, Norris gave up his editing job. He, Jeannette, and Billy moved to San Francisco, where Mrs. Norris had a house waiting for them—one of the properties that had come to her in the divorce settlement. Frank finished *The Pit*, and he and Jeannette were about to sail to Australia on vacation when she came down with appendicitis, requiring surgery. She had barely recovered when her husband suffered a similar attack, which he dismissed as indigestion. On October 20, 1902, his physician recommended that he, too, undergo an appendectomy, but Norris held out. On the morning of the 22nd, he awoke in great pain and was taken to the hospital, where the diagnosis was a burst appendix. He died three days later, at age thirty-two. The fault, if any, lay with the patient, but on hearing what had happened, Hamlin Garland said he wanted to collar Norris's doctor and tell him, "See what an irreparable injury to American literature you have wrought."

The Pit became a posthumous hit, with almost 100,000 copies sold in its year of publication (1903) alone. Later that year, Doubleday, Page followed up with a seven-volume *Complete Works*. It did not, however, include the trilogy's third volume, *The Wolf*, of which Norris had written not a word. In 1914 Frank's brother Charles oversaw the publication of a last novel, *Vandover and the Brute*—actually an apprentice work, most of which had been written while Frank was at Harvard and under the sway of Zola. A kind of inverted *McTeague*, *Vandover and the Brute* is about a high-society swell whose better self loses out to the beast inside him; Vandover and the brute, in other words, are the same fellow. (The book had returned from oblivion. After Norris's death, it went into one of several crates taken to a warehouse for storage. In 1906, the warehouse burned down in the aftermath of the San Francisco earthquake, and *Vandover* was thought to have been destroyed. But that particular crate had been transferred to another location shortly before the quake, and the manuscript was eventually found intact.)

Norris's rival Stephen Crane had died in 1900, from the effects of tuberculosis and malaria. He was twenty-eight.

Émile Zola was sixty-two when he predeceased Norris by a few weeks. A chimney in his house had clogged up, causing carbon monoxide to back up and poison the novelist in his sleep. There was speculation that one of his political enemies might have caused the "accident," but nothing was ever proved.

Collis Huntington, who had expected to live to a hundred, died at age seventy-eight in August of 1900, after a heart attack, while on vacation in the Adirondacks—too soon to be able to read the vibrant novel to which his outsized career and self-justifying remarks had made such vital contributions. Bierce sent him off with a mock epitaph:

> Here Huntington's ashes long have lain
> Whose loss was our eternal gain,
> For while he exercised all his powers
> Whatever he gained, the loss was ours.

Otherwise, however, his former nemesis ruled the deceased tycoon off-limits. "I do not speak ill of the dead," Bierce wrote to a friend in 1900, "—have, indeed, refused to write of the late C. P. Huntington."

Thirteen years after Collis's death, his widow, Arabella (his second wife), married his nephew Henry E. Huntington. Since Arabella and Henry had each been a principal heir to Collis's estate, their marriage resulted in a prodigious financial merger. Unlike Collis, the newlyweds had a robust philanthropic strain, which ultimately bore fruit in the Huntington Library, Art Collections, and Gardens—an admirable institution but none of Collis's doing.

After defeating the Southern Pacific, Bierce returned to the West Coast. For several years he lived mostly in Los Gatos, at the foot of the Santa Cruz Mountains, where the dry climate was easy on the lungs, and wrote fitfully for the *Examiner*.

Perhaps it was the letdown after such an exhausting match, or merely the fact that a satirist's pen can stay sharp for only so long, but Bierce—now almost sixty—was losing interest in "Prattle." Yet the old pro could still lash out eloquently when the spirit moved him. One series of outbursts put him at odds with Hearst again, this time over something more momentous than editorial meddling with his copy. While the publisher was doing his best to start a war with Spain over Cuba, his favorite columnist was savaging the idea in the *Examiner*. After Hearst got his way, Bierce wrote:

> We are at war with Spain to-day merely in obedience to a suasion that has been gathering force from the beginning of our national existence. The passion for territory once roused rages like a lion; successive conquests only strengthen it. That is the fever that is now burning in the American blood.

On another occasion, Bierce delivered one of his vintage put-downs, calling it "the Yanko Spanko war." Hearst, to his credit, let Bierce have his say.

In 1899, Bierce announced that he was moving back to Washington. Hearst still didn't want to lose him, so the *Examiner* gave Bierce a flattering send-off in an article that played up the transfer as vital to its coverage of the momentous issues pending before Congress. By now, however, Bierce was contributing less to newspapers and more to *Cosmopolitan*, a Hearst magazine that had joined the muckraking movement. This turned out to be a less-than-ideal match. Bierce believed that the rich had got that way because they were smarter than the poor, he feared labor unions and anarchists, and he scoffed at the notion that the nation's social problems lent themselves to ready-made solutions. Despite being something of a patron saint to the muckraking writers, he dismissed them as more interested in careerism than in righting wrongs. He resented being considered Hearst's hit man and used sassy language to turn down the publisher's request that he go after Joseph Pulitzer: "I don't like the job of chained bulldog, to be let loose only to tear the panties off the boys who throw rocks at *you*. You wouldn't like it yourself in my place. Henceforth I won't *bite anybody*; a nice quiet life for mine."

As the years went by, so little of what he wrote for Hearst got into print that Bierce offered to take a pay cut. "You haven't heard me shrieking about that, have you?" the publisher replied. At last, in 1909, Bierce severed ties with Hearst, and the paychecks, fully deserved or not, arrived no more.

Bierce's surviving son, Leigh, had modest gifts as a writer—and a drinking problem. After one bibulous night in New York City during the winter of 1900–01, he came down with pneumonia. Bierce went north to nurse him, but after a few weeks' illness, Leigh died. Two days later, in a letter to a friend, Bierce relied on understatement to soft-pedal his grief: "My boy died on Sunday morning. I'm a bit broken in body and mind." In 1904, Mollie Bierce, acting on the mistaken impression that her husband wanted his freedom, instituted divorce proceedings in Los Angeles, where she then lived. The decree was granted; she died of heart failure in 1905. (She seems never to have complained publicly of how summarily Bierce had rejected her.)

If anything, Bierce was touchier as an old man than he'd been as a young one, and friends who slighted him were apt to find themselves cut off. But he never lacked for replacements, especially younger writers seeking to learn from the master, and he carried on a friendship-by-correspondence with H. L. Mencken, the twentieth-century American writer who most resembles him as a satirist. Overall, Bierce's out-to-pasture years in Washington seem to have been pleasant enough. As he informed a friend back in California,

I live rather quietly—the life of an elderly and tolerably respectable clubman; loaf about the Capitol a little (a certain chair in the House restaurant is known as "Bierce's seat in

Congress") [and] have a little circle of friends of both sexes, to which I hope to add you some day, and busy myself with the small affairs that I care about. So I await the end, with absolute indifference as to when it shall come.

This period of leisure ended when Bierce immersed himself in a vanity project: selecting and seeing into print his *Collected Works* for the Washington-based publisher Walter Neale. Bierce labored hard over the project—"I'm cutting-about my stuff a good deal—changing things from one book to another, adding, subtracting, and dividing." The "stuff" ultimately stacked up as twelve volumes, though Neale stretched the contents by using a large font and generous margins. Bierce had sold himself on the idea that the assembled layer cake of his journalism would be greater than the sum of the myriad slices in which it had originally appeared, but the world could have done without much of the *Collected Works*. A "Best of" volume or two consisting of selected short stories, *The Devil's Dictionary*, the Civil War reminiscences, and the wittiest poems and fables would have sufficed.

Bierce had revisited Civil War battlefields from time to time, and now he dreamed of recapturing the spirit of his youth by going on one last adventure, perhaps to Central or South America. At the same time he dreaded the prospect of becoming a broken-down burden. Once, while visiting his daughter in Illinois, he drew her attention to a bent, shuffling old passerby and promised, "I'll never be like that!" When revolution broke out in Mexico, Bierce decided to pay that country a visit, after which he meant to travel farther south to the Andes, a mountain range he found alluring.

And so, at the age of seventy-one, he set in motion the most puzzling last act in American literature—one that perversely denied readers the opportunity to find out how the great student of death met his own. On October 2, 1913, he left Washington, alone, by train. After touring several Southern battlefields, including Chickamauga and Shiloh, he arrived in El Paso, Texas, where he crossed the border on December 16 and obtained credentials as an observer of Pancho Villa's army. In one of his last letters, Bierce had mapped out a possible ending to his life:

> Good-bye—if you hear of my being stood up against a Mexican stone wall and shot to rags please know that I think that a pretty good way to depart this life. It beats old age, disease, or falling down the cellar stairs. To be a Gringo in Mexico—ah, that is euthanasia!

In his last surviving letter, written from the Mexican state of Chihuahua, to a female friend on the day after Christmas 1913, he tried to set the record straight on his temperament:

> you . . . asked me in [your] letter to "confess" that I cared for human sympathy, sentiment and friendship. This to *me* who have always valued those things more than anything else in life!—who have the dearest and best friends of any man in the world, I think,—sweet souls who have the insight to take me at my own appraisement. . . . Evidently you share the current notion that because I don't like fools and rogues I am a kind of monster—a misanthrope without sentiment and without heart.

With that off his chest, he ended the letter by breaking off this friendship, too. Or, as he put it, "you go into the discard."

Shortly afterwards, at the end of 1913 or the beginning of 1914, euthanasia evidently came to the Gringo in Mexico—but how it did so is an unsolvable mystery. He never returned from Mexico, nor was ever heard from again. A reasonable guess is that he was killed during fighting in or around the city of Ojinaga and buried in a common grave.

William Randolph Hearst made little headway in his attempt to parlay immense wealth and influence into political power. In the first decade of the twentieth century, he ran promiscuously for office—mayor of New York, governor of New York, congressman, president of the United States—but all he had to show for his efforts in the end was a pair of terms in the House of Representatives. When he died in 1951, at the age of eighty-eight, he had outlived every other major participant in the Octopus conflict by almost forty years.

Despite the defeat of its funding bill and the death of the last surviving member of its Big Four, the Southern Pacific Railroad rolled on for a while. Not much changed under the leadership of Collis Huntington's widow and nephew, certainly not the company's attempts to pull the strings of California politics—until, that is, California progressives prevailed upon a San Francisco lawyer named Hiram Johnson to run for political office. As mentioned earlier, Hiram was the son of Grove Johnson, the Democrat whose steadfast support of the funding bill in 1896 had left him odd man out in the California congressional delegation. Father and son differed sharply on politics, and although Hiram was initially loath to abandon his law practice, in 1910 he accepted the Republican gubernatorial nomination. Once committed, he threw himself wholeheartedly into the race. "He toured the state in a bright red Locomobile roadster," wrote an historian, "announcing his arrival in isolated communities with a cowbell and speaking from the rumble seat of the car."

Not only did Johnson win; in office, he was true to his word, backing reforms that transformed California government. He pushed through constitutional amendments establishing the initiative, referendum, and recall as tools of direct democracy, as well as a series of measures to bring the railroads under control. The latter resulted in a new, more powerful state agency assigned to regulate not just railroads but all utilities. Longtime Southern Pacific chief counsel William F. Herrin was once asked how the railroad had stayed on top so long. "By controlling reform movements," he answered. But the combination of clamor for change and a governor who kept his campaign promises proved too strong for the post-Collis Southern Pacific. A similar upheaval had occurred at the federal level with passage of the 1906 Hepburn Act, which strengthened the Interstate Commerce Commission's authority over railroad rates, and under the leadership of President Roosevelt, who injected new life into the Sherman Antitrust Act. (The affinity between Johnson and Roosevelt led to the governor's being picked as the former president's running mate in his unsuccessful attempt to return to the White House on the Progressive ticket in 1912.)

During the same period, the Southern Pacific had been slowly losing its identity. Neither Arabella nor Henry Huntington cared much about running a railroad, and the Union Pacific, whose principal owner was now railroad magnate E. H. Harriman, began buying the company's stock. Harriman died before completing the project, but in 1911 the Union Pacific obtained working control of its old competitor for federal subsidies.

In a sign of how drastically times had changed, a takeover that might once have been admired by some and decried by others as one more blow in the ongoing battle for survival of the corporate fittest now provoked the federal government to file an action for restraint of trade. This and other, related suits wended their way through the courts for years, but eventually the Union Pacific was ordered to divest itself of the Southern Pacific. The decision was less than earthshaking, however—reined in by the new regulatory system in California, the Octopus had lost much of its squeeze.

As David Lavender noted, by burning their ledgers to preclude public scrutiny, "the Big Four condemned themselves to being judged by unfriendly figures only." Friendly or not, those figures speak volumes. Each of the Big Four left an estate of at least $20 million, a huge amount at the time (in the case of the enterprising and long-lived Huntington, the sum may have been three or four times as much), and it would be naive to overlook the chief source of those sums: federal subsidies pocketed by the Big Four by way of the Contract & Finance Company.

On the other hand, there may be something to the assertion made by revisionist historians that we've been oversold on the magnitude of the company's political power. One of those revisionists, R. Hal Williams, contended that

> the legend of railroad domination misjudges the independence and honesty of a generation of Californians and completely ignores the significant accomplishments of those decades. On the Pacific Coast men acted far more often in opposition to or in disregard of the railroad than in compliance with it, and their actions, not the dictates of the Southern Pacific Railroad, determined the direction of state politics.

During the funding controversy, Bierce himself had pointed to the strong maverick streak in his fellow citizens, declaring that by dint of hard work Congress might produce a bill acceptable to all Californians, but adding, "This I say, however, with a keen sense of the many difficulties that Californian human nature commonly interposes to an agreement on any proposition less simple than that twice two are four." These correctives to conventional wisdom apply more smoothly, however, to the final years of that "generation of Californians," when opposition to the Southern Pacific had risen to such a pitch that newspapers and the California delegation showed near unanimity in opposing the railroad's policies, than to the early and middle years, when the Big Four regularly blocked efforts at reform with well-placed payments to legislators, bureaucrats, and newspapermen.

And with that, I think, we come to the most damning item in the bill of particulars against the Southern Pacific: its poisoning of the body politic, as attested to by the Big Four themselves in their letters to David Colton and to each other. We'll never know how many construction firms the railroad stifled by steering all its business to its own Contract & Finance Company, or how many ranchers it hurt by charging unfair rates. But we can see the results of the Southern Pacific's suborning of lawmakers and regulators in the mess that is California politics today. A healthy republic should have no need of the initiative, referendum, or recall. (If a citizen has a promising idea for a new law, he ought to be able to persuade his assemblyman to introduce it as a bill. If a public official is seriously violating his oath of office, he ought to be impeached.) These Progressive-era safety valves were grafted onto the constitutions of California and other states in answer to the widespread conviction that big money had engulfed government, leaving the normal checks and balances useless when it came to loosening corporations' grips on the levers of power.

One effect of these well-meaning measures, more than a century later, is that a state with the world's eighth-largest economy finds itself tied in knots—awash in deficits, sometimes having to furlough its employees, shut its parks, and go for months on end without a budget—by unwieldy and clashing procedures, chief among them what *Newsweek* has called "a broken initiative process that puts high-stakes questions to an uncompromising electorate." Initiatives bypass the normal legislative process by which, as bills are refined and debated, diverse interests get to have their say. Instead, voters are presented with up-or-down votes on what are often raw and rigid ideas. And in an irony that the Big Four would have appreciated, gathering signatures to put an initiative on the ballot, buying ads to try to sway voters, hiring lawyers to contest alleged defects in elections—all these tasks have become so costly that large corporations enjoy a decided advantage whenever an initiative touches upon their prerogatives. Big money, in other words, still has California over a barrel, just as it did in the Gilded Age. The state has become a prisoner of its own reforms, especially those spawned by the frustration people felt in the late nineteenth century over how single-mindedly, and with so little regard for ethics, the Southern Pacific and other giant corporations pushed their agendas, until they came to resemble monsters.

If this is so, Ambrose Bierce's funding-bill articles and Frank Norris's *Octopus* share an unwitting flaw: bad timing. Had the funding-bill controversy crystallized, say, a decade earlier and had Norris taken up his great subject at the outset of his career, California lawmakers and other officials might have read their works, taken heart, and found the strength to reject the railroad's blandishments and impose a strong regulatory system before the corruption got out of hand. In doing so, they would have demonstrated that the Octopus was a few suction cups short of omnipotence and thus there was no need to tamper with the basic political structure. It didn't happen that way, however, and overall the tampering may well have done more harm than good.

More than a century after the death of the Big Four's last surviving member, the widespread distrust of representative government which is a legacy of the Southern Pacific and other nineteenth-century monopolies continues to roil American politics. Oddly, however, that distrust has lent itself to a widespread movement not to strengthen government so that it can do its job better, but to weaken it, gutting regulatory agencies and cutting taxes to the bone, all so that the marketplace can have its way—in other words, a recrudescence of Social Darwinism, though that term is rarely used anymore. This movement has been slowed, at least temporarily, by the commonly accepted diagnosis of the economic near debacle of 2007 onward: It originated in and spread from insufficiently regulated sectors of the banking and securities industries. Yet the warning remains in effect: At the beginning of the twenty-first century, the political climate is such that the United States is in danger of being dragged back into the era of the robber barons.

It's doubtful that such a development would have surprised Ambrose Bierce. For an inveterate cynic like him, irony was all in a day's work.

⇥ acknowledgments ⇤

Like *Mile-High Fever* before it, *The Great American Railroad War* owes a great debt to my spouse, Mike Bell, who repeatedly helped me narrow the gap between what I meant to say and what actually landed on the pages of my first draft.

It takes two coasts to make a book—or, at least, this one. Here in Washington, D.C., the support of David and Margaret Hensler has made me an immeasurably happier writer. In New York, Bob and Beth Sheehan lavished their hospitality on me. Up in the Berkshires, Dick Lipez and Joe Wheaton generously gave me a New England base. In Berkeley, Steve Weissman and Laura Mahanes made my Western research swing both feasible and fun, and Steve coached me on the theory and practice of California ballot initiatives. Between Sacramento and the Nevada border, Joe and Gail Hensler helped me get a sense of what the Big Four let themselves in for when they signed up to lay rails across the Sierra Nevada. In cyberspace, Art Taylor and Kyle Semmel asked such smart questions about my writing that I'm sure I learned more in the process than they did. And thanks to Heather Wheeler, without whose insistence that I read *The Octopus* this book might never have been written.

I am deeply indebted to S. T. Joshi and David E. Schultz, who some years ago went to the trouble of photocopying and transcribing all of Ambrose Bierce's funding-bill articles. In a handsome act of generosity, S. T. sent me both hard and electronic copies of their work, thereby sparing me many long and sick-making hours of watching microfilm shimmy across a screen in the Library of Congress. S. T. also read my Bierce chapters in draft and offered astute suggestions for improvement—all this while working on multiple projects of his own, including the recently published Bierce volume for the Library of America.

Bert Foer, one of the foremost experts on American antitrust law, graciously vetted my first draft. I'm lucky to have in my corner Marie Arana, Carolyn See, and Adam Goodheart, all of whom really know how to dish out the encouragement.

I have benefited from the published work of several historians and biographers, notably David Haward Bain, Terry Beers, Russell Duncan and David J. Klooster, S. T. Joshi and David E. Schultz, David Lavender, Joseph R. McElrath and Jesse S. Crisler, Richard Orsi, and John Hoyt Williams (for a full list of books consulted, see the bibliography). Thanks to Kathryn Santos at the California State Railroad Museum in Sacramento and Jeff Bridgers and Roslyn Pachoca at the Library of Congress for help in rounding up illustrations.

My agent, Mitchell Waters, and his assistant, Mark McCloud, have promoted this project with their customary brio. At St. Martin's Press, Michael Flamini and Vicki Lame have added to their luster as classy editors. Jessica Zimmerman, also of St. Martin's, gets the word out not only to the obvious places but also to others that a merely mortal publicist would overlook.

Finally, a word about *The Washington Post*. As a tool of the Huntington forces, it comes off rather badly in these pages—Ambrose Bierce went so far as to call it "the Huntington Post." But that incarnation of the paper is removed from the current one—at which I have been happily employed for getting on to thirty years—by more than a century and several degrees of ownership. I have no doubt that if the Graham family had been running the *Post* in 1896, the paper would have sided with Bierce.

⇒ notes ⇐

Introduction

2 "on an original investment": Hopkins, Ernest Jerome, ed., *The Ambrose Bierce Satanic Reader*, New York: Doubleday, 1968, p. 199.

3 "Yes, born East myself": Twain, Mark, and Warner, Charles Dudley, *The Gilded Age: A Tale of Today*, New York: Meridian Classics, 1985, p. 107.

1. Working on the Railroad

9 "When [Andrew] Jackson entered": McDougall, Walter A., *Throes of Democracy: The American Civil War Era, 1829–1877*, New York: Harper, 2008, p. 144.

10 "[it was] so big as to need": Adams, Henry, *The Education of Henry Adams*, New York: Penguin Classics, 1995, p. 231.

12 "a people's railroad": Bain, David Haward, *Empire Express: Building the First Transcontinental Railroad*, New York: Viking, 1999, p. 70.

12 "a clean thing": ibid., p. 82.

13 "Are the working men of the world": Lears, Jackson, *Rebirth of a Nation: The Making of Modern America, 1877–1920*, New York: Harper, 2009, p. 81.

14 "gave me my right to liberty": ibid.

14 "God has intended": Bellesiles, Michael A., *1877: America's Year of Living Violently*, New York: The New Press, 2010, p. 178.

18 "It's about time somebody else helped": Lewis, Oscar, *The Big Four: The Story of Huntington, Stanford, Hopkins, and Crocker, and of the Building of the Central Pacific*, New York: Alfred A. Knopf, 1938, p. 27.

18 "the worst place I ever saw": Bain, *Empire Express*, p. 98.

19 "His manners were so gentle": Rayner, Richard, *The Associates: Four Capitalists Who Created California*, New York: Atlas & Company/Norton, 2008, p. 33.

19–20 "the Government must come forward": Ambrose, Stephen E., *Nothing Like It in the World: The Men Who Built the Transcontinental Railroad 1863–1869*, New York: Touchstone Books, 2001, p. 83.

20 "The Western soil": Williams, John Hoyt, *A Great and Shining Road: The Epic Story of the Transcontinental Railroad*, New York: Times Books, 1988, p. 45.

22 "WE HAVE DRAWN THE ELEPHANT": Bain, *Empire Express*, p. 115.

24 "I knew how to manage men": Lavender, David, *The Great Persuader*, New York: Doubleday, 1970, p. 123.

25 "All that I have": Williams, *A Great and Shining Road*, p. 62.

25 "I had a blowout": Lewis, *The Big Four*, p. 43.

26 "did not ask him to do anything": Bain, *Empire Express*, p. 136.

26 "a casual observer would not be likely": Daggett, Stuart, *Chapters on the History of the Southern Pacific*, New York: Ronald Press, 1922, p. 59.

26 "$480,000 more in government bonds": Williams, *A Great and Shining Road*, p. 66.

27 "my pertinacity and Abraham's faith": Bain, *Empire Express*, p. 137.

28 "If old Huntington is going to sell out": ibid., p. 142.

28 "experience and capital": ibid., p. 143.

2. Hell-Bent for Promontory Summit

29 "I have gone to sleep": Williams, *A Great and Shining Road*, p. 92.

30 "awful lazy": Bain, *Empire Express*, p. 577.

30 "[There was] no earthly doubt": Williams, *A Great and Shining Road*, p. 89.

31 "I would have been glad": Bain, *Empire Express*, p. 195.

32 "dregs of Asia": Lavender, *The Great Persuader*, p. 161.

32 "They are laying siege": Williams, *A Great and Shining Road*, p. 100.

33 "hosts of Chinamen": Bain, *Empire Express*, p. 652.

33 "their quiet efficiency was astounding": Williams, *A Great and Shining Road*, p. 97.

33 "If we deny to the individual": Rice, Richard B., Bullough, William A., and Orsi, Richard J., *The Elusive Eden: A New History of California*, New York: Alfred A. Knopf, 1988, p. 248.

35 "one-eye bossy man": Williams, *A Great and Shining Road*, p. 181.

35 "On average, a Central Pacific railroad tunnel": ibid., p. 116.

36 "The snow would fall": Bain, *Empire Express*, p. 246.

38 "[The men toiled] with the regularity": ibid., p. 288.

38 "Make it as perfect": Williams, *A Great and Shining Road*, p. 159.

38 "[they] lived practically entirely out of sight": ibid., p. 143.

39 "A white column shot up": Bain, *Empire Express*, p. 319.

39 "It puts me out of all patience": Lewis, *The Big Four*, p. 79.

40 "It costs a fearful amount": Bain, *Empire Express*, p. 321.

41 "As each stepped forward": Lewis, *The Big Four*, p. 74.

42 "We will of course go right on": Bain, *Empire Express*, p. 365.

43 "It was beginning to look like a railroad": ibid., p. 369.

43 "I tell you, we have got the Union Co.": ibid., p. 366.

44 "no one else had suspected": Williams, *A Great and Shining Road*, p. 172.

44 "At last we have reached the summit": Bain, *Empire Express*, p. 412.

45 "We are expanding too much": ibid., p. 397.

45 "We can't expect to monopolize": ibid.

45 "I think if 1868": ibid., p. 431.

46 "As the Union Co. are so very corrupt": ibid., p. 453.

46 "when a cheap road will pass": Williams, *A Great and Shining Road*, p. 204.

46 "Floating in Congressional waters": Jacob, Kathryn Allamong, *King of the Lobby: The Life and Times of Sam Ward, Man-About-Washington in the Gilded Age*, Baltimore: The Johns Hopkins University Press, 2010, p. 100.

47 "And you know devilish well": Lavender, *The Great Persuader*, p. 174.

47 "circumstances arise sometimes when power": ibid., p. 384.

48 "Under this system": Williams, *A Great and Shining Road*, p. 208.

48 "the crossing of the Sierra mountains": ibid., p. 209.

49 "The train stopped": ibid., p. 227.

49 "I think you must have slept": Lavender, *The Great Persuader*, p. 234.

51 "We send you greeting": Bain, *Empire Express*, p. 476.

51 "We return your greeting": ibid.

51 "[There was] something tigerish": Lavender, *The Great Persuader*, p. 129.

52 "as soon as we get within say, four hundred miles": Bain, *Empire Express*, p. 475.

52   "It is in violation of the act of Congress": ibid., p. 489.

53   "I thought we had better take *high ground*": ibid., p. 492.

53   "a first-class man": ibid., p. 502.

54   "No surviving letters indicate": Lavender, *The Great Persuader*, p. 222.

54   "I will hold my grip": Bain, *Empire Express*, p. 523.

54   "By God, Charley": ibid., p. 556.

55   "deference to the great number": *San Francisco Examiner*, March 7, 1896.

55   " 'Now, gentlemen,' said I": Bain, *Empire Express*, p. 576.

56   "an outrage": ibid., p. 582.

56   "managed by a small clique": ibid., p. 599.

56   "It is but another name": ibid., p. 600.

57   "The laborers upon the Central Pacific": Williams, *A Great and Shining Road*, p. 220.

57   "Stewart . . . has always stood by us": Lavender, *The Great Persuader*, p. 241.

60   "I notice by the papers": ibid., p. 243.

61   "In conclusion, I will add": Bain, *Empire Express*, p. 665.

62   "There is henceforth but one Pacific Railroad": ibid., p. 667.

62   "the spirit of my brave husband": Williams, *A Great and Shining Road*, p. 267.

62   "a detriment, with the conditions": Bain, *Empire Express*, p. 670.

62   "Mr. President of the Central Pacific": ibid.

3. How to Be Very, Very Unpopular

63   "By engineers of repute": Williams, *A Great and Shining Road*, p. 275.

64   "We rejected the offer": Lavender, *The Great Persuader*, p. 212.

64   "No set of men": Daggett, *Chapters on the History of the Southern Pacific*, p. 182.

66   "THE KING OF FRAUDS": Bain, *Empire Express*, p. 676.

66   "I never dreamed of corrupting": ibid., p. 689.

66   "It's like the man in Massachusetts": ibid., p. 700.

67   "I wasn't worth a cent": Twain and Warner, *The Gilded Age*, p. 193.

67   "these hell hounds": Lavender, *The Great Persuader*, p. 291.

68   "The ultimate decision": ibid., p. 292.

68   "condemned themselves to being forever judged": ibid., p. 411.

68   "There are uglier buildings in America": www.sfgenealogy.com/sf/history/hgoe75/htm.

69   "being desirous of making the best possible impression": Lewis, *The Big Four*, p. 113.

69 "I will drop the obsequious smile": ibid., p. 114.

70 "seal him in": www.sfcityguides.org.

71 "With absence of shame and decency": Lavender, *The Great Persuader*, p. 303.

72 "By 1877 the Central Pacific": Daggett, *Chapters on the History of the Southern Pacific*, p.140.

73 "the railroad charged Nevadans": Elliott, Russell R., *History of Nevada*, Lincoln: University of Nebraska Press, 1987, p. 158.

73 "The railroads . . . raised their rates": *San Francisco Examiner*, March 8, 1896.

74 "California in the period from 1869": Orsi, Richard J., *Sunset Limited: The Southern Pacific Railroad and the Development of the American West 1850–1930*, Berkeley: University of California Press, 2007, p. 48.

75 "The events of the past year": Deverell, William, *Railroad Crossing: Californians and the Railroad 1850–1910*, Berkeley: University of California Press, 1994, p. 91.

76 "No government can last long": Lavender, *The Great Persuader*, p. 326.

76 "I am aware of the opinion": *Sinking Fund Cases*, 99 U.S. 700, at 767 (1878).

77 "Friend Colton": Beatty, Jack, *Age of Betrayal: The Triumph of Money in America, 1865–1900*, New York: Alfred A. Knopf, 2007, p. 254.

77 "Cannot you have [Governor] Stanford": ibid.

78 "It costs money to fix things": Williams, *A Great and Shining Road*, p. 129.

79 "no one outside the railroad employ": Deverell, *Railroad Crossing*, p. 51.

79 "for [the entire sixteen years of its existence]": *San Francisco Examiner*, February 28, 1896.

79 "The idea of a Railroad Commission": Deverell, *Railroad Crossing*, p. 59.

79 "IT IS REPORTED THAT YOU ARE IN THE FIELD": Lavender, *The Great Persuader*, p. 345.

80 ". . . it seems to be the general belief": White, Richard, *Railroaded: The Transcontinentals and the Making of Modern America*, New York: W. W. Norton, 2011, p. 192.

81 "throw Trinity Church": Lewis, *The Big Four*, p. 252.

81 "Mr. Stanford has about as much to do": Lavender, *The Great Persuader*, p. 360.

83 "The tentacles of the octopus": Morrow, William C., *Blood-Money*, San Francisco: F. J. Walker & Company 1882, p. 106.

83 "one of the cogs": ibid.

83 "I fear that blood must be spilled": ibid., p. 150.

84 "Stanford, the president of the company": Post, C. C., *Driven from Sea to Sea; or, Just a Campin'*, Chicago: J. E. Downey & Company, 1884, p. 260.

84 "the story is not yet finished": ibid., p. 335.

84 "He didn't see any use for hell": Royce, Josiah, *The Feud of Oakfield Creek: A Novel of California Life*, New York: Johnson Reprint Corporation, 1970, p. 85.

85 "the doctrine that vast public fortunes": ibid., p. 359.

85 "nobody could ever afterwards": ibid., p. 475.

85 "Royce sometimes felt": Santanaya, George, *The Genteel Tradition in American Philosophy* and *Character and Opinion in the United States*, New Haven: Yale University Press, 2009, p. 79.

85 "a perjurer and a liar": Robinson, John R., "The Octopus: A History of the Construction, Conspiracies, Extortions, Robberies, and Villainous Acts of the Central Pacific, Southern Pacific of Kentucky, Union Pacific and Other Subsidized Railroads," San Francisco, 1894, p. 39.

85 "For the past thirty years": ibid., p. 21.

86 "stolen and robbed the public": ibid., p. 4.

86 "The people have been and are now contributing": ibid., p. 115.

86 "they evidently lived happily": Lavender, *The Great Persuader*, p. 348.

4. Ambrose Bierce at a Low Point

89 "to [my father's] books": O'Connor, Richard, *Ambrose Bierce: A Biography*, Boston: Little, Brown, 1967, p. 11.

89 "With what anguish of mind": McWilliams, Carey, *Ambrose Bierce: A Biography*, Hamden, Connecticut: Archon Books, 1967, p. 26.

89 "Belief without evidence": All quotations from *The Devil's Dictionary* are from the Library of America volume *Bierce: The Devil's Dictionary, Tales, & Memoirs*, edited by S. T. Joshi, 2011. The entries are alphabetical, and no further citations to quotations from Bierce's *Dictionary* will be given.

89 "Early one June morning": *The Collected Writings of Ambrose Bierce*, Secaucus, New Jersey: The Citadel Press, 1946, p. 803.

89 "Having murdered my mother": ibid, p. 793.

90 "unwashed savages": McWilliams, *Ambrose Bierce*, p. 26.

90 "My poor Mother": Joshi, S. T., and Schultz, David E., eds., *A Much Misunderstood Man: Selected Letters of Ambrose Bierce*, Columbus: Ohio State University Press, 2003, p. 16.

91 "At one point in my green and salad days": Duncan, Russell, and Klooster, David J., *Phantoms of a Blood-Stained Period: The Complete Civil War Writings of Ambrose Bierce*, Amherst: University of Massachusetts Press, 2002, p. 316.

92 "At the battle of Gaines's Mill": ibid., p. 304.

92 "In those hours": McWilliams, *Ambrose Bierce*, p. 41.

93 "It was hazardous work": McElfresh, Earl B., *Maps and Mapmakers of the Civil War*, New York: Abrams, 1999, p. 35.

93 "the best hated man": Duncan and Klooster, *Phantoms of a Blood-Stained Period*, p. 222.

93 "While engaged in this duty": McWilliams, *Ambrose Bierce*, p. 55.

94 "this is a world of fools": *The Collected Works of Ambrose Bierce*, New York: The Neale Publishing Company, 1911, vol. X, p. 77.

94 "Heaven is a prophecy": McWilliams, *Ambrose Bierce*, p. 183.

94 "hater of mankind": Joshi, S. T., and Schultz, David E., eds., *Ambrose Bierce: A Sole Survivor: Bits of Autobiography*, Knoxville: University of Tennessee Press, 1998, p. 215.

94 "Do you think it philosophical": ibid.

94 "does it really seem to you": ibid.

96 "The fact that Henry Armstrong was buried": *The Collected Writings of Ambrose Bierce*, p. 416.

97 "to teach precision in writing": Bierce, Ambrose, *Write It Right: A Little Blacklist of Literary Faults*, Toluca Lake, California: Terripam Publishers, Inc., 1986, p. 6.

97 "Allude to": ibid., p. 11.

97 "Laundry": ibid., p. 40.

98 "It never seems to have occurred to him": Wilson, Edmund, *Patriotic Gore: Studies in the Literature of the American Civil War*, New York: Noonday, 1977, p. 631.

98 "'a liar, a scoundrel'": from a "Town Crier" column reproduced and bound into de Castro, Adolphe, *Portrait of Ambrose Bierce*, New York: The Century Company, 1929, after p. 22.

98 "Is President Grant to be allowed": ibid.

98 "An Episcopal clergyman in New York": ibid.

99 "Remember that it hurts no one": McWilliams, *Ambrose Bierce*, p. 93.

99 "My son, the gentleman whom you hold": O'Connor, *Ambrose Bierce*, p. 88.

100 "Do you know that I have the supremest contempt": McWilliams, *Ambrose Bierce*, p. 106.

100 "I need not attempt to describe my feelings": ibid., p. 104.

101 "that aggregation of shop clerks": Joshi and Schultz, *A Much Misunderstood Man*, p. 95.

101 "Bierce was the mildest and gentlest gentleman": McWilliams, *Ambrose Bierce*, p. 200.

103   "The personal property of the late Anthony Chabot": O'Connor, *Ambrose Bierce*, p. 117.

103   "HERE LIES FRANK PIXLEY": McWilliams, *Ambrose Bierce*, p. 157.

103   "The covers of this book": ibid., p. 287.

103   "the Public Executioner": ibid., p. 156.

104   "bankers, brokers": Hopkins, *The Ambrose Bierce Satanic Reader*, p. 34.

104   "I found a young man": *Collected Works*, vol. XII, p. 305.

105   "The wine of Arpad Haraszthy": O'Connor, *Ambrose Bierce*, p. 159.

105   "[Hearst] did not once direct": *Collected Works*, vol. XII, p. 305.

106   "Don't for heaven's sake": O'Connor, *Ambrose Bierce*, p. 185.

106   "always famous for her composed manner": Abbot, Willis J., *Watching the World Go By*, Boston: Little, Brown, 1933, p. 139.

107   "So much so, Sir": Lee, Hermione, *Biography: A Very Short Introduction*, Oxford, England: Oxford University Press, 2009, p. 51.

108   "going home to Jesus": Duncan and Klooster, *Phantoms of a Blood-Stained Period*, p. 116.

109   "among our three greatest writers": McWilliams, *Ambrose Bierce*, p. 219.

109   "I am sure Mr. Howells": ibid.

109   "I don't take part in competitions": ibid., p. 189.

109   "his eyes flashing": ibid., p. 115.

110   "Nothing matters": ibid., p. 193.

110   "Perhaps it is because I am a trifle dazed": ibid., p. 197.

110   "No, I'm not a great man": ibid., p. 200.

111   "His writing—with its purged vocabulary": Wilson, *Patriotic Gore*, p. 632.

111   "An opera, or an oratorio": *Collected Works*, vol. X, p. 236.

111   "the ordinary novel . . . objectionable": Kennedy, J. Gerald, ed., *The Portable Edgar Allan Poe*, London: Penguin Classics, 2006, p. 533.

113   "When two lines of battle": Duncan and Klooster, *Phantoms of a Blood-Stained Period*, p. 274.

113   "As a rule the Confederates": ibid.

113   "The soldier never becomes wholly familiar": ibid., pp. 247–48.

114   "The particular thing that they lose": ibid., pp. 313–14.

115   "a Federal sergeant": ibid., pp. 103–04.

116   "I had thought": Morris, Roy, Jr., *Ambrose Bierce: Alone in Bad Company*, New York: Crown, 1995, p. 224.

116   "show [me] a passage": ibid.

116   "That story has everything": ibid., p. 215.

117   "*The Red Badge* is all right": Crane, Stephen, *The Red Badge of Courage*, New York: Bantam Classics, 1983, p. vii.

117 "What reg'ment do yeh b'long teh?": ibid., p. 71.

117 "It is seldom indeed": Duncan and Klooster, *Phantoms of a Blood-Stained Period*, p. 220.

117 "the furnace roar": Crane, *The Red Badge of Courage*, p. 61.

117 "continued to curse": ibid., p. 122.

5. Anatomy of the Funding Bill

120 "There can be no question": Deverell, *Railroad Crossing*, p. 132.

121 "The entire state at the time": Older, Fremont, *My Own Story*, New York: Johnson Reprint Corporation, 1968, p. 21.

121 "This fellow is uncontrollable": de Castro, *Portrait of Ambrose Bierce*, p. 56.

122 "From the point of view of reason": Deverell, *Railroad Crossing*, p. 85.

123 "Within thee, as within a magic glass": Beers, Terry, ed., *Gunfight at Mussel Slough: Evolution of a Western Myth*, Berkeley: Heyday Books, 2004, pp. 91–92.

124 "Here Stanford lies": Grenander, M. E., ed., *Poems of Ambrose Bierce*, Lincoln: University of Nebraska Press, 1995, p. 113.

124 "To the removal of himself": Lindley, Daniel, *Ambrose Bierce Takes on the Railroad: The Journalist as Muckraker and Cynic*, Westport, Connecticut, Praeger, 1990, p. 84.

125 "the market price of our favor": ibid., p. 88.

125 "In assuming that we have either made": Hopkins, *The Ambrose Bierce Satanic Reader*, p. 198.

126 "What in the absence of competition": Lindley, *Ambrose Bierce Takes on the Railroad*, p. 98.

126 "in the past twenty years": ibid., p. 99.

127 "To see earnings divided": Daggett, *Chapters on the History of the Southern Pacific*, p. 379.

127 "I have an impression that nobody": Deverell, *Railroad Crossing*, p. 131.

128 "I know old Thurman well": Daggett, *Chapters on the History of the Southern Pacific*, p. 388.

129 "It is impossible to read": Myers, Gustavus, *History of Great American Fortunes*, New York: Modern Library, 1936, p. 523.

130 "It is not too much to say": *United States v. Stanford*, 161 U.S. 412, 430 (1896).

131 "Huntington wouldn't steal a red-hot stove," etc.: Stewart, Robert E., and Stewart, M. T., *Adolph Sutro: A Biography*, Berkeley: Howell-North, 1962, p. 201.

131 "The statement that Mr. Huntington wouldn't steal": Williams, R. Hal, *The Democratic Party and California Politics 1880–1896*, Palo Alto: Stanford University Press, 1973, p. 221.

132 "just one transcontinental line": ibid., p. 219.

132 "got a kind of craze on": ibid.

132 "If there is anybody who has done more": Lavender, *The Great Persuader*, p. 422.

132 "The new bonds": *San Francisco Examiner*, March 19, 1896.

6. Bierce at War Again

134 "Railroad combination so strong": *San Francisco Examiner*, January 21, 1896.

135 "I shall be glad": ibid.

135 "Ambrose Bierce knows the trail": ibid.

137 "Bierce on the Funding Bill: *San Francisco Examiner*, February 1, 1896.

138 "for three days or more of this week": ibid.

138 "to the general public here": ibid.

138 "an acute public apathy": ibid.

138 "the honest words": ibid.

138 "OUTSIDE OF A FEW DISAPPOINTED AGITATORS": ibid.

138 "If 'The Examiner' would care to blacklist": ibid.

138–39 "'The Examiner's' columns": ibid.

139 "believe that a corporation which for thirty years": ibid.

140 "In a newspaper controversy": Joshi and Schultz, *A Sole Survivor*, p. 207.

140 "no rules can be given": ibid.

140 "(1) by guarding your self-respect": ibid.

142 "on rolls of brown wrapping paper": Lindley, *Ambrose Bierce Takes on the Railroad*, p. 108.

143 "HUNTINGTON'S METHODS ALMOST BEYOND BELIEF": *San Francisco Examiner*, February 3, 1896.

143 "If [Williams] is not guilty": ibid.

143 "William Greer Harrison is to the fore": *San Francisco Examiner*, February 4, 1896.

144 "literary bureau": ibid.

144 "'I was not interviewed'": *San Francisco Examiner*, February 6, 1896.

144 "never in my life expressed an opinion": *San Francisco Examiner*, February 8, 1896.

144 "I do not see any harm": ibid.

144 "THE MOST BAREFACED OF ALL": ibid.

145 "HUNTINGTON LYING": *San Francisco Examiner*, February 2, 1896.

145 "Mr. Huntington is not altogether bad": ibid.

146 "inflated old pigskin": ibid.

146 "[Huntington] observed them doing Pierce": *San Francisco Examiner*, February 9, 1896.

146 "the illustrious Kentuckian": ibid.

147 "He who considers": ibid.

147 "the inscribed scribe of the Blue Grass Gospel": *San Francisco Examiner*, February 11, 1896.

147 "took his hand out of all manner of pockets": *San Francisco Examiner*, February 15, 1896.

147 "The spectacle of this old man": ibid.

148 "plunder by perjury": ibid.

148 "People who read 'The Examiner'" et seq.: *San Francisco Examiner*, February 16, 1896.

149 "My name . . . has been used": *San Francisco Examiner*, February 18, 1896.

149 "supremely distressed": ibid.

150 "the same men": ibid.

150 "Of our modern Forty Thieves": ibid.

150 "If there is in Washington one person": ibid.

150 "no selfish interest in the matter": *San Francisco Examiner*, June 30, 1896.

150 "It was absolutely impossible": *San Francisco Examiner*, February 19, 1896.

151 "quite sure that he had never seen [them]": ibid.

151 "There was not another member": ibid.

151 "Well, name your price": McWilliams, *Ambrose Bierce*, p. 240.

151 "Oh, I just wanted to see": ibid., p. 241.

152 "Mr. Collis P. Huntington": *San Francisco Examiner*, March 19, 1899.

152 "once in presence of three members": *San Francisco Examiner*, March 21, 1896.

153 "'If I did [read]'": *San Francisco Examiner*, February 15, 1896.

153 "Ambrose Bierce—who has to write": *Washington Star*, February 18, 1896.

153 "grand larceny trial": *San Francisco Examiner*, February 21, 1896.

153 "With such an intellectual giant": *San Francisco Examiner*, February 20, 1896.

153 "Now the Washington papers": *San Francisco Examiner*, February 25, 1896.

154 "modestly bent his goat-like head": *San Francisco Examiner*, February 28, 1896.

154 "On the whole we are making progress": *San Francisco Examiner*, February 25, 1896.

154 "as Chairman of the Committee on Visible Virtues": *San Francisco Examiner*, March 1, 1896.

154 "the ever-superserviceable": *San Francisco Examiner*, February 28, 1896.

154 "It is almost a foregone conclusion": *San Francisco Examiner*, March 1, 1896.

155 "one of the most elaborate": *San Francisco Examiner*, March 7, 1896.

155 "It is to be hoped": *San Francisco Examiner*, February 22, 1896.

155 "sat there in the presence of Senators": *San Francisco Examiner*, March 7, 1896.

155 "I cannot help feeling": ibid.

155 "goods from New York and elsewhere": *San Francisco Examiner*, March 8, 1896.

155 "by dint of patience and persistence": ibid.

156 "Nothing could be got out of [Huntington]": ibid.

157 "to get his story on record": *San Francisco Examiner*, March 12, 1896.

157 "One would have thought": *San Francisco Examiner*, March 13, 1896.

157 "A member of the committee": ibid.

158 "There are perhaps a hundred men": ibid.

159 "Afraid to Testify": *San Francisco Examiner*, March 16, 1896.

159 "Any statement that 'The Examiner'" et seq.: *San Francisco Examiner*, March 21, 1896.

159 "After some heated discussion": ibid.

159 "I have reason to think that Huntington": ibid.

160 "Pacific railroad matters": *San Francisco Examiner*, March 22, 1896.

160 "It is true that I have had to stop": Joshi and Schultz, *A Much Misunderstood Man*, p. 51.

161 "TORTURED BY FIERCE APACHES": *San Francisco Examiner*, April 1, 1896.

161 "THIS IS THE FUNDING BILL": *San Francisco Examiner*, March 31, 1896.

161 "'the Hubbard plan'": *San Francisco Examiner*, April 1, 1896.

161 "It will be observed": ibid.

161 "If there is no Pacific railroad legislation": ibid.

162 "There is now a reasonable hope": ibid.

162 "small army of high-priced attorneys": ibid.

162 "We are still a long way": *San Francisco Examiner*, April 5, 1896.

162 "The observer who pats himself on the back": *San Francisco Examiner*, April 7, 1896.

163 "the natural port of Los Angeles": *New York Journal*, May 4, 1896.

163 "hopes of his recovery": *San Francisco Examiner*, April 9, 1896.

164 "a faultlessly respectable person": ibid.

164 "It is clear now that one of the hardest blows": *San Francisco Examiner*, April 12, 1896.

165 "Congress was probably moved by the grandeur": *San Francisco Examiner*, April 21, 1896.

165 "The opposition to the railroad bill": *San Francisco Examiner*, April 22, 1896.

165 "As a single example": ibid.

166 "HUNTINGTON HAS A LOSING FIGHT": *San Francisco Examiner*, April 25, 1896.

166 "Huntington is a snake": ibid.

166 "My own opinion of Speaker Reed": ibid.

167 "They never open their mouths": Tuchman, Barbara, *The Proud Tower: Portrait of the World Before the War, 1890–1914*, New York: Bantam Books, 1971, p. 134.

167 "Having embedded that fly": ibid., p. 139.

167 "The others have taken it": ibid., p. 164.

167 "Open-minded members": *San Francisco Examiner*, April 25, 1896.

167 "The mystery continues": *New York Journal*, May 6, 1896.

168 "FUNDING DEALT ITS DEATH BLOW": *San Francisco Examiner*, May 7, 1896.

168 "[controverted] the effect of the repeated assertions": ibid.

168 "That's bully": ibid.

168 "The resolution distinctly foreshadows": ibid.

169 "very unwelcome": ibid.

169 "about given up hope": ibid.

169 "Tapeworm Boyd [squirming]": *San Francisco Examiner*, May 9, 1896.

169 "down on the floor": ibid.

169 "COLLIS DREADS A COMMISSION": *San Francisco Examiner*, May 10, 1896.

169 "Senator Jones was not in evidence to-day": ibid.

169 "To-day Mr. Huntington saw": *San Francisco Examiner*, May 13, 1896.

170 "The commission was thrust upon Huntington": *San Francisco Examiner*, May 14, 1896.

170 "the country has been shown": ibid.

170 "CLEVELAND WILL NAME THE BOARD": *San Francisco Examiner*, May 23, 1896.

170 "The close of the session is in sight": *San Francisco Examiner*, May 27, 1896.

172 "It was remarkable that a meeting called": *San Francisco Examiner*, May 30, 1896.

172 "our newspapers were almost a unit": ibid.

172 "when a great journal": ibid.

172 "the fitting, burning, liquid": ibid.

172 "The history of the contest": ibid.

173 "For the first time in its career": ibid.

173 "I feel rather like a fool": *San Francisco Examiner*, January 10, 1897.

173 "naturally cause other friends": White, Richard, *Railroaded*, p. 452.

174 "The *Examiner* has a very large circulation": Swanberg, W. A., *Citizen Hearst*, New York: Scribners, 1961, pp. 110–11.

175 "no evidence that [Hearst's] news": p. 118.

176 "These very men whom you are now scolding about": Daggett, *Chapters on the History of the Southern Pacific*, p. 405.

177 "with difficulty": O'Connor, *Ambrose Bierce*, p. 236.

177 "an enormously long stride": Lindley, *Ambrose Bierce Takes on the Railroad*, p. 115.

177 "[The defeat] marked the doom": McWilliams, *Ambrose Bierce*, p. 245.

178 "As far as my part in the inception": Lindley, *Ambrose Bierce Takes on the Railroad*, p. 127.

179 "These articles were extraordinary": McWilliams, *Ambrose Bierce*, p. 245.

180 "Americans knew that public freedom": Arendt, Hannah, *On Revolution*, New York: Viking Compass, 1965, p. 115.

7. The Beast Emerges from Within Frank Norris

181 "appears to have modeled human nature": McElrath, Joseph R., Jr., and Crisler, Jesse S., *Frank Norris: A Life*, Urbana, University of Illinois Press, 2006, p. xv.

182 "I am willing to forgo": ibid., p. 108.

183 "May we not say": ibid., p. 124.

183 "an 'honorable dismissal'": ibid., p. 112.

183 "emphasized the need": Hart, James D., ed., *A Novelist in the Making: A Collection of Student Themes, and the Novels* Blix *and* Vandover the Brute, Cambridge: Belknap/Harvard University Press, 1970, p. 13.

185 "thimble-headed bobbism": McElrath and Crisler, *Frank Norris*, p. 117.

186 "As is the rule": ibid., p. 178.

187 "a certain railroad with offices in Boston": Hofstadter, Richard, *The Age of Reform: From Bryan to F.D.R.*, New York: Alfred A. Knopf, 1955, p. 229.

187 "[the] association of poverty with progress": Klein, Maury, *The Genesis of Industrial America, 1870–1920*, Cambridge: Cambridge University Press, 2007, p. 135.

189 "the drama of a broken teacup": Howells, William Dean, *Criticism and Fiction*, and Norris, Frank, *The Responsibilities of the Novelist*, Cambridge, Massachusetts: Walker-de Berry, Inc., 1963, p. 280. (This unusual book is a dual volume.)

189 "he can tell nothing but something like what he has seen": Bierce, *Collected Works*, vol. X, p. 240.

189 "the kind of fiction": Howells, *Criticism and Fiction*, and Norris, *The Responsibilities of the Novelist*, p. 280.

189 "They must be twisted from the ordinary": Lenning, Arthur, *Stroheim*, Lexington: University Press of Kentucky, 2000, p. 187.

190 "But where can the man be found": Howe, Irving, *A Critic's Notebook*, New York: Harvest, 1995, p. 222.

190 "the passage of progress on its way towards the twentieth century": Zola, Émile, *La Bête humaine*, translated by Roger Pearson, Oxford, England: The World's Classics, 1996, p. xli.

190 "the evil beast": Zola, Émile, *Germinal*, translated by L. W. Tancock, Baltimore: Penguin Classics, 1964, p. 452.

191 "monster": Zola, Émile, *Au Bonheur des dames*, translated by Robin Buss, London: Penguin Classics, 2001, p. 17.

191 "flaming eye" and "the ravenous mouth of a furnace": Zola, *La Bête humaine*, p. 279.

191 "Upon the equator": McElrath and Crisler, *Frank Norris*, p. 182.

192 "the high spirits of an undergraduate humor magazine": Starr, Kevin, *Americans and the California Dream 1850–1915*, New York: Oxford University Press, p. 259.

192 "monster" and "leviathan": McElrath and Crisler, *Frank Norris*, pp. 212–13.

193 "Kearney street": Starr, *Americans and the California Dream*, p. 260.

193 "great whaleback steamer taking on grain": Hart, *A Novelist in the Making*, p. 30.

193 "You got off the train": McElrath and Crisler, *Frank Norris*, p. 207.

193 "And then, in that immense silence": ibid., p. 211.

193   "especially fond of a good joke": ibid., p. 259.

195   "The Young Personage": ibid., pp. 274–75.

196   "It was a trivial affair": ibid., p. 277.

196   "The firing of rifles on the battlefield": ibid., p. 290.

197   "Even though not a soldier": ibid., p. 313.

197   "at a little green parrot": ibid., p. 311.

198   "so big that it frightens me": ibid., p. 334.

199   "the idealisation of the ugly": Pritchett, V. S., *Complete Collected Essays*, New York: Random House, 1991, p. 453.

199   "the unplumbed depths of the human heart": Howells, *Criticism and Fiction*, and Norris, *The Responsibilities of the Novelist*, p. 282.

199   "mind was as his body, heavy": Norris, Frank, *McTeague: A Story of San Francisco*, New York: New American Library of World Literature, 1964, p. 7.

199   "It was the old battle": ibid., p. 28.

200   "The people about the [boarding] house": ibid., p. 239.

201   "And in some strange, inexplicable way": ibid.

201   "the only truthful literary method": Garraty, John A., and Carnes, Mark C., eds., *American National Biography*, New York: Oxford University Press, 1999, vol. 16, p. 498.

203   "was the child of my brain": Lenning, *Stroheim*, p. 104.

204   "The public, of course, will not see the underwear": Madsen, Axel, *Gloria and Joe*, New York: Berkley Books, 1989, p. 187.

204   "the history of each Stroheim film": Lenning, *Stroheim*, p. 156.

204   "I never truckled": ibid., p. 187.

205   "It has taken Stroheim 67 pages": ibid., p. 197.

206   "Fight! Fight!": Lingenfelter, Richard E., *Death Valley & the Amargosa: A Land of Illusion*, Berkeley: University of California Press, 1986, p. 446.

206   "all scenes of McTeague biting": Lenning, *Stroheim*, p. 219.

206   "morbid and senseless": Lingenfelter, *Death Valley & the Amargosa*, p. 446.

206   "made only one real picture in my life": ibid.

8. Norris Picks Up a Rake

209   "to study the whole question": McElrath and Crisler, *Frank Norris*, p. 340.

209   "Go back to California": ibid., p. 337.

209   "Whatever degree of animus Norris held": ibid., p. 342.

210   "The Wheat affair is building up": ibid., p. 343.

210   "good friends": ibid., p. 357.

211   "enlisted upon the other side": ibid., p. 341.

212   "Not the most gifted man that ever lived": Howells, William Dean, *A Hazard of New Fortunes*, New York: The World's Classics, 1990, p. 170.

214   "all of a sudden to a great big crushing END": Walker, Franklin, *Frank Norris: A Biography*, Garden City, New York: Doubleday, 1932, p. 266.

214   "It's a wonder I don't forget me own name": Norris, Frank, *The Octopus*, New York: Penguin Classics, 1986, p. ix.

215   "Fair!": ibid., p. 19.

216   "Presley saw again": ibid., p. 51.

216   "Think of it!": ibid., p. 71.

217   "I can't change": ibid.

217   "*The Company invites settlers*": ibid., p. 117.

217   "The presence of the railroad": ibid., p. 98.

217–18   "They agreed to charge but two-fifty": ibid.

218   "I'll bet I could sell": ibid., p. 97.

218   "the implacable, iron monster": ibid., p. 273.

219   "Matters are just romping right along": ibid., p. 296.

219–20   "'We want a man the railroad can't control!'": Beers, *Gunfight at Mussel Slough*, p. 188.

220   "serving writs in ejectment": Norris, *The Octopus*, p. 509.

221   "Shelgrim owns the courts": ibid., p. 104.

221   "infertile pate": *San Francisco Examiner*, February 2, 1896.

222   "the faintest suggestion of a lisp": Norris, *The Octopus*, p. 575.

222   "Control the road!": ibid., p. 576.

222   "colossal indifference": ibid., p. 577.

223   "The purpose for which Zola wrote his book": Howells, *Criticism and Fiction*, and Norris, *The Responsibilities of the Novelist*, p. 205.

224   "because the farmers of the valley": Norris, *The Octopus*, p. 608.

224   "The larger view, always and through all shams": ibid., p. 652.

224   "the most ambitious of American novels": Spiller, Robert E., *The Cycle of American Literature*, New York: Mentor, 1957, p. 157.

225   "There is something like Zola about Mr. Norris": McElrath and Crisler, *Frank Norris*, p. 380.

9. Mussel Slough Under a Microscope

227   "Hoh, yes, the Interstate Commerce Commission": Norris, *The Octopus*, p. 105.

227 "the average receipts": Daggett, *Chapters on the History of the Southern Pacific*, p. 351.

228 "Perhaps nothing engendered more hostility": Emery, Robert A., "Railroad Rates in *The Octopus*: A Literary Footnote," 64 *Journal of Transportation Law and Policy* 298, 302 (1997).

228 "[He] emphasized each word": Norris, *The Octopus*, pp. 349–50.

228 "Mr. Huntington was asked": *San Francisco Examiner*, March 8, 1896.

230 "The grant to the Union Pacific": Williams, *A Great and Shining Road*, p. 142.

231 "What we get by the sale": Orsi, *Sunset Limited*, p. 56.

231 "We want the country settled": Rice et al., *The Elusive Eden*, p. 224.

232 "In the fall of 1869": Beers, *Gunfight at Mussel Slough*, p. 70.

234 "blossom and bear": ibid.

234 "Few of the squatters": Orsi, *Sunset Limited*, p. 97.

234 "have entered on the railroad land": Beers, *Gunfight at Mussel Slough*, p. 167.

235 "secretly contracted with several hundred neighbors": Rice et al., *The Elusive Eden*, p. 221.

235 "uneasy about the land": Beers, *Gunfight at Mussel Slough*, p. 72.

235 "we wrote . . . to the railroad": ibid.

236 "There is but one price": ibid., p. 99.

236 "of questionable legal validity": Larimore, John A., "Legal Questions Arising from the Mussel Slough Lands Dispute," *Southern California Quarterly*, vol. 58, p. 93 (1976).

236 "Spare no pains": Rice et al., *The Elusive Eden*, p. 225.

236 "the Western Civil War": Brown, Richard Maxwell, *No Duty to Retreat*, New York: Oxford University Press, 1991, p. 91.

237 "Such were the mounting tensions": ibid., p. 101.

237 "into two hostile, violence-prone factions": ibid.

238 "would strike the first blow": Rice et al., *The Elusive Eden*, p. 223.

239 "an American community": Brown, *No Duty to Retreat*, p. 98.

239 "the railroad's [Mussel Slough] prices": Rice et al., *The Elusive Eden*, p. 226.

240 "slight reductions": ibid., p. 230.

242 "I think I had better go": ibid., p. 231.

242 "On peril of your life": ibid., p. 232.

242 "God damn you": ibid.

242 "Thinking the settlers had attacked the marshal": ibid.

243 "Instantly the revolvers and rifles": Norris, *The Octopus*, p. 521.

244 "the Mephistopheles who for his own aggrandizement": Rice et al., *The Elusive Eden*, p. 233.

244 "It is not denied that the corporation": Beers, *Gunfight at Mussel Slough*, p. 288.

244 "death struggle": ibid., p. 289.

244 "blond and quiet": Brown, *No Duty to Retreat*, p. 110.

245 "All good people sympathize": Beers, *Gunfight at Mussel Slough*, p. 164.

246 "The railroad sent armed thugs": McWilliams, *Ambrose Bierce*, p. 159.

246 "[It owns] more power": Miller, May Merrill, *First the Blade*, New York: Alfred A. Knopf, 1938, pp. 421–22.

247 "proprietor of a real estate business": ibid., p. 574.

247 "Mussel Slough Massacre": Hall, Oakley, *Ambrose Bierce and the Queen of Spades*, Berkeley: University of California Press, 1998, p. 7.

247 "The stuff of the novel": Didion, Joan, *Where I Was From*, New York: Vintage International, 2004, p. 40.

248 "lease agreements": ibid., p. 41.

248 "under [a] rather willful misapprehension": ibid.

248 "were of a type": ibid., p. 47.

248 "dissonance its author grasped": ibid., p. 48.

248 "shootout": ibid., p. 41.

248 "slaughter": ibid., p. 178.

250 "one of the loveliest cities": Brown, *No Duty to Retreat*, p. 126.

250 "an austere monoculture": ibid.

251 "reformer who is half charlatan": Wister, Owen, *Roosevelt: The Story of a Friendship, 1880–1919*, New York: Macmillan, 1930, p. 83.

251 "inclined to think": ibid., p. 84.

10. Endings

253 "Corner wheat!": Norris, Frank, *The Pit: A Story of Chicago*, New York: Penguin Twentieth-Century Classics, 1994, p. 308.

253 "Will it not go on": McElrath and Crisler, *Frank Norris*, p. 409.

253 "Whenever [Frank] stopped at my desk": ibid., p. 394.

254 "See what an irreparable injury": Norris, *The Octopus*, p. xxxiii.

255 "Here Huntington's ashes": O'Connor, *Ambrose Bierce*, p. 227.

255 "I do not speak ill of the dead": Joshi and Schultz, *A Much Misunderstood Man*, p. 70.

256 "We are at war with Spain": Morris, *Ambrose Bierce: Alone in Bad Company*, p. 231.

256 "Yanko Spanko": Berkove, Lawrence I., *A Prescription for Adversity: The Moral Art of Ambrose Bierce*, Columbus: Ohio State University Press, 2002, p. 27.

257 "I don't like the job of chained bulldog": Joshi and Schultz, *A Much Understood Man*, p. 161.

257 "You haven't heard me shrieking": O'Connor, *Ambrose Bierce*, p. 285.

257 "My boy died on Sunday": Joshi and Schultz, *A Much Understood Man*, p. 78.

257 "I live rather quietly": ibid., p. 99.

258 "I'm cutting-about my stuff": ibid., p. 188.

258 "I'll never be like that": McWilliams, *Ambrose Bierce: A Biography*, p. 315.

259 "Good-bye—if you hear of my": Joshi and Schultz, *A Much Understood Man*, p. 243.

259 "you . . . asked me in [your] letter": ibid., p. 244.

260 "He toured the state": Rice et al., *The Elusive Eden*, p. 336.

260 "By controlling reform movements": Deverell, *Railroad Crossing*, p. 171.

262 "the legend of railroad domination": Williams, *The Democratic Party and California Politics 1880–1896*, p. 231.

262 "This I say, however": *San Francisco Examiner*, April 1, 1896.

263 "a broken initiative process": Stone, David, *Newsweek*, October 26, 2010.

⚊ bibliography ⚊

Newsweek
New York Journal
San Francisco Examiner
Washington Star

Abbot, Willis J., *Watching the World Go By*, Boston: Little, Brown, 1933.

Adams, Henry, *The Education of Henry Adams*, London: Penguin Classics, 1995.

Ambrose, Stephen A., *Nothing Like It in the World: The Men Who Built the Transcontinental Railroad 1863–1869*, New York: Touchstone, 2001.

Arendt, Hannah, *On Revolution*, New York: Viking Compass, 1965.

Bain, David Haward, *Empire Express: Building the First Transcontinental Railroad*, New York: Viking, 1999.

Beatty, Jack, *Age of Betrayal: The Triumph of Money in America, 1865–1900*, New York: Alfred A. Knopf, 2007.

Beers, Terry, ed., *Gunfight at Mussel Slough: Evolution of a Western Myth*, Berkeley: Heyday Books, 2004.

Bellesiles, Michael A., *1877: America's Year of Living Violently*, New York: The New Press, 2010.

Bierce, Ambrose, *The Collected Works of Ambrose Bierce*, 12 volumes, New York: The Neale Publishing Company, 1909.

Bierce, Ambrose, *The Collected Writings of Ambrose Bierce*, Secaucus, New Jersey: The Citadel Press, 1972.

Bierce, Ambrose, *The Devil's Dictionary, Tales, & Memoirs*, New York: Library of America, 2011.

Bierce, Ambrose, *Write It Right*, Toluca Lake, California: Terripam Publishers Inc., 1986.

Brown, Richard Maxwell, *No Duty to Retreat: Violence and Values in American History and Society*, New York: Oxford University Press, 1991.

Crane, Stephen, *The Red Badge of Courage*, New York: Bantam Classics, 1983.

Daggett, Stuart, *Chapters on the History of the Southern Pacific*, New York: The Ronald Press Company, 1922.

de Castro, Adolphe, *Portrait of Ambrose Bierce*, New York: The Century Co., 1929.

Deverell, William, *Railroad Crossing: Californians and the Railroad 1850–1910*, Berkeley: University of California Press, 1994.

Didion, Joan, *Where I Was From*, New York: Vintage International, 2004.

Drabelle, Dennis, *Mile-High Fever: Silver Mines, Boom Towns, and High Living on the Comstock Lode*, New York: St. Martin's Press, 2009.

Duncan, Russell, and Klooster, David J., eds., *Phantoms of a Blood-Stained Period: The Complete Civil War Writings of Ambrose Bierce*, Amherst: University of Massachusetts Press, 2002.

Elliott, Russell R., *History of Nevada*, second ed., Lincoln: University of Nebraska Press, 1987.

Emery, Robert A., "Railroad Rates in *The Octopus*: A Literary Footnote," 64 *Journal of Transportation Law, Logistics, and Policy* 298 (1997).

Garraty, John A., and Carnes, Mark C., eds., *American National Biography*, New York: Oxford University Press, 1999.

Grenander, M. E., ed., *Poems of Ambrose Bierce*, Lincoln: University of Nebraska Press, 1995.

Hall, Oakley, *Ambrose Bierce and the Queen of Spades*, Berkeley: University of California Press, 1998.

Hart, James D., ed., *A Novelist in the Making: A Collection of Student Themes and the Novels* Blix *and* Vandover and the Brute, Belknap/Harvard University Press, 1970.

Hofstadter, Richard, *The Age of Reform: From Bryan to F.D.R.*, New York: Alfred A. Knopf, 1955.

Hopkins, Ernest Jerome, ed., *The Ambrose Bierce Satanic Reader*, New York: Doubleday, 1968.

Howe, Irving, *A Critic's Notebook*, New York: Harvest, 1995.

Howells, William Dean, *A Hazard of New Fortunes*, New York: The World's Classics, 1990.

Howells, William Dean, *Criticism and Fiction*, and Norris, Frank, *The Responsibilities of the Novelist*, Cambridge, Massachusetts: Walker-de Berry, Inc., 1962.

Jacob, Kathryn Allamong, *King of the Lobby: The Life and Times of Sam Ward, Man-About-Washington in the Gilded Age*, Baltimore: The Johns Hopkins University Press, 2010.

Joshi, S. T., and Schultz, David E., *Ambrose Bierce: A Sole Survivor: Bits of Autobiography*, Knoxville: University of Tennessee Press, 1998.

Joshi, S. T., and Schultz, David E., *A Much Misunderstood Man: Selected Letters of Ambrose Bierce*, Columbus: Ohio State University Press, 2003.

Larimore, John A., "Legal Questions Arising from the Mussel Slough Lands Dispute," *Southern California Quarterly*, vol. 58 (1976).

Kennedy, J. Gerald, ed., *The Portable Edgar Allan Poe*, London: Penguin Classics, 2006.

Klein, Maury, *The Genesis of Industrial America, 1870–1920*, Cambridge, England: Cambridge University Press, 2007.

Lavender, David, *The Great Persuader*, New York: Doubleday, 1970.

Lears, Jackson, *Rebirth of a Nation: The Making of Modern America, 1877–1920*, New York: Harper, 2009.

Lee, Hermione, *Biography: A Very Short Introduction*, Oxford, England: Oxford University Press, 2009.

Lenning, Arthur, *Stroheim*, Lexington: University Press of Kentucky, 2000.

Lewis, Oscar, *The Big Four: The Story of Huntington, Stanford, Hopkins, and Crocker, and of the Building of the Central Pacific*, New York: Alfred A. Knopf, 1938.

Lindley, David, *Ambrose Bierce Takes on the Railroad: The Journalist as Muckraker and Cynic*, Wesport, Connecticut: Praeger, 1999.

Lingenfelter, Richard E., *Death Valley & the Amargosa: A Land of Illusion*, Berkeley: University of California Press, 1986.

Madsen, Axel, *Gloria and Joe*, New York: Berkeley Books, 1989.

McDougall, Walter A., *Throes of Democracy: The American Civil War Era 1829–1877*, New York: Harper, 2008.

McElfresh, Earl B., *Maps and Mapmakers of the Civil War*, New York: Abrams, 1999.

McElrath, Joseph R., Jr., and Crisler, Jesse S., *Frank Norris: A Life*, Urbana: University of Illinois Press, 2006.

McWilliams, Carey, *Ambrose Bierce: A Biography*, Hamden, Connecticut: Archon Books, 1967.

Miller, May Merrill, *First the Blade*, New York: Alfred A. Knopf, 1938.

Morris, Roy, Jr., *Ambrose Bierce: Alone in Bad Company*: New York, Crown, 1995.

Morrow, William C., *Blood-Money*, San Francisco, F. J. Walker & Co., 1882.

Myers, Gustavus, *History of the Great American Fortunes*, New York: The Modern Library, 1936.

Norris, Frank, *McTeague: A Story of San Francisco*, New York: Signet Classic, 1964.

Norris, Frank, *The Octopus: A Story of California*, New York: Penguin Classics, 1986.

Norris, Frank, *The Pit: A Story of Chicago*, New York: Penguin Twentieth-Century Classics, 1994.

Norris, Frank, *The Responsibilities of the Novelist and Other Literary Essays*, New York: Haskell House, 1969.

O'Connor, Richard, *Ambrose Bierce: A Biography*, Boston: Little, Brown, 1967.

Older, Fremont, *My Own Story*, San Francisco, The Call Publishing Company, 1919.

Orsi, Richard J., *Sunset Limited: The Southern Pacific Railroad and the Development of the American West 1850–1930*, Berkeley: University of California Press, 2007.

Post, C. C., *Driven from Sea to Sea; or, Just a Campin'*, Chicago: J. E. Downey & Company, 1884.

Pritchett, V. S., *Complete Collected Essays*, New York: Alfred A. Knopf, 1991.

Rayner, Richard, *The Associates: Four Capitalists Who Created California*, New York: Atlas & Company/Norton, 2008.

Rice, Richard B., Bullough, William A., and Orsi, Richard J., *The Elusive Eden: A New History of California*, New York: Alfred A. Knopf, 1988.

Robinson, John R., "The Octopus: A History of the Construction, Conspiracies, Extortions, Robberies, and Villainous Acts of the Central Pacific, Southern Pacific of Kentucky, Union Pacific and Other Subsidized Railroads" (pamphlet), San Francisco: 1894.

Royce, Josiah, *The Feud of Oakfield Creek: A Novel of California Life*, New York: Johnson Reprint Corporation, 1970.

Santayana, George, *The Genteel Tradition in American Philosophy* and *Character and Opinion in the United States*, New Haven: Yale University Press, 2009.

Spiller, Robert E., *The Cycle of American Literature*, New York: Mentor, 1957.

Starr, Kevin, *Americans and the California Dream 1850–1915*, Oxford, England: Oxford University Press, 1973.

Stewart, Robert E., Jr., and Stewart, Mary Frances, *Adolph Sutro: A Biography*, Berkeley, California: Howell-North, 1962.

Swanberg, W. A., *Citizen Hearst*, New York: Scribners, 1961.

Tuchman, Barbara, *The Proud Tower: A Portrait of the World Before the War 1890–1914*, New York: Bantam Books, 1971.

Twain, Mark, and Warner, Charles Dudley, *The Gilded Age: A Tale of Today*, New York: Meridian Classics, 1985.

White, Richard, *Railroaded: The Transcontinentals and the Making of Modern America*, New York: W. W. Norton, 2011.

Williams, John Hoyt, *A Great and Shining Road: The Epic Story of the Transcontinental Railroad*, New York: Times Books, 1988.

Williams, R. Hal, *The Democratic Party and California Politics 1880–1896*, Palo Alto: Stanford University Press, 1973.

Wilson, Edmund, *Patriotic Gore: Studies in the Literature of the American Civil War*, New York: Noonday, 1977.

Zola, Émile, *Au Bonheur des dames (The Ladies' Delight)*, translated by Robin Buss, London: Penguin Classics, 2001.

Zola, Émile, *Germinal*, translated by L. W. Tancock, Baltimore: Penguin Classics, 1954.

Zola, Émile, *La Bête humaine*, translated by Roger Pearson, Oxford, England: The World's Classics, 1996.

⚜ index ⚜

Bierce, Ambrose (*continued*)
  Collected Works, 258
  cynicism and misanthropy of,
    mistakenly attributed, 93–95
  and defeat of the Funding Bill,
    172–73
  disappearance and presumed death
    in Mexico, 258–59
  early life, 88–95
  effectiveness of campaign against
    the SP, 179–80
  fictionalization about (by Oakley
    Hall), 247
  gossip columns of, 98, 102, 256
  Hearst's support of, 1, 256–57
  Hearst's telegram, summoning him
    to Washington, 134–35
  Huntington asks him to name his
    price, supposedly, 151–52
  interviews of, 153
  lampooning poems by, 123–24,
    219–20, 255
  last years, 255–59
  as literary critic, 111–12, 189
  literary output comprised solely of
    short pieces, 110–14, 180, 258
  in London, 99–101
  marriage and family, 99–101, 103,
    109–10
  meets ghost of his dead friend, 100
  meets Hearst and goes to work for
    him, 104–6
  praised in the *San Francisco
    Examiner*, 149
  pride in his work, 180
  pro-establishment temperament of,
    121, 256
  in San Francisco, 95–96, 98–99,
    101–6
  short stories, 89, 106–9, 111–12,
    192
  style of writing, 96–98, 140
  in Washington, 134–36, 160–61
  writing about CP and SP, 1–6, 73,
    79, 108–9, 122–26, 245, 262
  writing about Crocker, 124–25
  writing about Crocker's mansion, 68
  writing about Mussel Slough, 244
  writing about war, 112–16, 196
Bierce, Day, 100, 109–10
Bierce, Helen, 101
Bierce, Leigh, 100, 257
Bierce, Lucius Verus, 90–91
Bierce, Marcus Aurelius, 89

Bierce, Mollie. *See* Day, Mary Ellen
  "Mollie"
The Big Four (Lewis), 246
Big Four railroad magnates, 23, 60
  called "railrogues," 122
  estates of, 261–62
  flaunting their wealth, 65, 68–71
  lawsuits involved in, 67–68, 69–70,
    130
  solidarity of, 40
  unpopularity of, 23–24, 64–71, 73–74
Black, Jeannette, 198, 214–15, 252, 254
Black Hills, Dakota Territory, 102
blacks and black institutions, Colis
  Huntington's support for, 33
Blaine, James, 66
blasting powder, 35
Blickensderfer, Jacob, 43
Blind Husbands (film), 203
Blix (Norris), 198, 214
Blood-Money (Morrow), 83–84, 85, 230,
  245
Bloomer Cut, 32
blue tickets (free rides), 120
Bohemian Club, San Francisco, 101,
  184, 210, 213
bonds issued by federal government to
  railroads, 20–21
  distributed to railroads, upon
    performance, 25–27
  interest paid on, 21
  to be repaid with longer-term
    bonds, 132–33
bonds issued by railroads, priority of,
  over federal-government-issued
  bonds, 30–31
Boyd, John, 41, 142, 169
Braden (farmer), 242
Brannan, Sam, 67
bribery, 36, 47, 65, 77–78, 120–21, 125,
  158–60, 176
  bungled, 127–28
  defense of, 66
  end of the era of, 179
Briggs, Emily, 46–47
Broderick, David, 241
Brooks, James, 66–67
Brown, John, 91
Brown, Richard Maxwell, cited,
  236–37, 249–50
Browning, Orville, 49–50, 51–52, 54,
  55–59, 233
Bunyan, John, 211
Burnettized wood, 37, 46

Comstock Lode, 16–17, 23, 29, 31, 50, 95, 131
Confederate veterans in vigilante groups, 236
Congress, railroad interests in, 19, 136
Contract & Finance Company, 44, 67–68, 80, 81, 262
  books of, rewritten and originals burned, 68, 150–51, 261
  dividends, 127
  link with CP, 44, 67, 149–51
contracting, to owned subsidiaries, 24
Cope, Edward Drinker, 102
corporations
  Bierce's definition of, 123, 130
  limits on, 6
  resistance to, 237
corruption of public officials
  in California, 75
  Huntington's views on, 47
Cosmopolitan magazine, 256
Council Bluffs, Iowa, 20
Cox, Jacob, 234
Crane, Stephen, 116–18, 191, 195–96
  early death of, 255
Crédit Mobilier (French company), 44
Crédit Mobilier (U.S. company), 24, 36, 44, 45, 49, 57
  scandal of, 66–67
Crocker, Charles
  background of, 15, 17
  bet of, with Durant, 50, 59–60
  Bierce's campaign against, 124–25
  business affairs, 80
  complains about value of CP's land grants, 230–31
  at congressional hearings, 80
  in construction of CP, 24–26, 31, 36, 39, 46, 53–55, 59–60
  as CP officer, 19, 57
  friends of, 238
  his opinion of Stanford, 30
  as manager of men, 40–41
  mansion on Nob Hill, 68–71
  as negotiator for CP, 31
  sells out, then returns, 65–66
  as SP president, 75–76, 239–40
  target of criticism, 2
  at track inspections, 44, 49
  at transcontinental festivities, 60
  wealth of, 13, 68–71
Crocker, Edwin Bryant (E.B.)
  on CP board, 24, 30
  as CP lawyer, 41, 52–53

and finances, 45
  proposal on construction, 39
  proposal on laying tracks, 42–43
  retirement of, 61, 65
Crocker & Company, 44, 81
Crow, Walter J., 237, 241–43
  gunslinger prowess, 244
Cuba, 256
Curtis, W. B., 144
Custer, George Armstrong, 38

Daggett, Stuart, cited, 71–72, 127, 227
Darwinian evolution, 183, 187–88
Davenport, Homer, 135
Davis, Jefferson, 11
Davis, Richard Harding, 191, 195
Day, Mary Ellen "Mollie," 99, 109, 257
death, as literary subject, 107–8
Death Valley, filming in, 205–6
de Castro, Adolphe, 121–22
Democratic Party, 119, 136
De Quille, Dan, 96
Devil's Dictionary (Bierce), 1, 89, 123, 189
DeYoung, Charles, 98
Didion, Joan, 247–48
distance, annihilation of, with railroads, 10
Dodge, Grenville, 42, 56, 61
  and route of the UPC, 59
Doggett, Gertrude, 184–85, 198, 215, 254
Donner Lake, 35
Donner Pass, 13
Donner Summit, 37
Doubleday, Frank, 209, 214
Doubleday and McClure, 209
Doubleday & Page, 214–15, 254
doubling back shipping maneuver, 72, 155–56, 227–29
Doyle, John J., 235, 244, 248–49
Dreiser, Theodore, 191, 214–15
drills, steam-powered, 39
Driven from Sea to Sea; or, Just a Campin' (Post), 84, 85, 230, 245
Durant, Thomas C., 50, 52, 53, 60
  at transcontinental festivities, 61–62
Dutch Flat, California, 13, 34, 37
Dutch Flat and Donner Lake Wagon Road, 23, 31–32
Dutch Flat Swindle (so-called), 23, 29

Echo Summit, 58
economic debacle of 2007, 264